The Textual Sublime

Contemporary Studies in Philosophy and Literature 1
Hugh J. Silverman, Editor

The Textual Sublime

Deconstruction and Its Differences

Edited by

Hugh J. Silverman and Gary E. Aylesworth

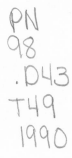
State University of New York Press

Published by
State University of New York Press, Albany

©1990 State University of New York

For information, address State University of New York
Press, State University Plaza, Albany, NY 12246

Library of Congress Cataloging-in Publication Data

The Textual sublime : deconstruction and its differences / Hugh J.
    Silverman and Gary E. Aylesworth, editors.
        p. cm.—(Contemporary studies in philosophy and literature
; 1)
    Bibliography: p.
    Includes index.
    ISBN 0-7914-0074-3.—ISBN 0-7914-0075-1 (pbk.)
    1. Deconstruction. 2. Criticism, Textual. 3. Literature—
    Aesthetics. 4. Literature—Philosophy. I. Silverman, Hugh J.
II. Aylesworth, Gary E. III. Series.
PN98.D43T49 1990   88-37124
801'.95—dc19   CIP

10   9   8   7   6   5   4   3   2   1

5-3-93

Contents

v

Acknowledgments

The essays in this volume were produced in connection with the eighth annual conference of the International Association for Philosophy and Literature (IAPL), which was held at the State University of New York at Stony Brook in May 1983. Most of the papers have been rewritten and molded to constitute a freestanding volume. Although the theme of the conference was "Deconstruction and its Alternatives," we have recast and narrowed its scope. In recasting the volume, we have endeavored to give it lasting effect with a general introduction (by Hugh J. Silverman, director of the conference) and preliminary remarks (by Gary E. Aylesworth, who was present at all stages of the conference and its aftermath). These introductory sections result from wide-ranging discussion and dialogue concerning the content, structure, and strategies for the volume. We have also included an extensive selected bibliography to enhance its value.

We are particularly pleased that this volume is the first in what is anticipated to be an important series of books resulting from conferences of the International Association for Philosophy and Literature. We are grateful to SUNY Press and its director, William Eastman, for agreeing to begin this new series; subsequent SUNY Press IAPL volumes are already in the making.

From the IAPL Executive Committee (James M. Edie, Mary Ann Caws, Donald Marshall, Charles Altieri, and Hugh J. Silverman) at the time of the conference, to the Stony Brook graduate students (including Leonard Lawlor, Kenneth Itzkowitz, and Gary E. Aylesworth—all of whom have now received their doctorates and are active in the philosophical profession) who read and discussed all of the more than one hundred papers that were submitted for the conference, to the undergraduates (including Jeffrey Gaines, John Hladky, and John Sekora—two of whom have gone on to graduate study in philosophy) who helped with local arrangements, to James Barry, Jr. and James Hatley who assisted us with some organizational and editorial matters at the publication stage, to the several hundred participants at the conference, and to the volume contributors who generously reworked their papers for publication, what we offer here is truly the result of a significant collective enterprise.

The editors would especially like to thank Sidney Gelber (then provost of the university) and Sandy Petrey (then dean of Humanities and Fine Arts) who first made it plausible and financially possible for a conference of such magnitude to be held at SUNY/Stony Brook. The encouragement of John H. Marburger III, president of the university, made the toil of working out local arrangements less onerous and more gratifying. Edward S. Casey (then chair of the Philosophy Department) provided both gracious acknowledgment of the work involved and the necessary financial commitment that helped support the conference. Their collective encouragement often kept the conference director from a state of total despair. For this and the many other respects in which she has kept balance, equilibrium, and efficiency, we are grateful to Mary E. Bruno who helped beyond the call of duty in sorting out some of the byzantine financial and organizational aspects of the conference. To Martha Smith and Virginia Massaro, who have always been there when we needed them for secretarial as well as basic human interest, we offer our special expression of gratitude. Finally, but not finally, we are deeply indebted to Patricia Athay for her critical, philosophically intense, and warm support over the years.

We hereby dedicate this volume to the memories of Eugenio Donato and Paul de Man. Within a year after the conference was completed, these two important figures had passed from the scene. Paul de Man was already not well (and was only able to send his paper, which was read by Peter Caws at the time), but Eugenio Donato participated actively and contributed to the high level of exchange. We hope that *The Textual Sublime* will serve as a small testament to the appreciation that they both deserve for their philosophical criticism in America. It is also hoped that the import and value of their contribution in the past two decades will not be tarnished by recent disclosures stemming from de Man's youth. Their critical acumen, their path-breaking effect, and their friendly human concern will not be forgotten by those who knew them.

Introduction

Hugh J. Silverman

Deconstruction has its differences. Some of these differences are conceptual, some internal, some critical, and some political. One of the principle differences that pertains to deconstruction is the philosophy-literature relation itself. One might, for instance, be led to ask: Is deconstruction a matter for philosophy or a matter for criticism? Is deconstruction identified with a philosophy or or with criticism? Can the literary text be read deconstructively without invoking deconstruction as philosophy? Can the philosophical text be read deconstructively without offering deconstruction as a critical activity? When deconstruction is invoked, what is the relation between philosophy and criticism? Do these differences make a difference or are they reducible to each other? If reducible, then even the most subtle differences simply disappear. In such a case, neither supplements the other, neither speaks for itself, neither has an identity of its own, and neither has its own space.

The textual sublime operates in this space of difference both establishing the identity of the critical text and the respects in which it raises philosophical issues that are not identical with the text, that lie at the margins of the text, and that open up the text to itself. As articulated here, the textual sublime is the concretization and thematization of deconstructive practice. The textual sublime is the articulation of deconstruction supplementing itself with both philosophy and criticism.

It would not take much to be convinced that philosophy is not reducible to literary criticism and that literary criticism has projects other than philosophy. Indeed most philosophers and most literary critics would be horrified at the very suggestion of identity. Yet deconstruction in literary study is often associated with philosophy, often determined as philosophical—or at least theoretical (and thereby not "literary," not even criticism). But if deconstruction is not criticism—that is, not of concern to teachers of literature—then it has no business talking about literary texts. As this volume will demonstrate, such an exclusion is hardly tenable.

Philosophy in general cannot account for the sublime in particular texts—that is the right and province of criticism alone. Yet the sublime, as one knows from even the most occasional reading of Kant and eighteenth-century critical theory, is a philosophical concept, a category of aesthetic judgment. Hence the sublime is of essential concern to philosophy. The sublime is that which marginalizes the literary text, takes it out of what it literally says and gives it another dimension, renders it more than "literary." The sublime opens the text to what is other than itself, to what only philosophy can name. Philosophy makes sense of the literary dimension of the literary text, but what it thematizes is not literary. What philosophy finds in the text is the sublime, which is a philosophical concept and hence already outside the domain of the literary text *qua* literary concern. Thus an irreconcilable difference arises: the literary seeks to articulate and express the sublime; philosophy names and appropriates the sublime for itself—in effect, philosophy removes the sublime from its proper place and makes use of it for its own purposes. But as Kant shows, the sublime is without purpose—and further opening the text to what is other than itself is rather a kind of purposiveness without purpose and therefore a return to the literary and the aesthetic as such.

Criticism wants to speak of the literary text in its detail, in its precision, in its multiple aspects. Philosophy wants to take up the literary text in its generality, in its role as an instance, as an occasion for something else. The textual sublime operates in the readings of texts, in the evaluation of their virtues, in the limitations of the critical approaches that seek to determine them. The textual sublime is the text protecting itself from the actions and attempts at closing it off, clarifying its meanings, reifying its vitality. The textual sublime gives hope to literary criticism because it defies reduction to simples, to concepts, to ideas, to textual components. The textual sublime gives purpose to philosophy, for without it philosophy itself would be of diminished interest; without it, philosophy would have only definite descriptions, concrete particulars, and determinate relations. Unlike the beautiful, the sublime is without boundaries. The textual sublime puts all claims to rigid limits under a shadow of doubt (and, among other things, opens the text to generalities).

Although the textual sublime is not offered as a formal concept in the essays that constitute this volume (though the discussion around Paul de Man's essay takes it up thematically), it is nevertheless a guiding theme. The textual sublime characterizes that space or domain in which the concern for the relations between philosophy and criticism are placed in question and examined in detail. As the text opens itself to what is other than itself, it marks the differential spaces of the text. The volume takes up the differences that operate not only between philosophy and literature, theory and criticism, reading and text, translation and original, but also between the Derridean and de Manian versions of deconstruction, between deconstruction and alternative critical practices. The essays in this volume are carefully linked so as to explore in detail these various differences inscribed within deconstruction itself.

The task of this volume is to examine deconstruction: its theoretical claims, its practical effects, and its textual interconnections. The book is organized into six interrelated parts: (1) deconstruction and criticism; (2) deconstruction and philosophy; (3) philosophy and criticism; (4) the rhetoric and practice of deconstruction: reading de Man; (5) deconstructing translation; and (6) alternatives to deconstruction. Each part develops aspects of the role of philosophy and literature in a deconstructive context. In what follows, the reader will find not only an overview of each section and the elements that link them, but also an explicit account of how the textual sublime operates throughout the volume. The preliminary remarks themselves explain in more detail how each section is organized. They also focus in on its key themes and unique contribution.

(1) In the first part, we look at deconstruction as a theoretical practice: what it is, what it is not, what it cannot be other than, what cannot be other than it. We will explore the choice of deconstruction and ask whether it makes a difference as a sociological or critical practice. The essays by Fynsk, Kinczewski, and Fischer show that not all readings are the same. As a concern of and for criticism, the question of deconstruction raises the issue of its alternatives. What is there about deconstruction that it might enjoin and articulate alternatives to itself? This marking of alternatives within the operations of the text itself is what we shall call the textual sublime. The task of a deconstructive criticism is to bring out these marks of alterity. But is there an agon, a discursive space, for critical readings and alternative theoretical practices as well? Critics of deconstruction will surely believe so (and this is the topic for the sixth part). They will want to say that deconstruction can be fought against, debated about, rejected out of hand. However, the agon is not only the event but also the site of the debate. The question is not whether deconstruction has alternatives but whether it makes sense to bring the whole concept of alternative into play in the first place. Here the debate must necessarily develop around what is textually sublime about any text and how it is the task of any deconstruction to make this consideration evident. This is the work of deconstructive criticism in its practice.

(2) The second part takes up the respects in which deconstruction needs philosophy, in which deconstruction demands a philosophical under-

standing in order to build a critical practice. Heidegger is invoked as the philosophical exemplar upon which Derridean deconstruction is constructed. But then, as Donato asserts, Heidegger was built on a Nietzschean frame. However, for a variety of reasons, the Nietzschean foundation is not a foundation at all. Not only is Nietzsche himself critical of the whole enterprise that seeks to establish foundations, but also, in the wake of Heidegger, Nietzschean thought takes the Derridean enterprise out from behind the veil, into the open, and gives it space. For Donato, history is not past, and closure is not the end. The Nietzschean text goes beyond its historical determinations— its sublimity has a force of its own.

Wood's response to Donato builds upon the separability of deconstructive strategies from the specific philosophical tradition upon which it depends. The idea that deconstruction obtains its identity from the particular historical line in which it is situated runs counter to deconstruction itself. It is not the Heideggerian or even Nietzschean debts that constitute deconstruction, but rather the set of moves and strategies that permit a reading of figures such as Nietzsche and Heidegger. Hence, although Donato wants to go beyond what separates philosophy and literature, he cannot do so without reading the texts of both and without examining (as he himself proposes) their ends, limits, and forms of closure. Hence the textual sublime rather than a textual history (such as literary history or the history of philosophy) is what is at issue in deconstruction.

By focusing on the question of "belonging," Chanter reviews both Donato's and Wood's texts and asks about the belonging together—or what she calls the "interlacing"—of Derrida's and Heidegger's texts. Like the laces of the peasant woman's shoes in Van Gogh's painting (according to Heidegger's reading), the texts are interwoven and interlinked. But the interlacing is not one of possession, or property, or owner's rights. The interlacing does not allow the responsibility to rest in Heidegger any more than in Derrida. What is textually sublime about this relation is that the difference between Heidegger's text and Derrida's text may be indistinguishable albeit still definitively a difference.

(3) In the third part, the theme of the sublime is taken up directly. The section begins with Harvey's account of the effective differences between the Derridean and de Manian enterprises—the one philosophical, the other critical; the one a strategy applied to the text, the other constituting the text; the one assymmetrical with respect to and inseparable from the text, the other supplementary to and a strategic repetition of the text. Harvey's reading of this opposition, lodged between deconstruction's dominant proponents and their practice, sets the frame for de Man's account of the sublime as a pragmatic and rhetorical feature, not as a dimension of a transcendental and critical philosophy.

De Man seeks to escape from the Kantian opposition between the dynamic sublime (the imagination stretching beyond its limits) and the mathematical sublime. In de Man's reading, Kant shifts from the sublime as a philosophical idea with its material-based other to a linguistic framework, where the sublime operates as a signifying function. For de Man, the sublime cannot stand off against the ideological and metaphysical, cannot be critical and transcendental, though nevertheless still philosophical. The sublime must, in the end, be a rhetorical, linguistic device, a trope that surpasses (or at least stands apart from) comprehension. The sublime cannot be either apprehension or comprehension, syntagmatic or paradigmatic, infinite or limited. The sublime must be tropological — that is, a feature of language at work.

Gasché, by contrast, is not worried that the sublime cannot be understood and read philosophically. He claims that the move to the linguistic is not necessary. For Gasché the sublime is an *Augenschein*, a presentation of ideas. The sublime does not exclude totality, rather it is a mood of what is as presented by way of negation, by way of alterity. The textual sublime is the text in the mode of a presentation of ideas with moods that are neither in harmony nor in conflict. The textual sublime calls for a presentation of moods that are other than what is presented as such.

(4) Where the third part indicates that the textual sublime is lodged insolubly somewhere between criticism and philosophy, part four takes up the practice of deconstruction as rhetoric on the one hand and as philosophy on the other. Furthermore, it takes up the work of de Man both directly and by contrast with some alternative critical practices. Jay, Caraher, and Felperin demonstrate facets of deconstruction as criticism in terms of the production-disclosure of the sublime in textual reading, in philosophical practice, and in the institution of criticism itself. Deconstruction is understood here as an activity that does not constitute itself as an alternative reading, that does not offer another way to analyze a text, that does not provide a positionality outside the text, that does not interpret the text by giving it meaning. Rather deconstruction reads a text such as Nietzsche's *Birth of Tragedy* as narrative, as a repetition of origins, as a reenactment of the problematic of tragedy at its birth in ancient Greece, in Schopenhauer, and in Wagner. In short, deconstruction reads narrative as textually sublime.

According to Jay, the reader is not a self or subject outside the text that is read. The reader and reading are themselves tropologically elaborated. The reader and the reading (figured as *prosopopeia*) are none other than the text itself — they do not constitute themselves as an alternative voice. They are the sublimity of the text itself.

By contrast, Caraher takes the philosopher philosophizing as the figure in the text. De Man (in "Shelley Disfigured") finds that the *philosophe*

Rousseau in Shelley's poem is without a face *(sans figure)* though also a significant figure in the text. Similarly, John Austin is the figure of the philosopher performing a theory of constatives and performatives. The performance inscribes the sublime into the text: the figure of the philosopher constating the distinction between constatives and performatives.

Between the philosophy of figures and the figure of the philosopher, Felperin offers an account of the institution of criticism. He shows that many of the students of de Man, Miller, Hartman, Bloom, and Derrida (the Yale School of the late 1970s and early 1980s) were actively engaged in a reading of literature at the interface between philosophy and literature, at the intersection of literature and social functions. Although philosophy as an academic discipline seemed (or seems) to be dissociated from the texts of social and cultural institutions, criticism could not (would not) insulate itself so thoroughly from those institutions. What philosophy might have been (might be) is, according to Felperin, linked to broader social issues through the practice of deconstructive criticism. However, only if criticism does not take itself as an institution can it operate deconstructively in relation to what it reads—and what it reads as text cannot be "simply" literary; it is also textually sublime.

(5) Where the previous section presents deconstruction as a rhetorical or critical practice (and not as linked to either criticism or philosophy), part five situates deconstruction in relation to the complex known as "translation." Translation is alternatively a task, an activity, and a performance, involving "complementarity" (Graham), "transitivity" (Allison), and "telelation" (Leavey). Each is a form of the movement of the textual sublime, both demonstrating the limits of the text and also taking the text outside itself.

With Benjamin, as Graham presents it, translation is complementary: both the original and the translated operate in relation to a "pure language." Deconstruction, as a complement to Benjamin's text, is itself not a reference to a unifying limit, but rather a supplement to that complementarity, the performance of the very limitations of a "pure language."

Allison takes propositions as a type for a sentence-token, as a meaning content of a judgment, as both a common meaning and its translation into another language. Although all these accounts fail, they do so because communication and language take shape in the use or practice of them. The transitivity of language cannot move into signification, for when signifying, it loses itself in the hermeneutic circle. The transitivity of language in the later Heidegger and in Derrida involves the actual performance or writing of the text—that is as the text is performed in one language or another. The transitivity of one language can *be* the transitivity of the other and vice versa. In translation, propositions are enacted in a particular language. What operates the difference as marked by the transitivity of each language is the textual sublime.

The task of translation is to move across, the "lation" is not just transitivity in a given text, but, as Leavey indicates, the passage of a "ghostly voice" by which one text haunts another. Here translation functions as an operation of the text's indecidability. Translation puts into practice what is already textually sublime about the text. Without the sublimity, the text would not be translatable. The stark individuality of the text would cut it off entirely from becoming a translated text. Without the sublimity of "lation," only what Allison calls the transfer of propositions through an ideal language would be possible. Translation relies upon an operation of the textual sublime in order to reformulate one text as another, as the juxtaposed translation, as an effect of what Leavey calls "telelation." This interruption of discursivity, this incursion into the limits of the text, this disclosure of the limits that are constituted by closure takes the text beyond itself—not to a higher level, not to a position that subsumes all others, not even to something new and adventuresome, but rather to the text itself. In translation, the text becomes itself *as other*. In translation, the textual sublime is rendered explicit, for translation is the realization of the sublimity of a text as a supplement to itself, as the event of the text as another text—that is, the 'same' text in another language.

(6) In the sixth and final section, three accounts of actual alternatives to deconstruction are offered. To the extent that the text is always a supplement to itself, the deconstructive text also sets off limits to itself as a critical practice. The deconstructive text produces non-deconstructive texts— that is, texts that themselves offer an alternative critical-theoretical product. In this last section, we have included three positions that mark themselves as 'outside' deconstruction, which claim to be *other than* deconstruction. Fynsk, Kinczewski, and Fischer (in the first section) examine what it would mean to be an alternative to deconstruction and show that what is outside deconstruction is already a constitution of deconstruction itself. The claim to otherness is in fact a reaffirmation of the same, for to be other means to determine that from which it is other. Easthope, Wurzer, and Villani show that alterity, conflict, and competition do not necessarily return to the same.

Easthope sets Althusserian structural Marxism against deconstruction. He claims that no matter how much deconstruction may attempt to show the disruption of discursivity in language, nevertheless structures do operate in textual as well as in broader political contexts. These structures with their particular determinations make sense of what is. They organize experience. And they show that language is ultimately, internally, and fundamentally discursive. In effect, the structural Marxian epistemology denies the importance of the textual sublime.

By contrast, following Wurzer, Adorno's aesthetic invokes *das Natur-schöne*—an idea directly associated with the sublime. However, the difference between the traditional German and particularly Kantian conception of the sublime *(das Erhabene)* as a description of the beauty and splendor of nature and the textual sublime needs to be clear. The text is not a representation of nature nor even an expression of nature. The text is also not what nature would be if it could be repeated in all its beauty. The text performs itself as other, as itself an alternative to *das Naturschöne*. In the text, *das Naturschöne* constitutes itself as a limit, as that which the text cannot be—even though *das Naturschöne* might operate as a postulate, description, proposition, or component *of* the text. At the limits of the text are its contexts. Beauty in nature operates where the text both inscribes it and, in another instance, displaces it to another text: an aesthetic text—that is, a text of judgment and the aesthetic itself. *Das Naturschöne* is a manifestation of the textual sublime only insofar as it marginalizes what is thematic in the romantic text. The romantic text introduces *das Naturschöne* as something special, as distinctly absent from the classical text and as occluded in the modern text. But as text the romantic text is no less sublime than any other text.

The poststructural text, according to Villani, is a response to the static structuralist idea of structure as the production of a "savage mind" (Lévi-Strauss), as the "zero degree of writing" (Barthes), as the other of desire or the *nom-du-père* in language (Lacan), or as the metonymical/ metaphorical moment of political economy. Villani's reading of Deleuze's poststructural text shows that the Barthesian zero degree must displace itself as the blank space that makes the next step in any game possible. The game—whether it be checkers, chess, bridge, musical chairs, twenty questions, or the like—always necessitates the next step: the empty space into which the structure will move in order to keep itself going. The poststructuralist text, then, is always becoming what it is not—namely its alternatives. The ultimate and repeatable sublime moment of the text is where and when it becomes other than itself. If poststructuralism is that space of alterity, then deconstruction simply becomes itself by moving toward such a space. The determination of the blank space is the undoing of deconstruction as a critical move. But it is an effect of deconstruction as well. The poststructuralist alternative to deconstruction is its sublime moment, its blank space—namely, the very difference that deconstruction itself scrutinizes, performs, and effects.

In this volume, we have brought together some formulations and dimensions of deconstruction and its practices. We consider whether deconstruction is as such a method, a program, or a formula for textual reading— in relation to philosophy, in relation to criticism, in relation to itself, in relation to translation, and in relation to alternative positions. The textual sublime—as the guiding theme of these essays—marks deconstruction and its differences, signals its identities and alterities, and highlights the subtleties of deconstructive textual readings. If there are to be differences with deconstruction—and there are surely many—they are formulated here as issues, characterized not with hostility, but with sympathy and respect, not with opposition but with careful, crucial, and critical understanding.

Part I

Deconstruction and Criticism

PRELIMINARY REMARKS

In 1979 the Seabury Press published a collection of essays under the title *Deconstruction and Criticism*. That volume has since become recognized as a landmark in the topography of contemporary letters. The controversy associated with deconstruction extends not just to the critical reading of texts, but also to the institution of criticism itself, and beyond, to the university and that genteel tradition of the West—to letters—and all that is signified by "writing" and "reading." Both the more narrow and the more general import of deconstruction are reflected in the following essays by Fynsk, Kinczewski, and Fischer.

In "The Choice of Deconstruction," Christopher Fynsk reflects upon the implications suggested by the title of the eighth annual IAPL conference: "Deconstruction and its Alternatives." As Fynsk points out, the title suggests that deconstruction might be "chosen" by the critic as one method among others, which would deny deconstruction's undoing of such traditional notions as "alternative" and "choice," enshrined as they are in the metaphysics of subjectivity. Thus the very title of an international conference, if accepted without comment, may co-opt the participants into discussing deconstruction in terms that would preclude a genuine appreciation of the issue. This point raises a question that implicates the institution of criticism itself—namely, Should deconstruction be discussed at all in terms other than its own? If so, what terms would constitute a vocabulary agreeable to all? If not, would not any "discussion" have to be itself a deconstructive performance? Inasmuch as deconstruction rejects any notion of "a vocabulary agreeable to all" in the first place, it seems to already decide the issue in its own favor. Or, more accurately, it prevents the issue from even being raised.

Fynsk suggests that an appropriate discussion of deconstruction, which would not play the traditionalist's game of argument and justification, nor lapse into a coy deconstructive performance, would attempt to understand deconstruction as a "passion" that signifies a historical determination. This suggestion brings into play the highly charged relation between deconstruction and its Heideggerian legacy. In Heideggerian terms, deconstruction could be explored as a *Geschick* (or *Geschenk*) of Being—that is, *not* as an alternative among others, but as a determining passion characteristic of a fundamental project of understanding. To affirm deconstruction then, would be to affirm the historical finitude that empowers deconstruction as well as any other interpretive enterprise.

This suggestion carries the discussion beyond the realm of literary criticism to a more philosophical consideration of hermeneutics and ontology. Although such considerations cannot be developed here, Fynsk's essay shows the importance of the philosophical aspects of deconstruction for its role in literary criticism. Although this connection will be examined explicitly in the following chapter, one should note that it seems to be implicit in any discussion of deconstruction or in any deconstructive performance.

Kathryn Kinczewski's article, "Is Deconstruction an Alternative?," takes the same point of departure as Fynsk, but remains within a more literary and linguistic purview. She compares the semiotic analysis of texts with the "alternative" of deconstructive readings. These positions are represented by Riffaterre and de Man, respectively. The issue is whether textual ambiguities can and ought to be structurally mastered (semiotics) or whether they ought to be appreciated as productively unmasterable (deconstruction). Further, there is the question whether semiotics, as a formal theory, can adequately account for the relations between the structures of a text and the moment of understanding that occurs only in a particular reading of the text. Kinczewski agrees with de Man that Riffaterre's semiotics is indeed a reinstantiation of formalism, and that it is inadequate to what actually occurs in reading. The deconstructive strategy, by contrast, insists upon the necessity of an aesthetic moment in interpretation. This presupposes a phenomenal irreducibility of the sign. The materiality of the sign, with its subsequent opacity, is for de Man a necessary darkness against which the illumination of understanding can occur. Where a formalist-semiotic analysis attempts to reduce the arbitrariness of the sign in favor of a structural system (the repetition of a word or a sentence), deconstruction celebrates the "arbitrariness" of the sign as necessary for particular illuminations. In retrospect, the sign is not arbitrary in the formal sense, but is an enabling moment for the possibility of structure per se. Thus, Kinczewski, in accord with de Man, rejects Riffaterre's employment of syllepsis as a means for mastering ambiguity, and upholds instead the "aporia of meaning" that is for de Man the possibility of particular readings, and the impossibility of *the* reading of a text.

Are semiotics and deconstruction "alternatives?" Kinczewski suggests that semiotics might exclude the hermeneutical procedures of deconstruction. However, deconstruction does not exclude semiotics. Rather, deconstruction preserves a semiotic moment within its own strategy, and thus cannot confront semiotics as an "other" in an ablolute sense. The deconstructive strategy, however, is more adequate to the problem of reading insofar as reading is irreducible to structures of repetition and closure.

In "Does Deconstruction Make Any Difference?," Michael Fischer returns to a consideration of the import of deconstruction for existing academic and social institutions. He offers the thesis that, contrary to popular claims for and against deconstructive practice, such practice does not threaten these institutions but makes them more secure. Citing Christopher Norris and J. Hillis Miller, Fischer suggests that the critical edge of deconstruction is addressed to values and concepts that are, in fact, rarely held. This significantly diminishes the revolutionary power that Norris, in particular, claims for deconstruction vis-à-vis existing institutions and traditional values based upon common sense. As Fischer remarks, "Deconstruction fails to explain why one should suspend the 'commonsense position': the motivation, and consequently the force, of deconstruction eludes me." Moreover, contrary to Norris's celebration of deconstruction as a liberation from oppressive conventions, he suggests that interpretive conventions are enabling precisely *because* they are constraining.

Fischer criticizes Miller's claim for deconstruction along similar lines. Where Miller offers deconstruction as a possibility for revising an arbitrary and ungrounded literary curriculum, Fischer notes that he also insists that any revised curriculum would necessarily suffer from an inherent arbitrariness itself. Granting this point, Fischer suggests that it would be best to leave the traditional, historically organized, curriculum as it is, rather than reinforce the illusion of nonarbitrariness that a deconstructively revised framework would promote. Insofar as this illusion is a natural by-product of deconstruction, the implication is that deconstruction simply reinforces the very arbitrariness of convention from which it overtly promises liberation.

A common question emerges from the three essays included in this part—namely, What is the nature of the relation between deconstruction and its other, whether that other is understood as an alternative critical method or the text (or institution) that is being read? Inasmuch as other critical methods are themselves extrapolated in texts, the question can be reduced to the problem of the relationship between deconstruction and the text per se. This relationship is one of sameness without identity: for in no case is deconstruction exclusively other than its text, nor is it a transparent repetition of the text. The essays in part I address, in various contexts, the dilemma of deconstruction as criticism.

                                                                    G.E.A.

1

The Choice of Deconstruction

Christopher Fynsk

"Deconstruction and its Alternatives"—I am surely not the first to pause over this title and ask: To what have we been called with the invitation to address this topic? I find it difficult to consider the choice of deconstruction—the title, after all, asks us to choose, or to entertain the choice—without questioning the stage or the scene that offers this choice.

The title, of course, suggests that the spotlight is on deconstruction. We are attending a premiere of sorts, for this is the first major colloquium in this country, to my knowledge, that has taken deconstruction as the focus of its attention. Of course the sensational quality of this event is tempered by the fact that deconstruction has occupied the institutional scene for well over a decade. But the title suggests that there is something new. It suggests that deconstruction has become an unavoidable alternative—*the* alternative somehow, that which raises the question of alternatives. If there is a sensational quality in the topic of this conference, I would argue that it lies in the fact that it should prompt us to ask, probably with a certain surprise: What situation has brought us to the point where we must choose? Who or what is demanding that we choose? Or another version of this question: Why has the question of deconstruction become so imposing? And who or what is imposing it upon us?

We may certainly read in the title the promise of a certain philosophical liberalism or catholicity. There is no doubt in my mind that with the title "Deconstruction and its Alternatives" the organizers sought to open the conference to those whose engagements or interests lead them to choose against deconstruction, or sought to create a context in which, through the free consideration of alternatives, a genuine choice, or at least a clear assessment, might be made.

5

But there is nevertheless a certain redundancy in the title. Would the freedom of the conference participants to question deconstruction from any number of viewpoints—any viewpoint of their choice—not have been preserved had the title been simply, for example, "Deconstruction"? Is not the invitation to consider alternatives, then, marked by a striking insistence —a desire to reassure the participants of their freedom? But where would that anxiety arise from, unless their freedom had in fact been threatened? Might the offer of alternatives be therefore a kind of *Verneinung* or *dénégation* prompted by the very act of posing deconstruction as an object of investigation? But why would this act prompt an anxious assertion of the continued validity of the academic prerogative of free and disinterested questioning? And would the threat be in deconstruction or in the act of posing deconstruction as an object of study?

I would suggest that both deconstruction, and the act of constituting it as an object of investigation, are the sources of the anxiety I hear in the title. I differentiate these two somewhat abstractly, for it is ultimately impossible to speak of the thing apart from its constitution as the object of a specular attention; but I will use this distinction for the sake of clarity and offer a few schematic notes.

To begin, consider that deconstruction itself is potentially threatening because it cannot be posed as the object of an either/or alternative. To speak of it as *one* entity is already extremely problematic, for the various practices of reading that identify themselves in relation to the term can hardly be identified with one another. (Perhaps I should note that the title of the conference may also be read in these terms: "Deconstruction and its Alternatives" names the multiplicity of versions or translations that constitute deconstruction as a general critical movement. Again, I do not know what the organizers meant with this title; I am analyzing its possible force.)

But should we restrict our analysis to only one usage of the term— that proposed by Derrida, for example, in the course of a reading of Heidegger—we would have to observe that deconstruction, as implying a theory of the constitution of any signifying process, and thus a theory of history and of the subject's implication in that history, cannot be the object of a disinterested theoretical examination. To pretend to stand apart from deconstruction and to assess it from a neutral or undefined position is to assume the position assigned to the subject of representation by the modern metaphysics of subjectivity—the very target of deconstruction. It is to understand deconstruction as a conception or view of the world (*Weltanschauung*) among others—all of which, as Heidegger argued in his essay "The Age of the World View,"[1] find their common ground (and thus the basis for comparison as alternative views) in their anthropological nature, in the fact that they proceed from a representation of man as the subject of representation and thus the measure of truth. Deconstruction, however, defines itself as a critique of the very structure of representation by which the subject assures its position in relation to what is. To represent deconstruction as one method among others that may be set forth within an either/or choice is to suspend its claims or presuppositions and to operate in terms that are radically foreign to it. To pose deconstruction as an alternative is to neutralize it and to preserve or shore up the position of the subject of representation.

The argument I am making here is really quite basic, but its implications are far from self-evident. To take seriously the thought of difference and the critique of representation is to bring into question the very acts of thought or of criticism, as well as the institution in which they are grounded. Deconstruction, as I want to argue, brings the questioner and his or her act of questioning into question. The resistance to deconstruction that is characteristic of its general reception has to do with the fact that it unsettles the secure position offered to the critic by the structure of representation as it has taken form in the modern world—or as it has given form to the modern world through the dominance of what Heidegger calls *Technik*.

The anxiety to which the title of this conference responds—if only in an effort to allay fears—derives, then, from the unsettling nature of the project of deconstruction. The title responds by offering deconstruction as the specular object of the institution's concern (the institution here being the IAPL as one representative of the university: a representative of both philosophy and literature). Institutionalization might in fact be defined in part as such a constitution of a specular object. The anxiety that may be read in the title indicates that the object of theoretical speculation, or "specularization"—they are the same thing in this operation—is particularly threatening. But a surplus of anxiety derives from the operation itself. For the effort to assure the participants of a certain freedom in questioning actually enjoins them to choose. The gesture of invitation that should guard or preserve those whom it invites from any binding imposition also constrains them to entertain a choice and either to commit themselves or to remain exposed in their neutrality or lack of position. As the title of what is presented at this conference it hides another sentence. "Here are your alternatives," it says: a phrase that one would expect to hear only in situations of urgency—when a decision must be made, when one is cornered. The title is a veiled demand—a demand that may be traced finally to the demand for justification that speaks in the principle of reason as Derrida, following Heidegger, has recently analyzed it.[2] The gesture that would reiterate freedom, then, binds. And although the reference comes a bit too easily these days, I think it would not be abusive to ask whether the title belongs to that category of speech acts that are constitutive of the double bind.

In any case, the title exposes the illusion of freedom that is part of the structure of representation and that would only have been better dissimulated had the title of the conference been "Deconstruction." As soon as deconstruction, or anything for that matter, is posed as an object of theoretical representation, a demand is made. The academic institution works powerfully and effectively in dissimulating that demand even as it functions as part of the apparatus that enforces it.

If deconstruction appears cagey, it does so because it skirts, or delimits, that demand in answering to what that which the principle of reason excludes or dissimulates. This refusal of deconstruction to account for itself or to justify itself is most visible in relation to the question of politics. One may indeed read the refusal in terms of a kind of escape from political responsibility; but such a reading ignores the critique of the fundamental categories of political thinking that traverses Derrida's work and that has been articulated recently and very forcefully by Lacoue-Labarthe and Nancy.[3] The analysis of the foundations of the political order in a discourse that disrupts the norms of conventional theoretical practice within the university is certainly a political act. (And I would add that it is an act that does not exclude more traditional *prises de position*—as one can see in Derrida's work over the past decade on the university.)

Clearly, this example shows that the apparent retreat or withdrawal from what generally passes for responsibility does not imply that the thinker who has chosen deconstruction is refusing to choose, and seeking to retain, the illusory freedom traditionally allowed to the philosopher or to those involved with literature. There *is* a choice; but it is not a free or undetermined one—or it is free in a sense that we have yet to think. We hear the choice in Derrida's frequent reference in recent years to a double affirmation: an affirmation that recites itself as it marks its relation to that which is affirmed (that *of* which it is an affirmation, and which makes it possible) but which in its alterity escapes objectification or constantly reserves itself, thus constantly calling for the affirmation. The abyss that we glimpse here belongs to what Heidegger calls the hermeneutic circle: the affirmation (and this is also one of Heidegger's terms: he speaks of *Selbstbehauptung*) opens, initially, to an engagement that has already been made, and thus the affirmation takes form in a structure of repetition.

These are notions that cannot be explored fully in the short time available here. But in order to begin to explicate them, and in order to suggest how deconstruction poses the necessity of thinking the *situated* nature of the act of thinking or questioning, I would like to stay within Heidegger's terms and suggest that we consider the critic's or philosopher's choice in relation to his or her passion. (And I am moving now from the choice of deconstruction to deconstruction's choice.) When

Heidegger comes to describe the necessity of situating the thinker and the necessity of bringing the act of thinking or questioning into question along with what is to be thought, he argues that we must be prepared to think knowledge as a passion. In the opening paragraphs of "What is Metaphysics?," for example, Heidegger argues that, because a metaphysical questioning must embrace the totality of what is (and as I argued in this context several years ago,[4] Derrida is doing no less, but also more, and in a way that makes it paradoxically less), the questioning itself must be taken up into the question. (Heidegger reiterates this motif with some frequency in the second essay of his *Nietzsche*, "The Eternal Return of the Same," when he attempts to show how the affirmation of eternal recurrence carries the thinker into what is to be thought, and thus into a repetitive affirmation. Were it not necessary to pass through Heidegger, Derrida, and perhaps Deleuze and Klossowski, I would suggest simply that the choice of deconstruction is to be thought in relation to what Nietzsche calls *amor fati.*)

But to continue with Heidegger's argument in "What is Metaphysics?," Heidegger writes the following after asserting the necessity of carrying the questioner into the questioning:

> From this we can conclude that metaphysical inquiry must be posed as a whole and from the essential position of the existence *(Dasein)* that questions. We are questioning, here and now, for ourselves. Our existence, in the community of researchers, teachers, and students, is determined by science. What happens to us, essentially, in the grounds of our existence, when science becomes our passion *(Leidenschaft)*?[5]

Heidegger is suggesting here that the passion for questioning is the mark of the questioner's implication in the act of questioning. "Dasein" names essentially the human situation in the event of history, and no thought of the history or topology of Being can proceed from any other topos. That knowledge should be a passion means that knowledge proceeds from within the structure of existence and as an existential project of Being. Passion marks the implication of Dasein in the activity of science (which in the sense Heidegger gives to the term is a relation to what is in its being).

The term 'passion' should not come as a surprise if we keep in mind the argument of the existential analytic. Human interest in metaphysical questioning—the human need and passion for knowledge—belongs to a concern for the possibility of Dasein. This concern defines the structural unity of Dasein's finite transcendence. The most intimate human interest, as Heidegger argues in his reading of Kant, focuses upon human finitude—its historical determination, where history is understood in relation to the ontological question of temporality. To bring to the foreground this interested or impassioned nature of philosophical questioning would then be to remark the necessary and essential finitude of this questioning (its determined or historical nature)—a finitude that cannot be mastered or overcome.

Indeed the strangeness of Heidegger's text—its unsettled, repetitive, even fragmentary nature—has to do precisely with such an assumption of the finitude from which it proceeds. After naming "care" the unity of the transcendental structure of the need for the comprehension of Being, Heidegger writes the following:

> In any case it remains to be considered that the working out of the inner-most essence of finitude required for the establishment of metaphysics must itself always be basically finite and can never become absolute. The only conclusion one can draw from this is that reflection on finitude, always to be renewed, can never succeed through a mutual playing off, or mediating equalization, of standpoints in order finally and in spite of everything to give us an absolute knowledge of finitude, a knowledge that is surreptitiously posited as being "true in itself."[6]

The passion for questioning answers to and turns upon this impossibility of inquiry securing for itself the position of subject as defined by the metaphysics of subjectivity. It is Nietzsche's lesson that this passion might be understood not as the experience of a lack or a negativity, but rather as an affirmation—an affirmation that does not lead the subject back to itself, but rather leads the subject to remark affirmatively the determination that gives it to be. A project of Being would be nothing other than the affirmation of an affirmation—the writing of a passion.

The resistance to deconstruction to which I have referred is a resistance to the notion of a writing that marks its own disappropriating conditions, and this, with increasing frequency, in the foregrounding of the passion in which it takes form—as in Derrida's La Carte Postale.[7] It is a resistance to a discourse that seeks to hold itself open to difference or alterity—to mark its finitude—as it holds in question the structures of closure and exclusion that are constituted whenever a discourse pretends to a mastery (always ideal) over a domain of what is.

I have left the term 'passion' somewhat open thus far in referring to Heidegger, because I would argue that Heidegger represses or elides certain dimensions of what he names with the term. He elides in particular the phenomena of mimetic desire, rivalry, and identification: phenomena that clearly structure in part Heidegger's own text, as one may see rapidly in his readings of Nietzsche and Hölderlin. A term like 'mimetic desire,' of course, must be redefined philosophically. But Heidegger's thought, if we follow certain leads given by Derrida among others, offers the means to think a term like mimesis (even though we are dealing here with the unthought of this thought) in terms other than those of the metaphysics of subjectivity, and to think together the various strands of the complex history of this term, almost all of which are knotted together in the text of Plato. I refer not only to mimesis in the original sense of the appearance or appearing of *physis*, and in what Heidegger describes as the derived sense of imitation, but also to the forms of identification that Plato warns against in the third book of his *Republic*.[8]

Heidegger offers the means of describing mimesis in terms of formal properties of art, and thus the means of accounting for the *conditions* of phenomena like capture or fascination. We see such a description, I would argue, in Heidegger's definition of the formal composition of the work of art in his essay "The Origin of the Work of Art." And by pressing those moments in the essay where Heidegger defines the finitude of Being in the necessity of truth's posing itself in the work, in the work's *Gestalt*, we recognize in the formal conditions that Heidegger is describing the presence of what Derrida has called the trace structure, or writing. These conditions, following Heidegger again, constitute the very possibility of reading the work in which they are set forth (and according to Heidegger, the work is a work precisely by virtue of such a setting forth). The work creates its readers, or "preservers," to use Heidegger's term. The reader's or spectator's fascination is nothing other than the opening of the reader's eye—the encounter with the conditions of the work's signifying structure. The work's address creates the possibility of affirmative response.

Unfortunately, it is impossible to develop here Heidegger's argument or even to begin what we might term its deconstruction—that is to say, a questioning of Heidegger's claims for the gathered, unified nature of the work in terms of Heidegger's own description in that essay of the finitude of truth, read in the light of the problematic of the trace structure. But a deconstructive reading would foreground Heidegger's claim that the event of truth in the work of art is a historical event—the event of history itself, or the opening of history—and it would seek the material conditions of that event (since in Heidegger's argument truth does not happen before or apart from its inscription in what he calls the earth: the inscription is initial). For Heidegger, art takes its possibility from language as *Dichtung*, and thus what we would search for, I think, would be what de Man has called the materiality of the letter, or what Derrida has called *écriture*, though I pose these terms as questions and would hesitate to identify them since the two notions of the materiality of language may well not be identical. The materiality in question, in any case, cannot be understood simply as substantial being or as a brute reality. It is the condition of what is often referred to, dogmatically, as the real.

In these last moments, I have raced through terms that require a far more patient attention: mimesis, history, writing, the real. But my aim has been simply to trace out some of the terms for understanding the assertion that the choice of deconstruction, or deconstruction's choice, issues from a passion that must be thought as the sign of a historical determination. The choice of deconstruction is an affirmation of history and as such it gives itself up to the possibility of dispossession and change. The practices of deconstruction as they are currently undertaken can hardly lay exclusive claim to the affirmation or choice to which I refer— they can hardly claim to be *the* voices or representatives of history (nor could they want to for reasons that should be obvious). Deconstruction opens upon the question of history—its affirmation moves within that question, but does not pretend to answer it: its answers simply repose it in the most rigorous ways possible. Surely there are other ways of moving within the question of history—just as the thought of finitude seems to suggest that there is more than one history. Any act of questioning may open a new history—though one can never choose in this matter. The choice of deconstruction is to refuse to stop questioning.

2

Is Deconstruction an Alternative?

Kathryn Kinczewski

Undertaking a rigorous investigation of signs and signification, semiotics produces a discipline which, ultimately, reveals the fundamental contradictions of the signifying process as we understand it. Semiotics leads, necessarily, to a critique of semiotics, to a perspective which shows the errors of its ways. But that perspective is never a viable alternative. It is not a position from which one could undertake an alternative analysis of signs and systems of signs, for the notion of analysis, of explanation, of production of models are all part of the semiotic perspective, and to undertake any of them is immediately to revert to that perspective. The alternative, then, is not a discipline, not another mode of analysis, but acts of writing, acts of displacement, play which violates language and rationality.

—Jonathan Culler, *The Pursuit of Signs:*
Semiotics, Literature, Deconstruction, p.42

Is deconstruction an alternative? "An alternative to what?" we might inquire at the very outset of this discussion, for an alternative consists of "an offer or statement of two things, so that if one is taken, the other must be left out" (Webster's *New International Dictionary*). Can deconstructive strategies of reading be considered to be a viable alternative to other methods of inquiry? Culler's answer, based on a reading of the above passage in *The Pursuit of Signs: Semiotics, Literature, Deconstruction*, would seem to be, and quite categorically, no! And yet the title of Jonathan Culler's work does read as follows: *The Pursuit of Signs: Semiotics, Literature, Deconstruction*. Wlad Godzich, for his part, in his introductory preface to the republication of Paul de Man's *Blindness and Insight*,[1] chooses to begin by addressing Michael Riffaterre's notion of a descriptive system in order to set Paul de Man's theoretical enterprise against a semiotic one—that is, against a method of inquiry that passes for possessing a certain amount of scientific rigor and that does not, as a 'science' of semiotics, put into question its own mode of inquiry. In de Man's essay on Riffaterre's work, originally entitled "Hypogram and Inscription: Michael Riffaterre's Poetics of Reading,"[2] de Man considers Riffaterre's "theory of poetic semiotics" to be "a model case for examining if and how the poetics of literary form can be made compatible with the hermeneutics of reading" (HI, 31). Based on these diverse modes of inquiry, are we not drawn to consider a semiotic reading as, possibly, an alternative to deconstructive strategies of reading? What is it that runs the risk of being "left out" in the alternative wager? On this matter de Man writes:

> More is at stake in this than the didactics of literary instruction or the possibility of literary history; at stake, first and foremost, is the category of the aesthetic as guardian of the rational cognition it appears to subvert and, beyond this, the destiny of cognition itself as it runs the risk of having to confront texts without the shelter of aesthetic distance (HI, 31).

An answer to the question, "Does either a semiotic reading or a deconstructive one constitute an alternative to be chosen?," might be sought in a study of de Man's summary review of Riffaterre's poetics of reading, which readily develops into a deconstructive reading of Riffaterre's writing style. The notion of an alternative (semiotics/deconstruction) will thus be explained, reworked, and, ultimately, questioned. Does this theoretical conjuncture constitute an alternative for literary theory and criticism? Is it a viable alternative?

As deconstructive critics, we could go back to de Man and to his notion that "at stake, first and foremost, is the category of the aesthetic as guardian of the rational cognition it appears to subvert" (HI, 31). The very concept of the alternative must be explained, reworked, and, ultimately, questioned. Should we continue to entertain the notion of an alternative or should we shift to an opposition to be reconciled dialectically—as Riffaterre's model of two readings would have it: a binary system in which the proper (intertextual) reading is said to cancel out the improper (ungrammatical, contextual) reading by means of syllepsis? Or as de Man would have it, does a deconstructive reading not persist in questioning "why the issue of methodology had to arise in the first place?"[3] Godzich writes: "For the practice of any methodological approach can be self-governing, whereas the question of the necessity of methodology raises the issue of what reading is" ("Introduction," p. xix).

Apparently, the theoretical imperative couched in de Man's deconstructive readings renders impossible any dialectical resolution to the alternatives and/or oppositions characteristic of semiotics and deconstruction. And yet, if an alternative approach could resolve contemporary literary debates, something would of necessity have to be left out: that is, something would be literally "out of place," and thus eradicated, effaced, forgotten. This broaches what de Man calls a challenge to understanding "that always again demands to be read." It also calls to mind the *Verrückung* (*déplacement*, shifting) of which Heidegger speaks in *What Is A Thing?*, especially in his opening remarks on "Philosophical and Scientific Questioning." He writes: "If one takes the every day representation as the sole standard of all things, then philosophy is always something deranged (*verrücktes*). This shifting (*Verrückung*) of the attitude of thought can be accomplished only after a jolt (*Ruck*).[4] The French translation of Heidegger's text is even more explicit: "*Si l'on tient la représentation quotidienne pour l'unique mesure de toutes choses, alors la philosophie est toujours quelque chose de déplacé. Ce déplacement qu'est l'attitude de la pensée ne peut être pris en charge que dans un écartement violent.*"[5] The need for something to be left out, when that "something" is nothing less than "the attitude of thought" that "always again demands to be read," produces a considerable amount of logical tension. In order to investigate and explore the validity of an alternative approach to contemporary discussions, let us consider Riffaterre's "theory of poetic semiotics" and de Man's "allegories of reading."

A number of issues arise in attempting to assimilate a semiotic poetics and a hermeneutics. The practice of reading and the theory of literature require a certain aesthetic in order to bring them together. Riffaterre's shift from structural stylistics' to a semiotics and, most recently, to a "hermeneutics of poetry"[6] and de Man's shift from a hermeneutic approach to a rhetoric of reading establishes the conditions for an analysis of "Sign and Symbol in Hegel's *Aesthetics*"[7] and "Hegel and the Sublime" (forthcoming). Riffaterre's assertive claim that "my sole aim is to enable all readers to follow the demonstrations based on texts" (*Semiotics of Poetry*, p. ix) is itself jeopardized by his own rather obsessive compulsion to integrate the hermeneutic activity of reading within his semiotic enterprise. De Man, for his part, seems relieved to finally ("at long last") identify Riffaterre's blind spot: namely, his "refusal to acknowledge the textual inscription of semantic determinants within a non-determinable system of figuration" (HI, 41).

De Man questions the compatibility of a poetics and a reading, stating that "a correct descriptive observation leads to fallacious hermeneutic conclusions" (HI, 43). However is not de Man's account of Riffaterre not also aberrant in its hermeneutic conclusions? Or does de Man's critique of Riffaterre's theory of poetic semiotics not set itself off from a discourse within which the very possibility of opting between a hermeneutics of poetry and a semiotics of poetry (or between a hermeneutics and a poetics of reading; between a theory of reading and a *paideia* of literature) is not itself addressed? Does the deconstructive maneuver, accomplished only after a jolt (a *Ruck*, "dans un écartement violent")—that distances itself from a discourse that fails to take into account a certain aesthetic needed to articulate the homogeneity between poetics and hermeneutics— thus avoid the errors of the semiotic perspective? The very limits of the distinction, which cannot be reduced to an opposition (between semiotics/hermeneutics or between a theory of reading/a *paideia* of literature), turns on the unmasterable distinction between the necessity and the possibility of allowing oneself what de Man has called "the shelter of aesthetic distance."

In a number of articles such as "Sémiotique intertextuelle: L'Interprétant," "Syllepsis," "L'Intertexte inconnu," "Interpretation and Undecidability,"[8] Riffaterre valiantly attempts to reconcile an aesthetics and a poetics of literature by proposing a method of literary study "that allows for a measure of theoretical rigor and generality (and which is therefore, to speak from an academic point of view, teachable) while leaving intact, or even enhancing, the aesthetic appreciation or the potential for historical insight that the work provides." This approach, however, never questions the phenomenality of reading as such. Instead, by means of recourse to the persistant persuasive power of a common aesthetic, Riffaterre tends to confuse a phenomenal, experiential, and empirical event with a nonphenomenal lingusitic structure. This blurs the distinction between a phenomenological (Husserlian) theory of language and a semiotic (Saussurean) one.

Is it not conceivable that Riffaterre's only too frequent recourse to a certain "consensus omnium" style of argument invites us to challenge the authority of this common aesthetic? To what extent does the tension that arises between a theory of reading and a *paideia* of literature reflect the systematic undoing of understanding? To what extent does the methodological rigor of a theory of reading produce a kind of "teaching of ignorance"[9] which systematically reenacts a deconstructive allegory of the undoing of understanding by reasserting the unmasterable distinction between meaning and signification characteristic of the sign? To what extent does a *paideia* of literature necessitate a certain propadeutic that, with relentless rigor, reveals a number of distinctions that remain obfuscated by a more general (and more appealingly teachable) theory of reading? And how is this unmasterability between the necessity and the possibility of definitive readings wedded, so to speak, with the strange bedfellows that are semiotics and deconstruction?

Thus de Man's critique of Riffaterre:

> In so far as it leads to the limits of its own theory, semiotics gives rise to a kind of interpretive activity, a Derridean *double science*, a deconstructive mode of reading, which works both within and against it. Deconstruction enjoys announcing the impossibility of the semiotic activity it inhabits as it undertakes the task it has set itself ... The tense interplay between the opposed yet inseparable activities of semiotics and deconstruction is already a major source of energy in literary studies, and it would be rash indeed to predict when or how its dominance will end (Jonathan Culler, *The Pursuit of Signs*, p. 43)

In "Hypogram and Inscription," originally published as a *Diacritics* review article, de Man regards Riffaterre's "entire enterprise as a sustained theoretical effort to integrate reading into the formal description of the text without exploding its borders" (HI, 31). According to de Man:

> All formalist theories of poetry sooner or later have to confront a similar problem: their adequation to the phenomenally realized aspects of their topic make them highly effective as a descriptive discipline, but at the cost of understanding. Formalism ... can only produce a stylistics (or a poetics) and not a hermeneutics of literature and it remains deficient in trying to account for the relationship between these two approaches (HI, 30-31).

Furthermore, although many have charted Riffaterre's theoretical itinerary in terms of a linear development from a stylistics in the *Essais de stylistique structurale* (Paris: Flammarion, 1971) to a semiotics in the *Semiotics of Poetry* (Bloomington: Indiana University Press, 1978) and finally to a hermeneutics of poetry in *La production du texte* (Paris: Seuil, 1979) as well as in the more recent articles cited above, de Man retraces the development of the Riffaterrean theoretical model only to find a reformulation of the initial formal postulate ("the determined, stable principle of meaning in its full phenomenal and cognitive sense" [p. 26]). De Man writes: "we in fact never left the field of formalist stylistics and the detour through semiotics has been an assimilation of semiotics to stylistics rather than the reverse" (HI, 39).

With reference to Riffaterre's "La trace de l'intertexte", de Man argues that "the system undone is that of the opposition between an aleatory (random) and a necessary intertextual relationship" (HI, 43). This very opposition that deconstructs Riffaterre's entire semiotic enterprise also provides an insightful narrative concerning the status of contemporary literary studies. Riffaterre repeatedly argues in favor of "the strict determination of textual markers," or in favor of rhetorical categories that are determined by grammatical structures, and the "imperative coercion of definitive readings" (see de Man, HI 35, 45, and 41, respectively). However, as Riffaterre is wont to say in his "Conclusion" to the *Semiotics of Poetry:*

> Reading is also unstable, and the interpretation is never final, because the text cannot be corrected or amended, and the ungrammaticalities, however, revealing they may be, however hermeneutically indicative, are still an obstacle (whether the obstacle blocks understanding or just looks like an abnormality, an error, a violation of the code rules). Because these ungrammaticalities threaten language as representation, the reader continually seeks relief by getting away from the dubious words, back to safe reality (or to a social consensus as to reality) [p. 165].

The opposition (aleatory/necessary) that structures Riffaterre's theory of poetic semiotics recalls a similar opposition that distinguishes between the semiotic and the symbolic function of art in Hegel's *Aesthetics.* As characteristic of the sign, Hegel insists upon "the *arbitrariness* of the relationship between the sensory component *necessarily* involved in any signification and the intended meaning" ("Sign and Symbol in Hegel," p. 766; emphasis mine). The symbolic function of art (with Hegel's theory of the aesthetic being predicated on a theory of art as symbolic) "consists precisely in the connection, the affinity and the concrete interpretation of meaning and of form" [*Aesthetics*, I, 395]. "*Das Symbol*," writes Hegel, "*ist nun zunächst ein Zeichen*," wherein "*zunächst*" can be translated by "next" or "first of all, chiefly, above all." One would be hard put to decide whether Hegel privileges the sign over the symbol, or vice versa. Undecidability reigns. Although, as de Man points out, " '*Das Zeichen,*' " says Hegel, "*muss für etwas Grosses erklärt werden*" —"the sign must be proclaimed to something great" ("Sign and Symbol in Hegel," p. 767). In Riffaterre's writings, the locus of undecidability (aleatory/necessary) is transmitted by a certain compulsion to repeat, redefine, and reformulate the crucial distinction between meaning and significance. The stakes are high, for the burden of Riffaterre's theory of poetic semiotics rests upon a full explanation of the way a poetic text carries meaning.

It would not be farfetched to say that Riffaterre's semiotic theory is predicated on a series of binary oppositions such as the following: mimesis/semiosis; first reading stage (heuristic)/second reading stage (retroactive, hermeneutic); practice of reading/theory of semiotics; poetics/hermeneutics. Another opposition to which Riffaterre might be less apt to acquiesce is that of a formalist, descriptive discipline (*paideia*)/"the textual inscription of semantic determinants within a non-determinable system of figuration."

Riffaterre sets up oppositions (which ought to be dialectically resolvable, culminating with the reader "converted to a proper reading when the structural equivalences become apparent all at once, in a blaze of revelation"—*Semiotics of Poetry*, p. 166) that are deconstructed (on the level of a theoretical model) by the specificity of a certain strategy of writing. De Man, for his part, in "Hypogram and Inscription," focuses on Riffaterre's reiterative attempts to bridge the gap between his magisterial theory of poetic semiotics and the textual strategies employed, the process of textual inscription; or, in other words, which is not the same thing, between signifying procedures and significance, poetics and hermeneutics.

Taking the hypogram (or paragram) as Riffaterre's theoretical model, de Man quotes from de Saussure's notes—this being the source of undecidability between anagram, paragram, and hypogram—in order to demonstrate the proximity in meaning of *hypographein* to the rhetorical figure *prosopopeia* [from *prosopon*, "mask or face," and *poein*]. De Man writes, "[Saussure] seems to be disturbed by the meaning of *hypographein* as 'signature,' but he also mentions a 'more special, though more widespread meaning as—to underscore by means of makeup the features of a face—(*souligner au moyen du fard les traits du visage*)'" (HI, 44). In Saussure's theoretical framework, the hypogram "underscores a name, a word, by trying to repeat its syllable, and thus giving it another, artificial, mode of being added, so to speak, to the original mode of being of the word" (HI, 44). The opposition between a proper, concrete meaning and a supplementary, artificial, figural one is precisely that which syllepsis attempts to reconcile. Nor is it without interest that syllepsis, a rhetorical trope, has been invoked in Riffaterre's more recent writings as a kind of go-between that has been called upon to mediate between Riffaterre's predominant theoretical borrowings from Saussure (i.e., the notion of the hypogram) and Charles Sanders Peirce (i.e., the notion of the interpretant). This completes Peirce's triadic semiotic model of logic, grammar, and rhetoric. However, we have come far afield from the realm of unproblematic, dyadic meaning—a grammar.

It is not surprising that Riffaterre follows with *A Grammar of Descriptive Poetry* and a *Typology of Intertextuality*. Riffaterre consistently maintains that grammar and rhetoric are distinct linguistic systems. This distinction becomes problematic when Riffaterre tries to reduce rhetorical figures to a typology of tropes (see, for example, his almost derisive use of syllepsis or catechresis) or when he evokes contempt for the widespread notion that the characteristic of poetic signification lies in its ambiguity: *"c'est-à-dire,"* he writes, *"l'empiètement d'un signifié sur l'autre pour un même signifiant"* (*La production du texte*, p. 29; emphasis mine). And yet the violent coercion of one *"signifié"* (one meaning) as it vies with another meaning, encroaching (cf. *"empiéter"*) upon the other's terrain so as to appropriate (*"empiéter"* also means "to usurp," "to arrogate to oneself certain rights that one does not possess") a single, unified meaning from a potentially polysemic signifier (this being its random, aleatory aspect) is part and parcel of a dramatically disruptive linguistic event that Riffaterre seeks to contain within certain well-defined perimeters. The threat of an ambiguous undecidability is to be held in check by the figure of syllepsis. Riffaterre writes:

> "Syllepsis" [is] the trope that consists in understanding the same word in two different ways at the same time, one meaning being literal or primary, the other figurative. The second meaning is not just different from and incompatible with the first: it is tied to the first as its polar opposite or the way the reverse of a coin is bound to the obverse—the *hymen* as *unbroken* membrane and as a *breaking through* of the barrier. The fact that *hymen* is also metaphorical in both its meanings is irrelevant to its undecidability. What makes it undecidable is not that it is an image but that it embodies a structure, that is, the syllepsis ("Syllepsis," p. 629; Riffaterre's emphasis).

A textual undecidability is thus domesticated by a descriptive formalism, but at the cost of understanding. Riffaterre substitutes a *structural* account for an aporia of meaning, as well he must if he is to remain faithful to his theory of poetic *semiotics*. Eco writes in *A Theory of Semiotics* (a work repeatedly cited by Riffaterre), "Semiotics treats subjects of semiotic acts in [this] way: either they can be defined in terms of semiotic structures or . . . they do not exist at all" (Eco, p. 316). And yet, Riffaterre seemingly goes out of his way to incorporate the theoretical insights of Saussure and Peirce within his semiotic enterprise, allowing them to *pierce* through the framework of his theory but only to the extent that Saussure's or Peirce's *breakthroughs* do not entirely *break through*, and thereby endanger, certain articles of faith of his magisterial poetics of reading.

Let us take an example. Reading for Riffaterre is often compared to puzzle-solving. He writes: "Suddenly the puzzle is solved, everything falls into place, indeed the whole poem ceases to be descriptive, ceases to be a sequence of mimetic signs, and becomes but a single sign, perceived from the end back to its given as a harmonious whole, wherein nothing is loose, wherein every word refers to one symbolic focus" (*Semiotics of Poetry*, p. 12). Riffaterre's appropriation (usurpation, *"empiètement"*) of certain theoretical notions (such as the hypogram or the interpretant) appears both entirely arbritrary—indeed, not only do many of his theoretical footnotes seem to provide little support for his theory of poetic semiotics,[10] some even confuse all the more a particularly fine point he is attempting to make—and nevertheless somehow coerced, necessary.

Although Riffaterre *says* that his "sole aim is to enable all readers to follow the demonstrations based on texts," his texts can be seen to *mean* otherwise and thus to dramatize an allegorical narrative by confronting the theory with the practice of reading. Riffaterre's initial theoretical axiom ("To put it simply, a poem says one thing and means another," *Semiotics of Poetry*, p. 1) can be seen to affect his own magisterial readings to the extent that he is no longer in control of the rhetorical trope (or "syllepsis") that he *says* "sums up the duality of the text's message":

> And now for a final rephrasing of my definition: *Syllepsis is a word understood in two different ways at once, as mean-and as significance.* And therefore, because it sums up the duality of the text's message—its semantic and semiotic faces—syllepsis is the literary sign par excellence.[11]

Riffaterre's compulsion to repeat the crucial distinction between meaning and significance lays bare the unbridgeable gap that separates *Zeichen/ Sinn/Bedeutung* (for Frege), the representamen/ interpretant/object (for Peirce), or the text/interpretant/intertext (for Raffaterre). To paraphrase de Man, far from closing off the tropological system, irony (that which says one thing and means another) enforces the repetition of its aberration.[12] For it is indeed ironic that Riffaterre's "final rephrasing" of his definition of syllepsis as the literary sign par excellence in effect points to "the trope contrary to the syllepsis, namely, the antanaclasis—*repeating the same word but with different meanings.*" Riffaterre goes out of his way to make this point in the very article that claims to demonstrate the sovereign status of syllepsis as the literary sign par excellence. Indeed, Riffaterre cannot but fail *not to leave out*—given the methodological rigor of his argument—what, with a certain ironic necessity *should have been left out* (that is, the moment of antanaclasis)if his theory of poetic semiotics were to remain theoretically intact in that everything would produce "but a single sign, perceived from the end back to its given as a harmonious whole, wherein nothing is loose, wherein every word refers to one symbolic focus." The logical economy of Riffaterre's theoretical enterprise invests heavily in a sylleptic structure. Syllepsis ought to produce an "epiphany of semiosis" in which every word refers to "one symbolic focus" (*Semiotics of Poetry*, p. 12), bringing about, instead, a modification of his semiotic theory. "*Il n'y a évidemment de scandale,*" writes Derrida in "Structure, Sign and Play in the Discourse of the Human Sciences," "*qu'à l'intérieur d'un système. . . .*" The moment of antanaclasis accomplishes the Heideggerian jolt (*Ruck, écartement violent*).[13]

The didactic successes of Riffaterre's poetics are compromised by his repetitive compulsion to respond to the challenge to understanding (a reading) that his own structural poetics brought about. At this point, the theory and the practice of reading no longer seem so exquisitely suited to one another but might more accurately be seen to vie with each other in an endless *lutte à mort*, an endless death struggle. And this unmasterable struggle merely repeats the tension that persists between the sign and the symbol inherent in language and, *a fortiori*, in the current polemics concerning literary theory and literary experience.

3

Does Deconstruction
Make Any Difference?

Michael Fischer

Despite the vast commentary on deconstruction, it is still not clear whether Derrida and his American allies expect practical results from their theorizing. As in any movement that has met with vitriolic opposition, the claims of deconstructionists reflect the often fierce accusations that these critics are answering. When self-described "conservative" opponents equate deconstruction with terrorism, the decline of the humanities, and the destruction of traditional values, many advocates emphasize its ludic, purely pleasurable fascination with the freeplay of language. The charge that the movement is dangerous thus generates the reassuring, often bemused, reply that it is not nihilistic, destructive, and so on.

Still other critics of deconstruction pounce on this defense as an admission of failure. For them, deconstruction is consequently the irresponsible pastime of jaded, escapist professors at elite universities, securely beyond the erosion of budgets, writing skills, and enrollments. To refute the charge that deconstruction is harmless, sympathizers urge that much more is at stake than the entertainment of a few professors—in fact, everything from the revival of literary criticism to political freedom. What at first looked like a child's toy turns out to be a real tool for tearing down repressive conventions and building a new kind of literary criticism.

Each of these responses uncovers something in deconstruction—its often alarming rhetoric, its love of verbal play, its frequent disregard for specific educational and political problems, its constructive intentions. Yet because each of these responses isolates one moment in deconstruction, none of them does justice to deconstruction as a whole, or, more

23

exactly, as self-generated, endless questioning. Pictured as a process, deconstruction is neither destructive nor harmless. Instead of threatening existing institutions, it leaves them more secure.

My examples of deconstruction here will be two texts that deserve more attention than they have thus far received: Christopher Norris's *Deconstruction Theory and Practice* (1982), a sympathetic study of Derrida and his American critics and advocates, and J. Hillis Miller's "The Function of Rhetorical Study at the Present Time" (1979), an application of deconstruction to the curriculum. Each seems to me symptomatic of larger tendencies in the work of Paul de Man, Geoffrey Hartman, and Jacques Derrida.

At first glance, Norris attributes enormous power to deconstruction, calling it in his introduction a technique for "making trouble" and "the active antithesis of everything that criticism ought to be if one accepts its traditional values and concepts" (xii).[1] He repeatedly praises its "unsettling power" (70), "exhilarating spirit" (92), and "liberating force" (21). In his account, deconstruction is tirelessly on the move, challenging, unmasking, combating, attacking, unfixing, undercutting, shaking, dislodging, wrenching, breaking down, defying, questioning, transforming, undoing, disturbing, undermining, annulling, unsettling, dismantling, collapsing, transgressing, opposing, resisting, subverting, and inverting. The targets of all this "perverse," "devastating," "dangerous," "sinister," "disconcerting" activity are nothing less than "every normal and comfortable habit of thought" (xii), "everything that criticism ought to be if one accepts its traditional values and concepts" (xii), "the whole traditional edifice of Western attitudes to thought and language" (29), "age-old conceptual limits" (57), "every last vestige of philosophic truth and certainty" (77), "the normative constraints of effective communication" (113), "the solemn inventions of Anglo-American academic discourse" (113), and "all proprietory limits" (114).

It is this kind of talk that has alarmed so-called conservative critics of deconstruction, especially historical scholars, who understandably see in such comments a massive repudiation of their work. But these critics of deconstruction resemble irate moviegoers who walk out on a film that is just getting started. After giving deconstruction such power, Norris proceeds to strip away its force, or at least to qualify its impact on the "traditional edifice" it seems to topple. In his view, deconstruction is "not to be taken as wholly undermining" the objects of its critique (48), whether Rousseau in the *Grammatology* or structuralism in "Structure, Sign, and Play" (deconstruction is not " 'post-structuralist' in the sense of displacing or invalidating the structuralist project" [54]). More generally:

> Deconstruction neither denies nor really affects the commonsense view that
> language exists to communicate meaning. It *suspends* that view for its own
> specific purpose of seeing what happens when the writs of convention no
> longer run. . . . This is not to say that [the deconstructionists'] questions are
> trivial or totally misconceived. They are . . . questions that present them-
> selves *compulsively* as soon as one abandons the commonsense position.
> But language continues to communicate, as life goes on, despite all the prob-
> lems thrown up by sceptical thought [128].

Skeptics since David Hume, in short, have realized that "life could scarcely
carry on if people were to act on their conclusions" (xii); deconstruction
is "likewise an activity of thought which cannot be consistently acted
on—that way madness lies—but which yet possesses an inescapable
rigour of its own" (xii).

These are the disclaimers that have provoked many activist critics to
conclude that deconstruction is therefore worthless, a fad that only a
dwindling number of well-established professors have the luxury to enjoy.
These opponents of deconstruction are as impatient as the conservative
readers mentioned earlier. I take seriously Norris's further point that the
deconstructionist's questions are neither "trivial" nor "totally misconceived," that they "present themselves *compulsively* as soon as one aban-
dons the commonsense position" (128). There is a potentially constructive side to deconstruction to which I will return.

But first I should note that my own dissatisfaction with deconstruction
begins with Norris's emphasis on "compulsively," which in my view tries
unsuccessfully to add urgency to an enterprise that lacks it. Deconstruction fails to explain why one should suspend the "commonsense position":
the motivation, and consequently the force, of deconstruction eludes me.

In part, deconstruction lacks a compelling rationale because it offers
liberation not from common sense but from extreme positions hardly
anyone holds. The movement is self-generated in that it sets up the targets
it knocks down. Commenting on Derrida's ascription of indeterminacy
to writing, Norris, for example, notes that "the effect is unsettling not
only for linguistics but for every field of enquiry based on the idea of an
immediate, intuitive access to meaning" (30). I do not know of any field
based on such an idea—linguistics included. In challenging the "idea of
an immediate, intuitive access to meaning," Derrida is not overturning
common sense but supporting it.

Similarly, Norris notes that the "deconstructive leverage supplied by
a term like *writing* depends on its resistance to any kind of settled or
definitive meaning" (31). A Derridean term like 'writing' or *différance*, in
other words, "cannot be reduced to any single, self-identical meaning"
(32). I do not know of any term that can be reduced to a single, invariable

meaning: the meaning of every term (including 'term') reflects the specific context in which the term occurs. The fact that the meaning of a word varies in this way shocks only those who "dream of a perfect, unimpeded communion of minds" (94). But for those who do not share this dream — and I would include most modern writers in this far from exclusive group — Derrida is smothering a hope that either never lived or died long ago.

Finally, borrowing an example from Roland Barthes to illustrate "the slippages of everyday referential meaning," Norris cites "the merest of telegraphic greetings: 'Monday. Returning tomorrow. Jean-Louis' " (112). Norris seems surprised that multiple ambiguities "lurk behind even such a simple and practical piece of language" (for example, "*Which* Jean-Louis? *Which* of the various Mondays on which the message might have been penned?" [112]). I am surprised by Norris's astonishment: precisely because the message is so simple, because it is "the merest of telegraphic greetings," its meaning is unclear. The sparseness of the text invites the playful speculation that Norris finds so bold.

I have been suggesting that hardly anyone holds the ostensibly "traditional," "commonsense" positions that deconstruction assaults. More importantly, no one needs these positions to resist conclusions that, in deconstruction, follow from the fact that we can never be absolutely sure about the meaning of a text. Deconstruction argues that interpretation is not simply difficult but impossible: the intent of Jean-Louis's telegram is a hole we can never fill. Derridean critics, in short, wake up from the "dream of a perfect, unimpeded communion of minds," only to find themselves cut off completely from the texts they thought they knew. As Norris puts it, commenting on Derrida's well-known contribution to *Deconstruction and Criticism*:

> The topic is ostensibly Shelley's poem "The Triumph of Life," which serves as a focus for the other contributors but which barely manages to peep through the tangles and cunning indirections of Derrida's text. He makes no pretence of "interpreting" the poem but uses its title and random associative hints as a springboard into regions of giddying uncertainty, where details merge and cross in a joyful breakdown of all proprietory limits. Any talk of meaning or structure is ineluctably "caught up in a process which it does not control," which for Derrida signals the total dissolution of those boundaries that mark off one text from another, or that try to interpose between poem and commentary [114].

Derrida does not choose to play with Shelley's poem; he has to, there being no "poem" or "meaning" for him to know.

"Knowledge" here entails total control, and much of Norris's energy goes into showing that authors cannot constrain the interpretation of their texts. A text, in other words, "ramifies" or "disseminates" an author's intent, forcing readers to see multiple possibilities and not a fixed "center" that governs the production of meaning. For Norris, metaphors get the better of what an author tries to say. On virtually every page, he speaks of "track[ing] down [a text] to its metaphors" (119), of "combat-[ing]" a text "by exposing its ruses of metaphor" (88), of "tropes taking over the business of narrative or logical argument, substituting a play of figural language that obeys its own laws of inverted cause-and-effect" (106). The "phraseology" of Marxist texts is in particular "revealingly loose and metaphorical" (79) (for Norris the two terms seem synonymous). Objecting to a passage from Terry Eagleton's *Criticism and Ideology*, Norris complains that "the argument here is entirely in the charge of its sustaining metaphors" (81); even Eagleton's "elaborate argumentation cannot conceal its dependence on these basic and proliferating figures of thought. . . . The Marxist model of representation, however refined in theory, is caught up in a rhetoric of tropes and images that entirely controls its logic" (83).

I agree with Norris that there is a logic of metaphor. In some versions of Marxism, for instance, 'base' generates 'superstructure' and various mechanical ways of relating the two terms. Sometimes, moreover, a metaphor can mislead an author. By making it hard to picture the independent force of art, the base/superstructure metaphor has (mis)led some Marxists into supposing that art, like a superstructure, lacks influence on the economic base that ostensibly buttresses it. But because metaphors can control an argument, it hardly follows that they have to. Some texts resist the "seductions of metaphor" (103) that all texts face.

Take one of Norris's own metaphors: "thinking is always and inseparably bound to the rhetorical devices that support it" (61). E. D. Hirsch's critique of deconstruction to the contrary, a deconstructionist would concede that the intent of Norris's assertion is at first glance clear: thought collapses without metaphorical supports, much as a house is no longer a house when its foundation crumbles. Thinking, in other words, always takes place through metaphors.

But the very metaphors in Norris's statement (a deconstructionist reading might add) enforce the separation between tropes and thought that Norris wishes to repress. "Devices" and "supports," like the foundation of a house, preexist what they support. Norris's statement accordingly implies a sequence: metaphors come before the thoughts that are then inseparably bound to them. Metaphors, to be sure, constrain thinking (the way a foundation limits what can be built on it) but metaphors do not constitute thinking.

One can deconstruct Norris's statement this way but I do not see any reason to take his comparison so literally. (Norris shrewdly points out that Derrida's readings are "perverse but utterly literal" [33]. I would say, perverse because invariably literal.) Norris's point in the statement I have been analyzing is that metaphors are like supports in some ways (i.e., without them, thought collapses), but unlike supports in other ways (i.e., metaphors are thoughts). One can read into Norris's tropes commitments that he does not endorse, but I find such an exercise gratuitous, inspired not by the text but by a dubious prior affirmation of the "bottomless relativity of meaning" (58). I can make this point, moreover, without falling back on the typically extreme position that Norris is attacking (here, the "repressive" claim that figurative language is only "a blemish on the surface of logical thought" [70]). One can grant that metaphors are powerful and even necessary without making them omnipotent.

As I conceded earlier, the deconstructionists' questions are not "totally misconceived," by which I mean that tropes can take over arguments and cloud an author's intent. But when deconstructionists turn this possibility into a necessity, they defuse their own enterprise—or admit to its lack of power—as shown by another glance at Jean-Louis's telegram, "Monday. Returning tomorrow. Jean-Louis."

According to Norris, we can "play with all the possible ambiguities that lurk behind even such a simple and practical piece of language," thereby defying "society," which "tries to bar such pleasurable vagaries by insisting on specific memoranda of dates, places, patronymics, and so forth" (112). I agree that an oppressive society may try to limit the liberties we take with such a text, but in my view conventions of interpretation may be enabling as well as constraining—more exactly, enabling because constraining—in the way, for instance, that tennis lessons, by curtailing our free play with the racket, permit us to hit the ball. (If I am anxious to pick up Jean-Louis at the airport, I may want to master the conventions that enable me to know what his telegram says.) But for Norris conventions are only repressive: "all social existence," he says at one point, "is self-alienating" (40), inimical to the creative play that readers always desire and texts always encourage. In Norris's argument, the theoretical impossibility of extracting a determinate meaning from a text becomes an ominous practical necessity, backed up by force, never by desire. What we cannot do in theory—settle on a meaning—we unfortunately have to do in practice, to pass the course, stay clear of the police, and so forth.

Norris, in short, concedes not only that there must be an authoritative, socially agreed upon reading of texts (or anarchy would result), but that this official reading must be arbitrary (given the radical undecidability of writing). It follows that either we placate authorities by acting as if their official interpretation is valid, or we play with texts as Barthes does, uncovering the possibilities that "society" suppresses. Instead of contradicting each other, these options occupy different moments in deconstruction. The first allows deconstructionists to get along in the world by honoring the consensus that they cannot overturn; the second allows them to live with their powerlessness by letting them feel superior to the "commonsense," "traditional" view which subscribes to the official reading that deconstructionists see through. Out of convenience or necessity, deconstructionists may acquiesce to the established version of things —as Norris admits, "life could scarcely carry on if people were to act on their conclusions" (xii)—but they know that the public understanding of reality is a mere contrivance, in Norris's words, "nothing more than an empty or fallible convention" (111). Deconstructionists may be compliant, but at least they are not duped.

Continually in motion, verbally assaulting all social conventions, deconstruction nevertheless goes nowhere—like running in place. Its place is the university, where most of its adherents work. Instead of endangering the university and, by extension, the larger society with which the university interacts, deconstruction leaves existing institutions more secure, as a brief look at my second example, J. Hillis Miller's "The Function of Rhetorical Study at the Present Time," shows.[2]

In part, Miller's essay is a perceptive, if by now familiar, comment on the plight of literary studies: put simply, the steadily declining number of students taking literature courses are understandably less prepared and less motivated than their predecessors. In Miller's opinion, we can take several steps to improve things. First, we should integrate the study of literature with our burgeoning programs in expository writing: "Learning to write well cannot be separated from learning to read well" (12). Secondly, we should reexamine our largely chronological "periodization" of literary history and the curriculum, considering more fluid models, like Harold Bloom's family romance or the dialectical scheme of Marxism: "By what right, according to what measure, guided or supported by what reason, is this framing [of historical periods] performed? What justifies it, as one justifies a line of type, rules it, and keeps it from straggling all down the page? Is periodization a free positing or the referential recording of a knowledge?" (14). Thirdly, we should ask the same questions of the boundaries we have drawn around genres, even around imaginative writing itself.

Deconstruction ("rhetorical study") motivates these questions. Like Norris, Miller tracks down texts to their metaphors, in this case the figures of speech that organize the curriculum (metonymy, for example, when the name of a monarch stands for an entire period, as in "Edwardian" or "Victorian"; metaphor when a stylistic feature assimilates the period to nature, making a period seem "rough, like an irregular pearl," in the case of the "baroque," or "self-born, born anew," in the case of "the Renaissance"). The figurative status of these categories prompts Miller to suspect their necessity:

Does the name of a period indicate its intrinsic essence, its very being, or is it a convenient fiction? . . . The question is whether the chosen part is genuinely similar to the whole, metaphorically valid, or whether it is a mere contingent metonymy, a piece of a heterogeneous mixture chosen arbitrarily to stand for the whole or to make a mélange without intrinsic unity seem like a whole [15].

As in Norris, deconstruction nullifies the skepticism it inspires, making the questions Miller asks of historical periods, genres, and literature disingenuous. Despite his holding out the possibility of "valid" categories, he knows in advance that all conceptions of literary history are merely convenient fictions, invented for "political purposes, according to one or another mode of figurative reduction," imposing coherence on the inaccessible facts (15). This knowledge (that all historical categories are "baseless" figures of speech) is somehow "not itself period-bound" but "part of any period in our history" (14). Miller notes that "the traditional historical organization by periods and genres should be dismantled only when we are sure we have alternatives that will be better" (17). But if all historical frameworks are as illegitimate as the "traditional historical" one, then it would seem best to leave things as they are. To the question, "Who has the right to name the period?," Miller answers, No one—or anyone. Any scheme for improvement is as groundless as the model it would replace.

A proposal that starts out promising change thus ends up discouraging it. Miller's analysis of the novel applies to his own deconstruction of the curriculum: "It is a throwing away of what is already thrown away in order to save it. It is a destroying of the already destroyed, in order to preserve the illusion that it is still intact" (16-17). Many of us suspect that the present historical organization of our subject matter is, in Miller's words, a "vast shifting fabrication." But after articulating this suspicion, Miller undermines it by concluding that all schemes suffer from the groundlessness that vitiates the present one.

As the texts I have been examining suggest, deconstruction does make a difference: it reinforces established political and educational arrangements rather than damaging them or simply leaving them as they are. The often noted assimilation of deconstruction by the university accordingly does not indicate the tolerance or self-destructiveness of the university but the conservatism of deconstruction. Instead of challenging what Norris calls the "solemn inventions of Anglo-American academic discourse" (113), deconstruction allows us to live with them.

Part II

Deconstruction and Philosophy

PRELIMINARY REMARKS

As is clear in the preceding section, the relation between deconstruction
and philosophy comes into question whenever deconstruction's deeper
implications are at issue. This relation is most pointedly evidenced in
Derrida's readings of Husserl, Heidegger, and Nietzsche. The relationship
between Derrida and Heidegger is especially problematical, in that, by
his own admission, Derrida's deconstructive practice is not completely
distinguishable from Heidegger's unbuilding (*Abbauen, Destruktion*) of
the history of ontology. Nevertheless, Derrida often appeals to certain
Heideggerian insights, while suggesting that Heidegger himself lapses
back into the metaphysics of presence, of logocentrism. This point is clear
in Derrida's criticism of Heidegger's reading of Nietzsche.

Where Heidegger takes Nietzsche to be the last metaphysician, in
that Nietzschean "Will to Power" (Being as becoming) is the historical
extension of the Platonic *eidos* (Being as the "outlook"—*Aussehen*—of
things), Derrida suggests that Nietzsche points the way beyond metaphysics insofar as he anticipates the active forgetting of the *Übermensch*.
The *Übermensch* would actively forget Being, with its attendant history
of concealment, which Heidegger would recover as the history of ontology. The Heideggerian destruction of this history, notes Derrida, is carried
out in the rhetoric of recovery and commemoration. Heidegger, he claims,
is nostalgic for Being, is oriented toward a lost presence, but a presence
nonetheless. Thus for Derrida Heidegger is himself implicated in that
which he would "destruct"—namely, the history of Being as presence.
Opposed to Heideggerian remembrance, Derrida sees in the texts of
Nietzsche an anticipation of the active forgetting of Being, which he valorizes as an "overcoming" of metaphysics more radical than Heidegger's
recovery of concealment *within* metaphysics.

In his difference with Heidegger over the interpretation of Nietzsche,
Derrida also criticizes Heidegger's appropriation of Hölderlin (instead of
Nietzsche) in his attempt to articulate a nonmetaphysical and nonhuman-
istic understanding of Being. Heidegger celebrates *Dichtung* (Poetry),
exemplified in Hölderlin, as a commemoration of Being's concealment
and an anticipation of a new epoch or *Geschick* from the origin of that
concealment. Derrida, on the other hand, takes the stylistic plurality of
Nietzsche's texts to be strategically superior to *Dichtung*, for the latter
remains oriented toward Being as a site of "origin." For deconstruction,
the stylistic plurality of a text disperses the very comportment of language toward Being that *Dichtung* preserves. *Dichtung* is logo-centric;
stylistic plurality is logo-semic. The latter, Derrida would suggest, is the
overcoming of metaphysics *par excellence*.

The relation between Derrida and Heidegger raises an important question as to the nature of deconstruction: Does deconstruction presuppose a philosophical problematic, or does it operate independently of that problematic?

In "Ending/Closure: On Derrida's Margining of Heidegger," Eugenio Donato introduces the question and affirms the first alternative. He begins by criticizing the popular association of Derrida with a movement in literary criticism, especially in the U.S.A. An accurate understanding of deconstruction, he suggests, must take note of Derrida's critique of Husserl in *Speech and Phenomena*. This critique, Donato maintains, is strictly philosophical and *not yet* deconstructive. Donato argues that *Speech and Phenomena* is a critique of the concept of "origin" in Husserl, such that perception is not originary, but is always already representation. This critique, he insists, is carried out philosophically, which is to say that it remains on the conceptual level. From this critique of the concept of "origin," Derrida introduces the nonconcept of *différance* and the notion of the closure of the history of metaphysics. From here, Derrida engages Heidegger's problematic of the end of metaphysics. Donato insists that Derrida becomes truly deconstructive in *Of Grammatology*, where he first introduces the notion of deconstruction as a strategy for reading Heidegger. "It is the need to read Heidegger," says Donato, "that requires a deconstructive strategy."

For Donato, *Of Grammatology* is an attempt to specify the nature of a post-Heideggerian philosophical discourse. This is evident, he believes, where Derrida displaces the Heideggerian notion of the *end* of metaphysics with the notion of *closure*, allowing Derrida to situate Heidegger within the tradition whose end Heidegger announces as the possibility for his own project. Furthermore, the reading of "end" via "closure" is concomitant with the displacement of Heideggerian ontological difference with deconstructive *différance*. *Différance*, notes Donato, both precedes and succeeds difference, mirroring the relation between Heidegger and Nietzsche. Donato's position is that the issue of "literariness" (stylistic plurality) arises necessarily out of a philosophical problematic, where it enables Derrida to place Nietzsche hypothetically "beyond" the closure of metaphysics.

In his reply to Donato, David Wood questions the necessity of linking deconstruction to a philosophical discourse. He suggests, pace Donato, that deconstruction can be abstracted from Derrida's reading of Husserl, Nietzsche, and Heidegger, and that literary critics need only isolate the formal schemata of these readings in order to develop a deconstructive method. The possibility of such schemata, argues Wood, is indicated in Donato's own abstract account of Derrida's notion of text. Furthermore, Wood claims that Donato is unfaithful to deconstruction's antipathy toward the serial ordering of historical sources. Does not Donato, he asks, attempt to establish a logical order between *Speech and Phenomena* and *Of Grammatology?* Finally, Wood argues that Donato has brought in the notion of literariness in Nietzsche from Lacoue-Labarthe, as if he were equating Lacoue-Labarthe and Derrida. Writing, says Wood, is the issue for Derrida, not literariness, and "writing is prior to the distinction between philosophy and literature." Wood maintains, therefore, that deconstruction is not bound to philosophy, nor to the distinction that would separate philosophy from literature.

Tina Chanter discusses the relationship between Derridean writing and Heideggerian philosophy in "Derrida and Heidegger: The Interlacing of Texts." Chanter argues that Donato's account of the issue is weakened in neglecting to examine any specific reading by Derrida of a Heideggerian text. She maintains that the most illuminating example of such a reading is found in *"Restitutions de la vérité en pointure,"* where Derrida explores Heidegger's famous essay "The Origin of the Work of Art" *(Der Ursprung des Kunstwerkes).*

Heidegger's exemplary art work is Van Gogh's painting of an old pair of shoes. He describes them as belonging to a peasant woman, for whom they are inconspicuously serviceable while she works in the fields. In the painting, however, they emerge from serviceability into their truth as earth-bound entities that support, and are supported by, a world of meaning. The painting, as a work of art, presents the shoes as an emergent "strife between earth and world," and in so doing presents *itself* as a site where "Being sets itself into work." Chanter recalls that in "Restitutions" Derrida considers the meaning of "belonging" insofar as Heidegger describes the shoes as belonging to the woman, or as earth belongs to world, or truth to work, or Heidegger's text to the tradition of aesthetics that it would supercede. Chanter suggests that, in an important sense, Derrida's text also belongs to that of Heidegger, even when he shows how Heidegger repeats the itinerary of traditional oppositions in his "nontraditional" discourse.

Derrida conveys this notion of belonging through the figure of the shoe laces that weave in and out of the eyelets bored into the leather. In such a way, Derrida remarks, Heidegger's text is both within and without a tradition of discourse that precedes it. For example, although Heidegger claims that Dasein is more fundamental than sexual difference, he nevertheless resorts to a female figure to convey Dasein as existing "outside" the truth—that is, in the world of serviceability, as opposed to the world of the painting. As Chanter points out, this figure repeats the traditional opposition of male/female, where the female is outside the truth and must relinquish her belonging(s) to the male, the possessor. Thus Heidegger's text is laced into the tradition, just as the peasant's world is laced into the world of art. This prompts Derrida to ask whether they are not finally indistinguishable. Likewise, Chanter notes that Derrida both criticizes and assents to Heidegger's complicity in the tradition, and so interlaces his own text with Heidegger's. As Derrida writes in *Of Grammatology*, "This would perhaps mean that we do not go beyond a period whose closure we can sketch."

Thus, insofar as deconstruction applies itself to philosophical texts, it would seem inseparable from a philosophical (Heideggerian) problematic, as Donato suggests. Moreover, the fact that Derrida works from out of a Heideggerian discourse is more than incidental. Derrida's connection with Heidegger is clearly constitutive for deconstruction as applied by Derrida himself. Nevertheless, the deconstruction of such notions as "property" and "belonging" would also unhinge this connection. Whether deconstruction can be schematized away from its philosophical origins is another question, but it cannot be identified with those origins. Chanter's emphasis upon the double meaning of interlacing is therefore appropriate. The relation between deconstruction and philosophy cannot be unequivocally determined.

G.E.A.

4

Ending/Closure: On Derrida's Margining of Heidegger

Eugenio Donato

The wasteland grows.

—Nietzsche

For that is what we are now; men who have leapt.
... And where have we leapt? Perhaps into an abyss?
No! Rather onto some firm soil. Some? No! But on
that soil upon which we live and die, if we are
honest with ourselves.

—Heidegger

*La proximité de deux languages, ça ne veut rien dire;
il y a là toute l'énigme de la traduction.*

—Derrida

Let it be said at the outset that this essay will not have the absurd
pretention of reading Derrida's relation to Heidegger. That task is, at the
present crossroads of critical theory, urgent and necessary, yet probably
impossible. Not only is this task complex, but more pertinently, in addition to the systematic discussions of Heidegger extending from the earlier
Of Grammatology and *Margins of Philosophy* to the reading of Nietzsche
in *Spurs* and the more recent playful and "literary" references in *La Carte
postale*, some three thousand pages representing lectures and seminars on
Heidegger remain unpublished. Given Derrida's practice of closely relating

his publishing to his teaching and lecturing, both the importance of Heidegger's works and Derrida's decision to withhold his reading are in themselves significant.

At the present time, the task of interpreting Derrida's reading of Heidegger would be comparable to that of interpreting Heidegger's reading of Nietzsche without the benefit of his Freiburg lectures (published in expanded form under the title of *Nietzsche*). The endeavor of reading Derrida's reading of Heidegger belongs to an indefinite future. Nevertheless, paradoxically, in the remarks that follow, I should like to underscore the necessity and timeliness of such an impossible task.

Judging from the recent controversies and publications surrounding "deconstruction," it is safe to assume that there is such a thing as deconstructive criticism and that, whatever deconstructive criticism is, it stems in great part from the works of Derrida—I am using the vague expression "works" rather than the word "theory" because, given the nature of Derrida's philosophical enterprise, one would have to put the word "theory" between brackets. To leave the word unbracketed would imply an interpretation of Derrida's writings that would considerably simplify their translation into a literary theoretical idiom.

Deconstruction exists today as a specifically American or Anglo-Saxon phenomenon—quite distinct from, say, a continental philosophical idiom inspired by Derrida. As such, it owes much to De Man, Hillis Miller, and Bloom, making it a predominantly literary practice. Even the few Anglo-Saxon philosophers who have been willing to give Derrida a sympathetic reading—I am thinking particularly of Rorty—do so partly because literary criticism, when tied to a continental philosophical grounding, offers a possible alternative to the exhaustion of common language philosophy that still dominates the American philosophical establishment.

Broadly characterized as a theory of literary texts and literary criticism, deconstruction is far from being synonymous with Derrida's philosophical—or for that matter literary—aims and practices. Deconstruction is better described as the product of the grafting of a theoretical translation of Derrida's writings onto a number of native literary practices or, as some would no doubt prefer to see it, as the contamination of a native critical idiom by a set of foreign, pernicious philosophical positions and practices. Given the tone of the controversies that have surrounded deconstruction—think of the inane and uninformed pronouncements of a Denis Donoghue in the *New York Review of Books* or a Donald Reiman in the *Times Literary Supplement*[1]—it is not difficult to imagine that the influence of Derrida on literary criticism is perceived in many academic halls as the arrival of an intellectual plague—the example of Freud should not be forgotten. The association of deconstruction with a single institution, the presumed existence of a Yale school, the publication of *Deconstruction and Criticism*, far from clarifying the issue of the relation of Derrida's writings to literary deconstruction have only muddied the waters to such an extent that, many a subtle difference being erased, a clear, speculative image such as Jonathan Culler's *On Deconstruction* has become possible. That rare protests (such as those of Rodolphe Gasché) against the identification of American literary deconstruction with Derrida's philosophical strategies have not received the attention they deserve is itself significant.[2]

The subtitle of Jonathan Culler's book—*Theory and Criticism after Structuralism*—implicitly echoes Frank Lentricchia's book *After the New Criticism*, which, with its confused genealogies and attempt to situate deconstruction in a continuous history of American criticism, is more interesting as a symptom of a problem than as an accurate description or nuanced solution. No doubt Culler sets the story straight and succeeds in giving a clear, succinct, if partial, account of American literary deconstruction. The question I wish to raise concerns some implications of this seemingly innocent translation of a continental philosophical problematic into an American literary idiom.

Gasché's essay had cogently argued for the necessity of recognizing a particular philosophical tradition in order to correctly situate the originality of Derrida's enterprise. Specifically, for Gasché, Derrida's notion of a deconstructive philosophical reading has its roots in a reflexive critique of phenomenology. Gasché, then, would place Derrida in a history that would minimally coinvolve the names of Husserl and Merleau-Ponty.[3] Assuming for a moment, and for the sake of argument, that Gasché indeed succeeds in identifying the correct history that subtends Derrida's enterprise, how can Culler, who devotes roughly one hundred forty pages of a three-hundred-page book to exploring Derrida's position, write: "I will not attempt to discuss the relationship of Derridean deconstruction to the work of Hegel, Nietzsche, Husserl, and Heidegger"?[4]

If Derrida had written only his *Introduction to Husserl's Origin of Geometry* and his *Speech and Phenomena*, would we see him today as the philosopher most responsible for philosophical deconstructive reading, and by implication, deconstructive literary criticism? Perhaps. Derrida's comment on the "Introduction" to his translation of *The Origin of Geometry*, from the privileged position of *Of Grammatology*, offers a critique of "origin" as a main theme of his earlier work and, no doubt, this critique is a by-product of deconstructive readings. Nevertheless, Derrida himself, in *Of Grammatology*, where he introduces the term "deconstruction," refers back to the "Introduction"—or more precisely, his treatment of the theme of origins in the "Introduction"—as a *critique* and not as a deconstruction: "As for this critique of the concept of origin in general (empirical and/or transcendental), we have attempted elsewhere to indicate the scheme of a possible argument."[5]

Again, if we turn to *Speech and Phenomena* and read the extraordinary note to the chapter entitled: *"le vouloir-dire comme soliloque"*—"the will-to-signify as soliloquy"—in which Derrida states his ultimate intention in writing that particular essay, it is not clear that the analysis is really "deconstructive" in the sense offered in *Of Grammatology*. Specifically, the note reads (in part):

> By affirming that *perception does not exist* or that that which is called perception is not originary, that, in a certain fashion, everything "begins" with "re-presentation" (a proposition that evidently can only be sustained by the erasure of these two concepts: it means that there is no "beginning" and that the "representation" of which we speak is not the modification of a "re-" which comes after or over an originary presentation) and by re-introducing the difference of the sign at the heart of the "originary," we should not take a step back from transcendental phenomenology towards either an "empiricism" or a "Kantian" critique of the pretension to an originary intuition. We have thus indicated the initial intention—and the distant horizon—of the present essay[VP, 50].

Derrida's assertion that perception does not exist, or rather, that perception is not originary but always already a re-presentation, stems from a philosophical critique of a number of concepts that constitute the very ground of Husserlian phenomenology. Specifically, *Speech and Phenomena* constitutes a radical critique of, on the one hand, the "presence of meaning to a full and originary intuition" (VP, 3), necessary to the constitution of an ideality that could be repeated indefinitely in the identity of its presence, and, on the other, of the possibility or meaning of a *Bedeutung* that is "immediately present to the act of expression" (VP, 86).

Had Derrida stopped writing after *Speech and Phenomena*, the consequences of his work would have been crucial for both philosophy and literary criticism. The latter would have had to come to terms with a new analytics of representation subtended by specific temporal strictures that would determine its properties. It would also ultimately ground a specific notion of representation that would play a role similar to that of presence in phenomenology.

Speech and Phenomena announces a number of themes that became central in Derrida's later writings. In *Speech and Phenomena* Derrida underscores the metaphysical tenor of Husserl's valorization of voice over writing. For Derrida, the materiality of language and the notion of "sign" in the Husserlian text open a moment of crisis for phenomenology—"the moment of crisis is always that of the sign" (*VP*, 91). Furthermore, in *Speech and Phenomena* Derrida introduces the "non-concept" of *dif-*

fèrance. Finally, at the end of *Speech and Phenomena* Derrida introduces the notion of the closure of the history of metaphysics which is so central to Derridean deconstruction. With this notion of closure he enteres into his dialogue with Heidegger and, in particular, with the latter's problematic of the *end* of metaphysics:

> Within the interior of the metaphysics of presence, of philosophy as knowledge of the presence of the object, as the being-close-to-itself of knowledge in conscience, we believe, quite simply, in absolute knowledge as the *closure*, if not the end, of history. We believe in it literally. We believe that *such a closure has taken place*. The history of Being as presence, as presence to itself in absolute knowledge, as self-consciousness within the infinity of *parousia* — that history is closed. . . .
>
> Within the opening of this question, *we no longer know*. This does not mean to say that we know nothing, but instead that we are beyond absolute knowledge . . . towards that from which its closure announces itself and decides itself [VP, 115].

This assertion of the closure of the history of metaphysics leaves Derrida with his suggestive description of a future project: "For that which 'begins' then, beyond absolute knowledge, *unheard-of* thoughts are needed that search for themselves across the memory of old signs" (VP, 115).

Yet if this quest for "unvoiced" thoughts — brought about by a reading and rewriting of old signs — points toward Derrida's *Of Grammatology* and his deconstructive readings/writings, it does not yet constitute deconstruction per se. What separates *Speech and Phenomena* from *Of Grammatology* is that, in the former work, the difference between the *closure* of metaphysics and Heidegger's *end* of metaphysics is not yet clearly marked and problematized. This not yet problematized relationship between the philosophical before of metaphysics and the "unheard-of thoughts" of its different future separates the two texts.

From *Of Grammatology*'s privileged position, the metaphysical "before" of phenomenology and the "after" of deconstruction will depend upon each other:

> In the originary temporalization and movement of the relationship to the other, such as Husserl effectively describes them, the non-presentation or the de-presentation is as "originary" as the presentation. *That is why a thought that thinks the trace can neither break with or be reduced to a transcendental phenomenology*. . . . In the deconstruction of the arche, we do not proceed to a choice [G, 91].

But then this interdependence of deconstruction on phenomenology is itself related to a more problematical relationship between a Heideggerian *end* of metaphysics and a Derridean *closure* of metaphysics. Only after Derrida introduces the notion of deconstruction in *Of Grammatology* (chapter one), via the problem of reading Heidegger, can he take a deconstructive, rather than critical, stance toward Husserlian phenomenology and begin to weave his complex "plot for philosophy."

Before raising the problem of Derrida's reading of Heidegger, I should like to add that the reason for marking the distance between *Speech and Phenomena* and *Of Grammatology* (as well as the attempt to localize the question of deconstruction within the Derridean corpus and the specific thematic through which that question is introduced), is that most readings of Derrida (including Culler's) and the notion of deconstruction as a tool for a critique of Western "logocentrism" could be derived from Derrida's critique of Husserlian phenomenology and its analytics of representation. This hardly accounts for the need to introduce a strategy of deconstructive reading/writing.

Of Grammatology has been read repeatedly as a philosophical critique of the implicit presuppositions, and scientific pretentions, of structuralism and semiology as linguistic models dominating the French intellectual scene in the 1960s. *Of Grammatology* is to have uncovered their metaphysical presuppositions and localized their pertinence to a philosophical history that they had feigned to discard or superced.

While *Of Grammatology* was indeed responsible for inaugurating what today we loosely name poststructuralism, and if indeed Derrida's critique of philosophical presuppositions concerning the representational system of modern linguistics is crucial to his reputation outside French philosophical circles, it is hardly clear that this is his most central philosophical concern. Derrida's own description of his intention in writing *Of Grammatology* locates its finality elsewhere:

> Thus we draw together this concept of trace with that which is at the heart of the latest writings of Emmanuel Levinas. . . . In agreement here—and not in the thought of Levinas—with a Heideggerian intention, this notion means, sometimes beyond Heideggerian discourse, the shaking of an ontology which, in its most intimate course, has determined the meaning of being as presence and the meaning of language as the full continuity of speech. To render enigmatic that which we believe to understand by the names of proximity, presence (the close, the proper, and pre- of presence), such would be the ultimate intention of this essay. This deconstruction of presence passes through the deconstruction of consciousness, and therefore through the irreducible notion of the trace (*Spur*) as it appears in the discourse of Nietzsche [G, 108].

The ultimate intention of the essay, then, has absolutely nothing to do with linguistics, structuralism, or semiology. Derrida's immediate aim,

beyond stating the necessity for philosophy to read its own tradition—
that is, to read a continuity established by betrayals and translations—is
the reading of Heidegger and of his project for an ontology that situates
itself beyond a Nietzschean end of metaphysics.

The reading of Heidegger requires a deconstructive strategy—"style"
would perhaps be more exact. If Derrida's deconstructive reading of
Heidegger necessarily involves Nietzsche, it is because Heidegger locates
Nietzsche at the *end* of metaphysics—where any ulterior metaphysical
stance is only a local repetition of a previously exhausted position.

That *Of Grammatology* is meant to define the nature of philosophical discourse *after* Heidegger, and that the critique of a certain linguistic
imperialism is only a thematic strategy within this ultimate project is
evident in the "Exergue" from *Of Grammatology*, (and particularly its
first chapter). Here Derrida introduces the word 'deconstruction' for the
first time in relation to his proposed reading of a philosophical tradition
dominated by the names of Hegel and Heidegger.

The three guiding themes enumerated at the beginning of the "Exergue"
to describe the "order" of logocentrism could be related specifically to
Heidegger. The first—namely, the necessity of understanding the concept
of 'writing' "in a world in which the phonetization of writing must dis-
simulate its own history in its very production" (G, 11)—refers to the
logic of Being as described by Heidegger, a logic that must occult itself in
the very production of the history of its metaphysical misreadings. The
third deals with the problem of the concept of science and clearly implies
the necessity of questioning Heidegger's localizing the presuppositions of
science within the previous metaphysical position and its imperviousness
to the question of the meaning of Being. For Derrida, the proliferation of
scientific languages, and particularly the desemanticized syntactic "writing" of mathematics, should point beyond the closure of metaphysics,
which a traditional philosophical discourse cannot fully take into account.

However, the second guiding theme seems to be particularly relevant
for the rest of the Derridean project. In his words:

> The history of metaphysics which, in spite of all differences, and not only
> from Plato to Hegel (passing even through Leibniz) but also, beyond its
> apparent boundaries, from the presocratics to Heidegger, has always assigned
> the origin of truth in general to the logos: the history of truth, of the truth of
> truth, has always been, with the exception of one metaphorical diversion
> that we shall have to take into account, the denigration of writing and its
> repression outside of the "plenitude" of speech [G, 11-12].

Clearly, Derrida's project is to rewrite the "history" of philosophy as
it is proposed by Heidegger. Indeed, as is well known, for the latter there

are two distinct "histories of philosophy": one that starts with Plato and ends with Nietzsche, and which constitutes the history of metaphysics properly speaking, and another that precedes and follows the history of metaphysics—namely, that of the presocratics and Heidegger's own ontology. The latter depends in part upon a dialogue with the genuine origin of philosophy as opposed to the false beginning inaugurated by Plato.

My only reason for summarizing Heidegger's position is to underscore the relevance for Derrida of the distinction between *end* and *closure*. Derrida's *closure* is a reading and displacement of the Heideggerian notion of *end*. The rewriting of the *end* of metaphysics into its closure necessarily problematizes its concomitant notion of origin. Some thirteen years after *Of Grammatology*, Derrida returns to this question of the complex relationship that endings maintain with origins and insists again on the need to distinguish between *end* and *closure*. In *"D'un ton apocalyptique"*—and this very title is suggestive with regard to any assertion of an *end*—he writes: "The ending has always begun, yet one must distinguish between end and closure" (F, 464).

The displacement of the concept of *end* to that of the closure of metaphysics, as the preceding quote clearly indicates, forbids us from thinking of the temporal and spatial patterns involved within such a displacement in terms of any simple, linear, or hierarchical notion of history. For the notion of *closure* brought about by a reading of the notion of *end* complicates not only the ordinary notions of a "before" and an "after" necessary to any uncritical "history" of philosophy or literary theory, but also problematizes Heidegger's notion of the conceptual priority of the prosocratics over the platonic "fall" and his assumed privileged belatedness with regard to Nietzsche—the thinker in whom, for Heidegger, metaphysics runs its full course and exhausts its philosophical content.

If until now I have emphasized the problem of reading as central to an understanding of the relationship of Derrida to Heidegger, if I have made this relationship central to the understanding of Derrida's notion of a deconstructive (style of) reading, and if I have underscored Heidegger's use of his belatedness with respect to Nietzsche and Derrida's more problematical belatedness with respect to Heidegger, it is because, to a literary critic like myself, the most suggestive way of understanding Derrida's central confrontation with Heidegger comes from the perspective of a Bloomian problematic of influences and misreadings.

Derrida's "plot for philosophy" in some ways resembles Bloom's "plot for poetry." Minimally, the belated Heidegger can only become a strong philosopher by misreading his strong antecedent, Nietzsche. Heidegger's reading of Nietzsche as the *end* of metaphysics effectively allows the former, by claiming a continuity with the presocratics, to become the precursor of his own precursor. In other words, the temporality that subtends the notion of *end* in Heidegger is metaleptic.

On the surface, Derrida's gesture of misreading the notion of the *end* of metaphysics as the *closure* of metaphysics seems to redouble the Heideggerian gesture. The very displacement of the Heideggerian necessity of a *destructive* reading into *a style of deconstructive reading*, a displacement inseparable from the displacement of the concept of *end* relative to that of *closure*, has an immediate consequence. This consequence is spelled out early in *Of Grammatology* and systematically developed in various articles following its publication. It demonstrates a number of ways in which Heidegger's work is still in nostalgic complicity with the metaphysical system whose end he had proclaimed.

It is not my purpose to analyze each specific reading of Heidegger by Derrida. It is enough to recall that Derrida, from the very first chapter of *Grammatology*, clearly states the motifs in Heidegger's thought that place him in the continuity of the very metaphysics he denounces. For instance, for Derrida Heidegger's recourse to a certain notion of "truth"—even if it concerns the truth of Being—is in continuity with the onto-theology he wishes to supercede:

> All the metaphysical determinations of truth, and even the one Heidegger reminds us of, beyond the onto-theology of metaphysics, are more or less immediately inseparable from an instance of the logos, or of a rationality thought within the lineage of the logos, in whatever way it is conceived. . . . Yet, within this logos, the originary and essential tie to the *phone* has never been broken [G, 21].

If phonocentrism and logocentrism are inseparable, then both can be shown to determine Heidegger's ontology:

> Logocentrism would therefore be responsible for the determination of the being of that-which-is as presence. Inasmuch as such a logocentrism is not completely absent from Heideggerian thought, it perhaps retains that thought within the period of onto-theology, within the philosophy of presence, that is to say, within philosophy itself. This would perhaps mean that we do not go beyond a period whose closure we can sketch [G, 23-24].

Clearly, then, the notion of *closure* allows Derrida to place Heidegger in a tradition whose *end* determines the possibility of his discourse. The notion of *closure*, which reads the Heideggerian notion of *end*, is, inseparable from the displacement—or perhaps I should say the misprision—of another Heideggerian concept—namely, that of an ontico-ontological difference into what Derrida chooses to name *différance*. Derrida's most synthetic statement—where he interweaves all these themes—is again situated in the first chapter of the *Grammatology*. This passage deserves to be quoted in its entirety not only because it clearly locates the Derridean reading of the Heideggerian project, but also because it indicates one of the main thrusts of Derrida's own deconstructive motifs:

> To come to recognize, not within but at the horizon of the Heideggerian paths, and yet in them, that the meaning of being is not a transcendental or transtemporal signified (even if it was always dissimulated within a temporal period), but already, in a properly *unheard of* meaning, a determined signifying trace, amounts to the affirmation that within the decisive concept of an ontico-ontological difference, *all must not be thought of in a single trait*; Being and that-which-is, ontical and ontological, would be, in an originary style, *derived* with regard to difference; and by that relationship which later on we will call *Différance* [G, 30].

And the passage concludes stating that through the Heideggerian notion of difference and its erasure, "we shall later on be able to attempt to put *différance* and writing in relation to each other." That is, only through the notion of *différance*, which determines Heidegger's original gesture and its erasure, can a deconstructive style of reading come about.

By redoubling the Heideggerian gesture, his notion of *end* is displaced so as to include, within the space it determines, the conceptual system that generates it in the first place. Derridean *closure* is in part the consequence of the necessity for the end to repeat itself and to include that which pretends to overrun its borders. Within this limited horizon, the function of Derrida's *différance* follows the same metaleptic logic as Heidegger's difference. Toward the end of the article "Différance," Derrida affirms that "Différance, in a certain and rather strange manner [is] older than either ontological difference or the truth of Being" [M, 23].

If Derridean *différance* precedes and follows Heideggerian difference, it is because the latter differs from the former inasmuch as neither "before" nor "after" are "absolutes," but are effects produced by a system of *closure* that knows itself for what it is. It differs from difference and, by its repeated gesture, ruins the related notions of origin and end: "Beyond Being and that-which-is, this difference differing (itself) incessantly would trace itself. This *différance* would be the first or the last trace if one could still speak of origins and of endings" [M, 77-78].

We may at this point return to a Bloomian "plot for philosophy" and read Derrida's strong reading of Heidegger as the repetition of Heidegger's strong reading of Nietzsche. Yet that repetition implies a difference: a difference which, as we have seen, affects the very notion of difference. If Bloom's map is suggestive for an understanding of Heidegger's reading of Nietzsche, it does not completely account for Derrida's reading of Heidegger. If Bloom's model repeats itself from strong poet to strong poet, that repetition is a repetition without a difference/*différance*—however one may wish to spell that word at this point. This is not to suggest that an understanding of Derrida's strategy in reading Heidegger would in any way invalidate Bloom's model. On the contrary, it complicates it to the extent that Bloom's map would describe one specific case of a more general model.

As I said earlier, Heidegger's concept of the end of metaphysics rests upon his reading of Nietzsche. Two questions necessarily come to mind: the first is strictly a Bloomian question; namely, if Heidegger has to undertake a strong belated reading of Nietzsche, what are his specific "dialectics of revisionism?" The other concerns the function of Nietzsche in Derrida's reading of Heidegger. Each of these questions is too complex to be given the attention it deserves in this context. I will, nevertheless, attempt a partial answer, aware that certain generalizations inevitably run the risk of oversimplification.

Minimally, for the Derrida of the *Grammatology*, Nietzsche does not quite exhaust or bring metaphysics to an end in the Heideggerian sense. For Derrida, Heidegger, from one perspective, is right; yet by and through the Heideggerian reading, and only in that way, a certain aspect of Nietzsche becomes irreducible to Heidegger's very reading. Only by abandoning Nietzsche to a Heideggerian reading may one come to recognize a specific aspect of his work as "post"-Heideggerian, "past" the *end* of metaphysics, and, in a certain sense, also "past" any closure of metaphysics. In Derrida's words:

> Perhaps we should not withdraw Nietzsche from a Heideggerian reading but on the contrary abandon him to it completely, subscribing to this interpretation without reserve, in a *certain fashion* and up to the point where the content of the Nietzschean discourse being almost lost for the question of Being, its form regains its absolute strangeness, where his text finally calls for another type of reading, more faithful to his type of writing [G, 32].

Only through Heideggerian reading would "reading and therefore writing, texts, . . . be for Nietzsche 'originary' operations." But Nietzsche's position with regard to Heidegger—and also to Derrida—is paradoxical. For, in a Bloomian vocabulary, we can say that, on the one hand, Nietzsche is indeed Heidegger's strong precursor permitting the latter to become a strong philosopher by reading, in the former, a formal philosophical *end*. Nevertheless, Heidegger, as a strong precursor of Derrida, permits the latter not only to be a strong philosopher by displacing a problematic of *ending* onto one of *closure*, but Derrida does so by displacing Heidegger's precursor to the position of a successor. Nietzsche is thus both "before" and "after" Heidegger, and only because Nietzsche is "after" Heidegger, can Derrida also be "after" Heidegger. Ultimately, in fact, a certain Nietzsche is situated possibly even after Derrida—that is, after the *closure* of metaphysics.

Derrida's reading of Heidegger implies a strategic positioning of Nietzsche. This reading complicates considerably the temporal modes and spatial topology between precursor and successor as well as between the notions of *end* and *closure*. Derridean deconstruction and the concept of *text* reside in this complex of temporality and topology. If every *closure* necessarily inscribes an *end* within itself, it is also true that every end, by being also a closure, cleaves from itself a certain part of itself which is not to be held accountable for the mastery implied by an end.

The names Nietzsche, Heidegger, and Derrida also stand for what Derrida would have us recognize as different moments belonging to any literary or philosophical textual practice. Indeed, every text exists by a redoubled series of readings/writings, which depend upon and constitute a unique system of temporal and spatial hierarchies in which "before" and "after," "inside" and "outside," "form" and "content," and the like, are destabilized by their own redoubling within a system that is always simultaneously a reading and a writing.

Given the complexity of this logic, every "reading" would seem to have two possible strategies. The first would inhabit a text from the inside — that is, "attempt a break and a decomposition without a change of ground, by repeating what is implicit in the founding concepts and in the originary problematic, by utilizing against the edifice the instruments or stones available in the house — that is, in language as well" (M, 162).

The other alternative would pretend that a reading can place itself in an absolute exteriority. But such an exteriority is always only an apparent effect of a *trompe l'oeil*, for "the simple practice of language ceaselessly reinstalls the new terrain into the oldest ground" (M, 163).

The opposition between the two styles of reading is a false one. Every reading must "interweave the two motifs" and "speak several languages and produce a plurality of texts at the same time." But, then, Nietzsche and Heidegger are only names of *texts*.

At this juncture, it is impossible to describe the logic of a *text* in terms of a before and an after, an inside and an outside, and so forth. The best metaphorical approximation to describe the temporal structure of this logic is perhaps that offered by Derrida himself when punning on the word *veille*:

> Should we read Nietzsche, with Heidegger, as the last of the great metaphysicians? Or should we, on the contrary, understand the question of the truth of Being as the last sleeping gasp of the superior man? Should we understand the *eve* as the guard standing watch over the house or as the awakening to the day that comes, at the eve of which we are. . . . We are perhaps between these two eves [M, 163-64].

We may turn now to our first question asked in a Bloomian key—namely, if a deconstructive reading depends upon a model generated by Heidegger's reading of Nietzsche, and Derrida's reading of Heidegger's reading of Nietzsche, what are the "dialectics of revisionism" in Heidegger's reading of Nietzsche?

The answer to this question is not simple. In his own reading of Nietzsche, Derrida will point to what he calls a "process of propriation"[6] and to a "gambit of the gift" (*coup de don*) as that which in the text of Nietzsche will necessarily escape Heidegger's reading:

> If the opposition of *to give* and *to take*, of *to possess* and *to be possessed*, is nothing more than a kind of transcendental snare which is produced by the hymen's graphic, the process of propriation would then escape all dialectics as well as any ontological decidability [M, 86].

Hence, Heidegger's ontological question concerning the "truth of being" is incapable of reading that component of Nietzsche's text that will inscribe, by a necessary reversal, Heidegger's own problematic:

> The question of the meaning or of the truth of being is not capable of the question of the proper, of the undecidable exchange of the more into the less, of the to give for taking, of the to give for keeping, of the to give for hurting, of the *coup du don*. It is not capable because it is already inscribed in the process of propriation [E, 86-87].

The preceding remarks do not exhaust Derrida's reading of Heidegger's Nietzsche in *Eperons*. Derrida, in fact, suggests that in *Time and Being* Heidegger comes to recognize the philosophical irreducibility of this "process of propriation" and "submits" (*soumet* is in italics in the text) it to the very question of Being, and in a belated recognition, accepts that the "giving" (*donner, geben*) and the "donation" (*donation, Gabe*) implied in the *es gibt sein* "no longer allow themselves to be brought within Being, within the horizon, or derived from the meaning of the Being of truth." In other words, Derrida recognizes in Heidegger's text a textual process that remains irreducible to his fundamental ontology.

Inasmuch as the "process of propriation" of Nietzsche's text remains a blind spot for Heidegger—at least in his *Nietzsche*—he fails to read it because his original philosophical undertaking is already a textual component of Nietzsche's writing. Derrida's reading of Heidegger's reading of Nietzsche is not quite reducible to a canonic Bloomian form. If we wish to maintain the Bloomian form of the question, then we must ask what—specifically in the text of Nietzsche—Heidegger refuses to read or chooses to misread. The answer to this question is not provided by Derrida but by Lacoue-Labarthe who, in a series of readings inspired by Derrida, attempts to answer precisely what, in Nietzsche's text, is necessarily erased as the *end* of metaphysics in Heidegger's reading of his predecessor. It would be an impossible task to summarize adequately Lacoue-Labarthe's decisive readings of Heidegger's reading of Nietzsche.[7] In this context, suffice it to say that the axis to Lacoue-Labarthe's texts is a meticulous demonstration of the effects of the literary forms, the textual presentation, the *Darstellung*, the fictioning, in short, the literariness of Nietzsche's texts in general and of *Zarathrustra* in particular.

Heidegger's contempt for what he calls literature, and his stated requirement to separate a poetical idiom, a privileged *Dichtung*, from literature is well known. For Heidegger, the poetic, as distinct from the literary, should stand in a privileged proximity to thinking. *Denken* and *Dichtung* belong to each other and are always distinct from the fictional and the literary. To quote one passage from among many, Heidegger writes in *What is Called Thinking?*:

> Homer, Sappho, Pindar, Sophocles, are they literature? No! But that is the way they appear to us, and the only way, even when we are engaged in demonstrating by means of literary history that these works of poetry really are not literature.
>
> Literature is what has been literally written down, and copied, with the intent that it be available to a reading public. In that way literature becomes the object of widely diverging interests, which in turn are once more stimulated by literary means—through literary criticism. . . . The poesy of the Occident and European literature are two radically different forces in our history.[8]

Nietzsche, however, is literary, and literary with a vengeance. Heidegger has to neutralize this dimension of his work in order to read his predecessor's writings as the final document of Western metaphysics. For, as Lacoue-Labarthe would have it, if Nietzsche did succeed in speaking "another language," it is because "the concept of *fiction* escapes conceptuality itself" and cannot be "understood within the discourse of truth."[9] In fact, the problematical nature of the literary dimension of Nietzsche's texts allows Derrida to place him strategically in a hypothetical future beyond the closure of metaphysics.

The problem raised by Derrida's strategy concerns the specificity of the idioms of philosophy and literature. If, as I suggested earlier, the result of Derrida's reading/writing strategy for deconstruction is to produce a notion of text in which temporal and spatial oppositions are reinscribed into each other, then a stable distinction between philosophical and literary idioms becomes untenable. And if, in turn, the notion of text liberates literary criticism from any normative function, it also precludes literary criticism—deconstructive or othrewise—from ever finding a ground for its practice independent of its formative strategics of reading/writing.

As a tentative conclusion, I shall simply raise a few further questions. Are we literary critics yet ready to read Derrida? And have we, beyond our traditional and institutional constraints, learned to write in a "plural language"? If one of the lessons to be learned from Derrida's practice of reading and writing is that the temporality and philosophical moments, to neatly display their temporal order and sapiential hierarchy, then should we not also admit that any attempt to define a concept of deconstruction based on Derrida's writings is by its very nature a misguided enterprise?

The corpus of writings we call Derrida still remains for us a precursor as well as a successor text, inasmuch as Derrida's philosophical enterprise implies the practice of a literary idiom. In this, perhaps, he is an exemplar. For is not the text, the literariness of literature, the literary "thing" that grounds our literary reading/writing as literary critics, the very quest— the always/already improbable future—of our impossible practice?

5

The Possibility of
Literary Deconstruction:
A Reply to Eugenio Donato

David Wood

One of Professor Donato's central claims is that 'deconstructive criticism' has lost sight of the philosophical ground from which it grew and on which the legitimacy of its practice depends. Linked as it must be to the texts of Derrida, the problematic of deconstruction draws on the work of Nietzsche and Heidegger, a tradition that literary deconstruction chooses by and large to ignore. In particular Derrida's development of complex strategies of writing must be seen as a response to Heidegger's discussion of the end of metaphysics.

It would be a standard procedure of misreading to represent my actual partial reading as complete, adequate, even absolute, thereby to disguise even from myself, the blind spots, the lacunas. Perhaps, then, I am throwing away at least one of my chances by openly declaring that I shall not be making responsible responses to many of Professor Donato's terminal questions. When he asks, for example, "Are we literary critics yet ready to read Derrida?" I suddenly feel my competence droop. I shall leave most of this bowl of cherries to those true practitioners of deconstructive literary criticism whom he may have provoked.

In my own response I should like to focus, first, on Donato's account of Derrida's relation to Heidegger. He began by claiming that it was an impossible project, but quite a bit of it leaked out nonetheless. Secondly, I shall consider Donato's claims about the significance of this relationship for the practice of deconstruction. I shall argue that Donato's own ability to give, for example, an abstract and quasiformal account of Derrida's understanding of *text* undercuts the claim that Derrida's rereading of Heidegger is of vital concern to deconstructive practice. And although agreeing with much of what he says about the Heidegger/Derrida relationship, I hope he will not mind my muddying the clarity of his story with a few reservations.

My first reservation concerns the important claim that because most readings of Derrida and deconstruction could be derived from Derrida's critique of Husserl in *Speech and Phenomena*, and because deconstruction proper begins with *Of Grammatology*, these readings are fundamentally limited. In particular, he argues, they do not grasp the continuing if problematic dependence of deconstruction on phenomenology, which gets worked through in *Of Grammatology*[1] for the first time, and consequently can supply no motivation for the complex strategies of writing and reading that Derrida employs.

I would be the last to deny that Derrida's debts at the level of strategy have a large Heideggerean component (though a full story would have to mention Nietzsche, Bataille, Hegel, and many others). As he himself writes, "What I have attempted to do would not have been possible without the opening of Heidegger's questions"[2] and specifically it is Heidegger "who recognizes that economically and strategically he had to borrow the syntactic and lexical resources of the language of metaphysics . . . at the very moment that one deconstructs this language" (p 10). But if it is true that "most readings of Derrida" can be derived from *Speech and Phenomena*, it is surely in part because although we do not get there the fully elaborated account of the problematics of closure, these problems are implicit in this book.

It concerns, after all, Husserl's confirmation of the most basic metaphysical value—that of presence—despite having set himself the goal of breaking once and for all with metaphysics. Indeed Derrida explicitly mentions (chap. 1, note 5) Heidegger as the source for this ironic judgment on Husserl's efforts, and suggests that Heidegger himself was not so simply self-snared. Donato mentions Derrida's references to the strategic need for *unheard-of* thoughts 'beyond' absolute knowledge only so that he can marginalize them as a mere 'extension' of Derrida's critique rather than as deconstruction proper.

Donato is not saying that deconstructive readings actually have been drawn only from *Speech and Phenomena* because he further wants to contend that although *Of Grammatology* has also been read, it has been read eccentrically. It is not, he claims, as so many believe, ultimately concerned with structuralism, linguistics, or semiology, but rather with the deconstruction of presence. But I wonder how far Donato would want to press this formulation. He insists on the *central* concern of *Of Grammatology*, he cites Derrida's own authorial reflections as evidence, and he supposes that a strict hierarchy of intentions can be established between the book's ultimate intention and those that are derivative and secondary. Do not each of these moves involve recourse to values (centeredness, authorial presence, a rigid hierarchy of intentions), which deconstruction would be the first to question? And while we are about it, we might add that the rigid distinction between *Speech and Phenomena* and *Of Grammatology* seems to presuppose what might be called a precritical adherence to the unity of particular texts, and to a belief in their proper ordering. And does not Derrida contest each of these principles (and precisely in relation to his own texts) at the beginning of *Positions:* "In what you call my books, what is first of all put in question is the unity of the book," (p, 3) and "It would be impossible to provide a linear, deductive representation of these works that would correspond to some logical order." (p. 4) But is that not exactly what Donato does: set up a logical order?

Donato finds further evidence for his own reading of *Of Grammatology* in the exergue, and its three guiding themes. He quite properly demonstrates their echoing of Heideggerean themes, more or less directly. But I fail to see the need to drive a wedge between Derrida's critique of linguistics and his account of the historically momentous repression of writing and the promotion of the plenitude of speech. I completely agree that Derrida is rewriting Heidegger here. But the way he is doing this is to push the word *writing* as far as it can go, and so it is surely unconvincing to try to treat his accounts of those tendencies in linguistics that exclude or repress writing as secondary or derivative. They are part of where this exclusion occurs.

Donato makes a great deal of the distinction between end and closure. And in the movement from Heidegger's 'end' to Derrida's 'closure' much is condensed. But before looking at that movement, I want to ask one small question about Donato's *formulation* of what he calls Derrida's immediate aim in *Of Grammatology*. It is perhaps just a slip but if so it ought to be corrected. He says that Derrida's immediate aim is "the reading of Heidegger and of his project of an ontology that would situate itself beyond a presumed Nietzschean end of metaphysics." It ought, for the record, to be said that Heidegger comes to explicitly reject such a characterization of his project as an 'ontology'. This is most explicit in his late (1949) introduction to *What is Metaphysics?*, originally published twenty years earlier. The first step in what he calls the attempt to recall the truth of Being is to leave the realm of all ontology, and Derrida himself, in the very chapter that Donato is dealing with, dates this repudiation of ontology from Heidegger's *Introduction to Metaphysics* (1935). Donato could respond that in some loose sense Heidegger still seeks an ontology just insofar as he seeks "the truth of Being." And he might suppose that he could get Derridean support for this claim via Derrida's reading of Heidegger's fundamental commitments as metaphysical (and hence perhaps ontological). But, as I shall show, Derrida's final position on Heidegger cannot be resolved so easily.

What about the end/closure relation? This is especially important for Donato because the dismantling of ordinary temporal sequence and the topology of limits built into the idea of closure can be used to restructure our ways of thinking of the 'order of priority' of Nietzsche, Heidegger, and Derrida. Now I must confess at the outset that some of my difficulty with what Donato says about the end/closure relation may well be the result of my own personal obtuseness. But there are places at which I think my reactions have a more general significance. I would have welcomed, for example, some explicit account of what Donato takes the difference to be. The closest he comes to such an account is to say that "the displacement of the concept of *end* to that of the *closure* of metaphysics . . . forbids us from thinking of the temporal and spatial patterns within such a displacement in terms of any simple, linear, or hierarchical notion of history." I think Donato is right—there is a crucial displacement taking place between end and closure, but it is one that preserves an identical insight about the problematic nature of the situation of philosophy at the end/closure of metaphysics. To demonstrate this I should like to juxtapose quotations from Heidegger and Derrida:

> Metaphysics cannot be abolished like an opinion. One can by no means leave it behind as a doctrine no longer believed and represented . . . If this is so, we may not presume to stand outside of metaphysics because we surmise the *ending* of metaphysics. For metaphysics overcome in this way does not disappear. It returns transformed. —Heidegger, "Overcoming Metaphysics."[3]

> Perhaps . . . one does not leave the epoch whose closure one can outline . . . The movements of belonging or not belonging to an epoch are too subtle . . . for us to make a definite judgement. —Derrida (G, 12).

In my view, Derrida is hardly going beyond a translation of the word *end* with that of *closure*. And their prescribed remedies for this problematic situation also run parallel. For Heidegger what is needed is a new way of thinking; for Derrida a new way of writing. But setting up of such parallels is not enough. The point at which Donato's emphasis upon displacement illuminates his point that Derrida plays topological havoc with the relation between the inside and the outside of the closure. At this point it would seem that Heidegger recognizes the problems of transition from the epoch of metaphysics to any beyond, but Derrida problematizes more thoroughly the very notion of the beyond.

One of the important consequences of this distinction for Donato is that it allows him to account for Derrida's placing of Heidegger within the very metaphysical tradition he announces. I think the argument is this: that Derrida's complex topology of closure in some sense encompasses Heidegger's simpler version of ending. And corresponding to

Heidegger's oversimplification of the end is his restoration of the value of origin in the shape of a certain 'truth' (= the truth of Being). If one were forced to say yes or no to the question "Does Derrida ultimately treat Heidegger as a metaphysician?," one would probably have to say yes, but I think Donato overstates the case and oversimplifies Derrida's treatment of Heidegger. It is not just that Derrida says many different things about Heidegger oscillating between speechs for the defense and for the prosecution—even in the short span of *The End of the Book and the Beginning of Writing* (G, 6-26). Here he at least temporarily rescues Heidegger from the charge of having produced a new philosophy of presence by pointing out that for Heidegger it is not Being, but *the question of Being*, that is basic. When he does develop a critical line on Heidegger, it is invariably accompanied by devices of moderation and hesitation. Consider the passage Donato quotes (G, 23). I would stress the words "would . . . be," "inasmuch as . . . ," "not completely," "perhaps," "would perhaps." The fact is, Donato somewhat later admits when he mentions Derrida's discussion of Heidegger's position in *Time and Being*, that there is evident in Heidegger's own development a self-reflective or perhaps self-deconstructive movement in which the force of most, if not all, of Derrida's partial readings is deflected.

Donato's complex account of the strategy involved in Derrida's readings of Heidegger's reading of Nietzsche, by which Derrida's releases Nietzsche from Heidegger's reading of him, is quite fascinating. Consider the point at which Donato, invokes Lacoue-Labarthe's reading of Nietzsche to fill out Derrida and then seems to equate or at least assimilate the two. It may seem a minor point but if Lacoue-Labarthe wants to claim that Nietzsche's *literariness* places him beyond the closure, it is the status of Nietzsche's writing as *writing* that is important for Derrida. And insofar as *writing* is prior to the distinction between philosophy and literature, Donato's point that Derrida's strategy makes the relationship between philosophy and literature problematic can be made with even greater force. It precludes the ever recurrent possibility of writing Nietzsche off as a 'mere' literary figure, a poet in disguise.

In this response, I have wanted in large measure to endorse Donato's account of Derrida's indebtness to his confrontation with Heidegger, especially with regard to his development of complex strategies of reading and writing. Perhaps simply as a mark of my own involvement in this issue, I have strewn my response with detailed reservations. I shall, however, question more radically what I take to be one of Donato's conclusions—the need for deconstructive criticism to grasp the Heideggerean (and Nietzschean) origin of Derrida's deconstructive strategies. Perhaps suprisingly coming from a philosopher (of sorts) I remain unconvinced by this claim.

Early on in his paper, Donato used Gasché's fine account of the importance of the reflexive critique of phenomenology in situating Derrida, as an object lesson in the dangers of philosophical innocence. But Gasché (in "Deconstruction as Criticism," 1979) had diagnosed specific short-comings, even *errors*, as directly attributable to the obscuring of this back-drop of phenomenological critique. De Man, for example, had mistakenly identified deconstruction with self-reflexivity, which was not just confu-sion, but a return to a pre-Derridean philosophy of the subject and of consciousness. However, my point is that Donato does not offer us any account of particular errors that the neglect of Heidegger (or the frame-work in which the end/closure of metaphysics is discussed) has gen-erated in deconstructive criticism. Consequently his account lacks a cer-tain motivation.

But if we accept something like Gasché's (1979) position—the need to read Derrida via his critique of phenomenology, adding, as Donato will, the further need to understand his strategies in relation to Heideg-ger—are we then bound to sympathize with the rhetorical thrust of Donato's question to Culler: How can he spend one hundred forty pages explaining Derrida while explicitly stating at the outset that he will not attempt to discuss the relationship of Derrida to Hegel, Husserl, Nietzsche, or Heidegger?

The question "How can he do this?" can be given a straight answer. At the very same place where Donato quotes Culler as tacitly admitting the relevance of that history he states that *he* will not be providing it. He refers us instead, not unintelligently, to Gayatri Spivak, and yes, Gasché.

This of course leaves us with the question—How could his one hun-dred forty pages have any coherence to anyone who had not already read Spivak and Gasché? And here a certain, perhaps limited, defense of Culler's enterprise (and others like it) can be mounted. It goes like this: to a certain extent one can give abstract accounts of the logic or strategy of deconstruction as Derrida practices it. One can recount Derrida's under-standing of textuality and the complex topology of limits. Culler, for example, on the first of these one hundred forty pages, quotes Derrida's account (in *Positions*) of the general strategy of deconstruction, an ac-count which could be represented formulaically as the reversal and dis-placement of a conceptual hierarchy. But Donato himself provides us with further examples, admirably formulated. Consider the following:

> Every text exists by a redoubled series of readings/writings which depend upon and constitutes a unique system in which the temporal and spatial hierarchies of "before" and "after," "inside" and "outside," "form" and "con-tent," etc., are destabilised by their own redoubling within a system that is always simultaneously a reading and a writing.

This is meant to convince us of the need to read Derrida's texts as redoublings of Heidegger, Nietzsche, et. al. (which indeed they are). But if our interest is not in reading Derrida for its own sake, but in doing as Derrida does, why can we not take this abstract account of the complex topology of any text and apply to in our deconstructive practice. Or, to be more accurate, why cannot those who practice literary deconstruction do this?

Perhaps I am misguided in suggesting that we can distinguish the historical source of Derrida's ideas from their analytical form. I would insist, however, that Derrida's success as a reader of texts is in large measure a consequence of his recepivity to the complex topologies and temporalities of textuality in general. These schemata, if they may be called that, are in part what makes it possible for him to read Nietzsche, Husserl, and Heidegger in the way he does, and they are by no means the exclusive property of these philosophical texts. Analogues to many of them can be found in Escher's lithographs, in the structure of certain logical and mathematical paradoxes, in the psychoanalytical study of dreams, and so on.

Speaking, I hope, not just autobiographically, the moments of insight (and indeed of frustration) in reading Derrida are always associated with having "grasped" (or failing to grasp) the formal scheme organizing his writing at a particular time (the words "formal" and "grasp" both being written under erasure!).

My conclusion, then, is that if reading Derrida involves grasping the dependence of his own reading on the elaboration and recognition of certain formal schemata (e.g., the complex topologies of enclosure), then, as these can be grasped and applied independently of a detailed knowledge of their embodiment in, say, the problematic of the end of metaphysics in Heidegger, we have a straight answer to how Culler (and others) can do what they do. And I might add that much of what Donato says when discussing the logic of closure seems to point to the same conclusion. Unless and until a return to the Heideggerean framework of Derrida's strategic problematic is adequately motivated by a detailed account of the general intellectual impoverishment or particular deficiencies within literary deconstruction, I am not convinced of its necessity.

6

Derrida and Heidegger:
The Interlacing of Texts

Tina Chanter

The Donato/Wood debate raises the question of property. Eugenio Donato criticizes Jonathan Culler for not taking account of Heidegger, Hegel, Nietzsche, and Husserl in his explanation of Derrida's position. But in his own attempt to correct that neglect, at least in regard to Heidegger, and only to some extent in regard to Nietzsche, Donato claims that Derrida moves beyond Heidegger's achievement. Although Culler himself does not provide a full discussion of the philosophical importance of Heidegger for Derrida, this is not because he deems it unnecessary. Indeed, as David Wood points out, Donato refers his readers to Rodolphe Gasché, who stresses the importance of Heidegger's thinking for Derrida.

Wood on the other hand, "perhaps surprisingly coming from a philosopher" as he himself acknowledges, is not convinced of the "need for deconstructive criticism to grasp the Heideggerian (and Nietzschean) origin of Derrida's deconstruction strategies." Wood therefore undertakes a "certain, perhaps limited, defense" of projects such as Culler's. Wood suggests that there is nothing to prevent practitioners of deconstruction from taking as their model an "abstract account of the complex topology" of a text, such as Culler provides. (According to Wood, Donato also produces such an account, albeit gratuitously.) Noticeable by its absence in this strange network of allegiances is the drawing of any conclusion about the effect Derrida's notion of writing might have upon the very idea of indebtedness of allegiance. Even Wood fails to draw out the significance of his own acknowledgment that the way in which "Derrida is rewriting Heidegger ... is to push the word *writing* as far as it can go." (Perhaps this is partly due to the apparently unproblematic use of the idea of a "practitioner" of deconstruction. Has Derrida not learned from Heidegger that

rules of practice are not easily separable from those of theory, indeed that
they are not easily discernible at all?)

Wood says that it is "seeing how the text works" that illuminates or
frustrates. Despite Wood's denial that he is distorting Derrida by considering separately the "historical source" and the "analytical form" of his
ideas, I suspect that the kind of defense he wants to make for Culler
cannot be sustained without violation. Surely to attend to what is stimu-
lating (or frustrating) in a text cannot be achieved merely by a 'formal'
grasp of organizing schemata devoid of historical understanding? (Even
Wood's proviso that the words 'formal' and 'grasp' should be understood
as "under erasure" provides no help so long as we have to be shown how
to read these terms under erasure. Rather the proviso indicates a tension.)
Wood concludes his reply to Donato with the words:

> Unless and until a return to the Heideggerian framework of Derrida's strate-
> gic problematic is adequately motivated by a detailed account of the general
> intellectual impoverishment or particular deficiencies within literary decon-
> struction, I am not convinced of its necessity.

I do not comply with this demand for a catalogue of errors in existing
attempts at literary deconstruction, any more than Donato does. An
appreciation of the differences between Derridean strategy and traditional
methods of reading seems to be lacking. Is not Derrida's way of taking up
Heidegger precisely an attempt to avoid conceptualizing the intellectual
pattern of a text's logic by purely analytic criteria, while avoiding a naive
endorsement of historical allegiance to one's precursors? Derrida takes
over from Heidegger a changed relation to the tradition. The inheritance
of the tradition is no longer a matter of historical accident simply to be
observed by those who inherit it. The way in which Derrida understands
his relation to Heidegger and, through Heidegger, his relation to the rest
of the tradition, cannot be thought apart from his rethinking of the historical relation itself—that is, through such notions as the trace.

One of the chief reasons why Donato does not elucidate the complexities of the Derrida-Heidegger relation satisfactorily, and cannot do
so within the scope of his essay, is that the task he sets for himself excludes
the analysis of any "specific reading of Heidegger by Derrida," even
though his argument seems to demand it. Despite his acknowledgment
that "displacement of the Heideggerian necessity of a *deconstructive* reading into a *style of deconstructive reading*," is "spelled out in the first
chapter of *Of Grammatology* and systematically worked out in a number
of articles that followed its publication," Donato offers us no sustained
treatment either of the displacement or the style of deconstructive reading. Instead, in order to uphold his claim that Derrida shows how the

Heideggerian notion of truth is basically metaphysical, Donato appeals to Derrida's 'closure' as having superseded the 'end' of philosophy that Heidegger announced.

Although there is no doubt that Derrida links Heidegger with logocentrism—and in claiming this Donato appropriately cites the sentence, "All metaphysical determination of truth . . . and even the one . . . that Heidegger reminds us of, are more or less inseparable from the instance of the logos"[1]—there are some important questions left open. Does Derrida not recognize that logocentrism characterizes not only Heidegger's thinking—and that of the whole tradition—but also his own thinking? Insofar as Derrida draws upon the language of the tradition, he cannot distance himself from it, even though his use of traditional language asserts and tries to maintain his distance. Referring to the 'concept of the *graphie*' and the '*instituted trace*' Derrida says:

> My efforts will be directed toward slowly detaching these two concepts from the classical discourse from which I necessarily borrow them. The effort will be laborious and we know a priori that its effectiveness will never be pure and absolute. (G, 68/46)

This observation confirms that when Derrida suggests that "one does not leave the epoch whose closure one can outline," he has in mind not only Heidegger but, equally, himself. If this is so, an alternative to Donato's view must be found.

Donato's claim can be summarized thus: in comparison to the Heideggerian 'end,' Derrida's notion of 'closure' is a relative success. As we have seen, Donato's distinction requires that the Heideggerian notion of truth be metaphysical. One could show, through a reading of Heidegger's essay "The Origin of The Work of Art", for example, that Heidegger's interpretation of truth as *aletheia* does not depend upon a metaphysical conception of presence. In fact, presence-to-self is singled out by Heidegger as a difficulty in *Being and Time*, particularly when he calls into question the problematic relation of Being to human being.[2]

What does it mean for Derrida to explore "enigmatic" terms such as presence and one's own (*propre*). This is to follow a direction signaled by Derrida in a passage near the end of part one, chapter two, of *De la Grammatologie*, where he writes:

> The word *trace* must refer itself to a certain number of contemporary discourses whose force I intend to take into account. Not that I accept them totally. But the word *trace* establishes the clearest connection with them and thus permits me to dispense with certain developments which have already demonstrated their effectiveness in those fields. Thus, I relate this concept of *trace* to what is at the center of the latest work of Emmanuel Levinas and his

critique of ontology: relationship to the illeity as to the alterity of a past that
never was and never can be lived in the originary or modified form of presence. Reconciled here to a Heideggerian intention—as it is not in Levinas's
thought—this notion signifies, sometimes beyond Heideggerian discourse,
the undermining of an ontology, which, in its innermost course, has determined the meaning of being as presence and the meaning of language as the
full continuity of speech. To make enigmatic what one thinks one understands by the words "proximity," "immediacy," "presence" (the proximate,
proche, the own, *propre*, and the pre-of presence), is my final intention in
this book [G, 103/70].

Derrida pushes beyond Heideggerian discourse here, but at the same
time embraces a "Heideggerian intention" in preference to a Levinasian
framework. (This is not to deny that he finds in Levinas much that is
congruent with his own thought—particularly, as in the passage quoted
above, with respect to Levinas's notion of the trace.) Although he testifies
that there are points at which he leaves Heideggerian discourse behind, it
is not yet clear how Derrida claims to be going beyond Heidegger—unless
it is in the very task of rendering "enigmatic" terms such as 'presence' and
'proximity,' thereby occluding the desire for the clarity that Heidegger
may still have held as an ideal. In order to catch sight of Derrida's relation to Heidegger, perhaps the best way is to consider those essays in
which Derrida develops his attempt to render presence "enigmatic" in his
reading of specific Hedeggerian texts.

To keep this task within the limits of the present study, I will focus
on a particular text: Derrida's *"Restitutions de la vérité en pointure,"* a
reading of Heidegger's "Origin of the Work of Art." By examining this
essay I hope to shed some light on a problem that is central to Donato's
paper but not raised there as such. It is the question of who has responsibility for a text, a question that for Derrida is ultimately a question of
the text, or of writing itself. In "Restitutions" Derrida addresses the question as to who may be answerable for a text, the question as to whose
property it may be.

In this essay, Derrida takes issue with Meyer Schapiro's paper, "The
Still Life as a Personal Object—A Note on Heidegger and Van Gogh."[3]
The most basic criticism Derrida raises against Schapiro is that the essential point in Heidegger's discussion of Van Gogh's painting, *Old Shoes*, is
the status of the painting as an example. Schapiro neglects this exemplary
status of Van Gogh's painting.

Heidegger initially adopts Van Gogh's painting of some old shoes to
serve as an example of equipment or products; they are exemplary for
their product quality. The old shoes serve their function in the appeal that
Heidegger makes to his readers' understanding of the familiar. When
Schapiro insists that there is evidence for the shoes having belonged to

Van Gogh himself, and not to a peasant, as Heidegger's discussion of the painting supposes, he misses the point. Heidegger refers to the shoes in Van Gogh's painting as an illustration of what everybody takes for granted. The owners of the shoes is of no importance; they simply serve as an example of something useful. Schapiro cannot see this, because he divorces this formal element of Heidegger's essay—his identification of the shoes with the peasant—not only from the context of the peasant's world, but also from other formal elements of the essay. For instance, the shoes appear not only as useful, but also as mere things on the one hand, and a work of art on the other. The relationship between these three aspects of the thing, the mere thing *(das blosse Ding)*, the thing as product, and the thing as work, is, Derrida says, like a lace:

> Each 'thing,' each mode of being of the thing, passes inside then outside the other. We will often avail ourselves of this figure of the lace: passing and re-passing through the eyelet of the thing, from outside in, from inside out . . .[4]

The figure of laces weaving in and out of the shoe leather, through the eyelets, illustrates for Derrida a movement that he will also call the work of the trace (R, 346/35). In describing the existing relationship between the three modes of the thing's being that Heidegger discusses, and by reference to the trace, Derrida places a new emphasis on the relationship between the shoes in Van Gogh's picture and the shoes outside the picture— that is, the relationship between the shoes as unused, abandoned, unlaced, bare, and the shoes as clothing for the peasant woman, the shoes as invested, inhabited, informed by the body (R, 302/7).

In his reading of "The Origin of the Work of Art," Derrida uses this difference between inside and outside to comment on sexual difference. Derrida notices Heidegger's dependence upon the "sex of reattachment," as he calls it (R, 349/37), whereby the owner of the shoes is recognized only in neutral terms when the shoes appear 'in' the picture—that is, as a product characterized by usefulness. However, considered 'outside' the painting, the shoes become the clothing of a peasant woman. "There's almost a rule in the peasant woman's appearing" says Derrida (R, 350/38). He continues:

> Heidegger designates as such the woman who wears *(la porteuse)* the shoes outside the painting (if we can say that), when the lace of discourse passes outside the edge of the frame, into this outside-the-work, *hors-d'oeuvre*, that Heidegger claims to see presented right in the work. But each time he speaks of the exemplary product *in* the painting, he speaks in a neutral, generic, i.e., in grammar, masculine way: *ein Paar Bauernschuhe*, a pair of peasant shoes. Why are the feet of the thing, here some shoes, thus presented as the feet of a (peasant) woman? [R, 350/38].

In another, more recent, essay Derrida makes tangible his conjecture that sexuality is important, if unthematic, in Heidegger's philosophy. Derrida says in "Geschlecht"[5] that "it is by the name of *'Dasein'* that I would introduce the question of sexual difference" (GS, 421/58). In the same essay Derrida asks about the effect of Heidegger's subordination of sexual difference to ontological difference:

> Is it not to remove sexuality from every originary structure? Deduce it? Or in any case derive it, confirming all the most traditional philosophemes, repeating them with the force of a new rigour? [GS, 428/79].

This last question recalls a commitment that Derrida makes to Heidegger in "Restitutions" by way of a strange acknowledgment:

> I've always been convinced of the strong necessity of Heidegger's questioning, even if here he repeats, in the worst as well as the best sense of the term, the traditional philosophy of art. And perhaps even to the extent that he does so [R, 299/5].

If we read this passage as a statement of the situation in which every attempt to exeed the limits of metaphysical philosophy finds itself circumscribed by, or drawn back into, the tradition it seeks to transgress, then the sentence with which Derrida follows his recognition of the necessity of Heidegger's questioning carries a sense that is not at first obvious. The sentence runs: "But each time I perceived the famous passage on a 'well-known painting by Van Gogh' as a moment of touching, laughable, and symptomatic collapse, signifying—Signifying what?" (R, 299/5). The passage Derrida has in mind is the one he makes so much of a little further on, and is, as Donato points out, the only passage Derrida quotes at length. Derrida makes this lengthy passage available to his readers in French, German, and English; I will not quote it in its entirety, but identify it only by recalling that is is puncuated with the words *"und dennoch!"* It is the passage where Heidegger describes the peasant's relationship to her working shoes, a passage Derrida thinks is full of pathos.

Of what is this laughable collapse a symptom? Of the tradition? Or of Heidegger's repetition of the tradition? Or of the rigor with which Heidegger repeats the tradition? Heidegger's treatment of the pair of shoes, provoking Derrida's laughter, does not invite absolute ridicule. If we take Derrida at his word, perhaps in the end the laugh is on us. For at every moment Derrida takes back what he says; he shows up Heidegger's writing as ludicrous, embarrassing. But at the same time, Derrida shows that the "absurd" passage is pivotal to Heidegger's discussion of the origin of the work of art. The difference between the familiarity with which the peasant knows her shoes, on the one hand, and the truth that emerges for the thinker confronted by Van Gogh's painting, on the other hand, is crucial to Heidegger's essay. Thus Derrida's ridicule of Heidegger finds its corollary in the respect he accords Heidegger. In acknowledging the strategic importance of Heidegger's evocation if the peasant's world of toil, Derrida has effected a reversal of his own judgment.[6]

That Derrida goes back on what he says is not to be taken lightly, but neither is it an excuse to dismiss his apparent contradictions as canceling one another out. The statements counter one another, but weave a pattern as they do so. The patterns that Derrida creates demand a different kind of reading, and, what is perhaps most difficult, a different kind of questioning. Whatever the direction of this new way of questioning, it will surely have to go beyond the tradition of metaphysics, though it will be bound by metaphysical thought in its very attempt to break the boundary. Acknowledging the need for this new way of questioning, we begin to see Derrida's reading of Heidegger's discussion of the origin of the work of art as a writing of woman into Heidegger's text. The naming of *Dasein* becomes for Derrida a way of thinking what Heidegger leaves unsaid.

Could it be that one of the undercurrents of "Restitutions" is Derrida's concern that the community of preservers and creators, envisaged by Heidegger's *"The Origin of the Work of Art"* as the keepers and makers of art, entails a division of the sexes that embraces a traditional male/female hierarchy? Is the peasant woman, who knows her shoes only in their reliability as she works, prevented from knowing them in their truth, as they appear to someone who looked at Van Gogh's painting of her old shoes? Could one of Derrida's more pointed questions to Heidegger be the following: Must woman, when it comes to truth, be kept in the background? In *Spurs*,[7] Derrida takes up Heidegger's reading of Nietzsche on the question of woman. He suggests a metaphysical necessity in the disappearance of woman; and her disappearance opens metaphysics to a thinking not governed by the metaphysical—though it would always have to be encompased by it.

Derrida writes:

> Just as there is no such thing, then, as a Being or an essence of *the* woman of the sexual difference, there is also no such thing as an essence of the *es gibt* in the *es gibt Sein*, that is, of Being's giving and gift. The "just as" finds no conjuncture. There is no such thing as a gift of Being from which there might be apprehended and opposed to it something like a determined gift (whether of the subject, the body, of the sex or other like things—so woman, then, will not have been my subject) [S, 120/121].

Historically woman has been excluded, for the most part, from own-
ership and prevented from filling the role of proprietor. If we wonder
why woman is compared to the *es gibt Sein*, the answer for Nietzsche, on
Derrida's reading, is that woman dissimulates, and is dissimulated by, the
tradition. Derrida says:

> Either, at times, woman is woman because she gives, *because she gives* her-
> self, while the man for his part takes, possesses, indeed takes possession. Or
> else, at other times, she is in fact *giving herself for*, is simulating, and conse-
> quently assuring the possessive mastery for her own self. The *for* which
> appears in the "to-give-oneself-for," whatever its value, whether it deceives
> by giving only an appearance of, or whether it actually introduces some
> destination, finality, or twisted calculation, some return, redemption, or gain,
> into the loss of proper-ty (*propre*), this *for* nonetheless continues to withhold
> the gift of a reserve [S, 108-10/109-11].

The passage provides a context for understanding Derrida's refusal
of a simple genealogy of origins and property, his refusal of the origin as
such. He says in "Restitutions":

> Now it seems clear to me that the *Origin* is also read as an essay on the gift,
> *Schenkung*. . . . Before applying these "concepts" (gift or abyss, for example)
> to the debate (indeed to such an object as Heidegger's text would be), per-
> haps we'd better begin by deciphering them and restoring them *in* Heidegger's
> text [R, 333/24-5].

In deciphering and restoring, Derrida appeals to a tendency in Heidegger's
own thought (if we could still talk in terms of property as if it were
unproblematic). Derrida finds in the Heideggerian notions of authentic-
ity, propriety, and proximity a 'dehiscence,' an 'oblique movement,' the
'abyssal structure' (S, 116/7). Derrida sees just such an oblique movement in Heidegger's account of the old shoes in Van Gogh's painting. The
movement of the laces weaving in and out of the shoes leads Derrida to
this question: Does this weaving of laces join the peasant world to the
world of art so that they are henceforth indistinguishable? (R, 347/36).
Given that his questioning is not limited to properties of things, but
extends to things as property per se, to the question of property itself, we
are compelled to ask: Is there any disfunction in the difference between
Derrida's 'own' text, "Restitutions," and Heidegger's text, *"The Origin of
the Work of Art"*?

Part III

Philosophy and Criticism

PRELIMINARY REMARKS

This part is in many ways a continuation of the first two. Here the essays by Harvey, de Man, and Gasché reiterate questions as to whether deconstruction changes or simply reinstantiates its text, whether deconstruction is a method of criticism among others, and whether deconstructive practices are necessarily bound to a philosophical/metaphysical problematic. This last question leads to its reversal, as suggested in the essay by de Man: Can deconstructive criticism identify and resolve aporias in philosophical texts? In his criticism of Kant's text on the sublime, de Man claims that when a conceptual resolution of a philosophical problematic becomes impossible, the materiality of the text provides the only way out, thus transposing the problematic into the domains of grammar, rhetoric, and textual mechanics. Here the critic holds the advantage over the philosopher. The philosopher is bound to structures and strategies of textuality over which he has no control, but which the critic can reveal and identify. This account of the relation between philosophy and criticism is the central focus of the present section.

In the preceding section the Donato-Wood debate reveals a tension between deconstructive criticism and philosophical discourse in the texts of Derrida. Irene Harvey's essay, "The Difference between Derrida and de Man," clarifies this issue in terms of a distinction between the two foremost strategists of deconstruction. Harvey reminds us that there is no such thing as deconstruction per se, for, being neither an object nor a method, it has no essence. Furthermore, the differences between Derrida and de Man are both theoretical and practical. In carefully distinguishing de Manian from Derridean deconstruction, Harvey allows us to situate more precisely the point of contention between de Man and Gasché.

According to Harvey, de Man claims that textuality is *inherently* deconstructive, whereas for Derrida deconstruction is a strategy of reading that is applied to the text. That is to say, de Man finds deconstruction to be a constituting structure of the text itself, where Derrida seeks to trace a nonstructural "play of the supplement" (or *différance*), which occurs between the text and its reading.

For de Man, the deconstructive reading seeks to reveal its own structure in the text, and from here to show that deconstruction is coextensive with all use of language whatsoever. Thus a deconstructive reading ineluctably repeats the linguistic categories of the text, whose structure is self-deconstructive to begin with. Therefore, the difference between a deconstructive reading and its text is only ironic, in that the deconstructive reading thematizes aporias implicit in the text, while formally and practically repeating these same aporias itself. Any deconstructive reading, then, is "text-productive," and is subject to the mechanics of self-deconstruction at work in the text "originally." As conceived by de Man, deconstruction is an endless reiteration of itself.

Derrida, on the other hand, seeks to move from the text and its structure to the play of *différance*. As Harvey points out, this play is nonstructural, but it allows for structure in the text. It is not reducible to a code, a grammar, or a mechanical operation. Rather, *différance* is a play of presence and absence in the constitution of textual identities, insofar as these identities must both include and exclude differences. The play of inclusion and exclusion, or effacement, leaves its trace in the text, and deconstruction seeks to produce and to reveal this movement. Contrary to de Man, Derridean deconstruction does not return to the original predicament of its text. Instead, it moves toward a level of constitution that is "prior" to, although only traceable within, the text. In this respect, says Harvey, Derrida's enterprise is more philosophical, for it seeks the conditions of textuality per se, whereas de Manian deconstruction is text-bound and inseparable from literary criticism.

In the essay entitled "Phenomenality and Materiality in Kant," de Man confirms this characterization of his work. Here he accomplishes his deconstructive reading of Kant's *Critique of Judgment* via a series of reductions. The first reduction moves from the conceptual level of philosophical discourse to language as a formal system, governed by the rules of tropological substitution. From the rhetoric of tropes, de Man moves to the performative function of language, and then from the performative function to the material mechanics of the text. De Man offers each reduction as the "resolution" of an aporia that occurs at the immediately preceding level. Ultimately, claims de Man, the materiality of Kant's text "resolves" the conceptual aporia presented by the analytic of the sublime. Thus the issue of a philosophical problematic is shifted to a problematic of language, and then to a problematic of the text. This vindicates the activity of textual criticism against the claim of "transcendence" on the part of a discourse that would characterize itself as "purely philosophical."

In his response to Paul de Man, Rodolphe Gasché challenges de Man's interpretation of the phenomenality (and hence materiality) of the sublime. This issue is crucial, for it decides the success or failure of Kant's strategy for articulating the relation between pure and practical reason, and such articulation is the guiding problematic of the *Critique of Judgment*. Where de Man finds a breakdown in Kant's strategy, leading to an aporia that is resolved only at the level of language, Gasché finds Kant's strategy to be sound, requiring no reduction from the level of concepts. For Gasché, philosophy is therefore vindicated over the reductive claims of textual criticism.

The point of contention between Gasché and de Man is focused upon Kant's suggestion that the sublime can be phenomenally presented by the sky or ocean. Such presentation is possible, says Kant, if we regard these phenomena "as poets do," by attending only to "what the eye reveals" (*was der Augenschein zeigt*). For de Man, the *Augenschein* is purely material, involving no reflexive judgment or semantic depth. It is reducible to the mathematization of pure optics, and therefore constitutes a formal materialism. This contradicts all of Kant's earlier analyses of the sublime as a presentation of ideas. Gasché counters that the *Augenschein* only shows itself, whereas the sublime is properly interpreted as the mood (*Stimmung*) of the mind in its contemplation of the ocular vision. The sublime is not presented in the "material" phenomenality of the ocean, for example, but the sublime is the *act* of finding the ocean sublime. As Gasché reads Kant, the phenomenality of the sublime always already involves a reflective, aesthetic judgment. In this case, the "immediate intuition" of the *Augenschein* is immediate in a negative sense. In seeing nothing determinate, the *Augenschein* is freed from the concepts of understanding and is given over to reason. Instead of marking a breakdown in Kant's discourse, the *Augenschein* achieves a presentation, albeit a negative one, of the faculty of ideas. And so the contradiction attested to by de Man does not arise; the strategy of Kant's philosophical discourse is completable at the conceptual level.

The differences between de Man and Gasché over the reading of a specific text, although illuminating, do not settle the more general question as to the relation between philosophy and criticism. This relation hinges upon the degree to which textual meaning is bound to textual mechanics. De Man would insist that the bond is complete, but a more philosophical reader would allow for the independence of concepts from specific textual configurations. Derrida's affiliation with philosophy is confirmed in his notion of *différance*, which although not a concept, is not bound to any textual structure. Thus, in regard to deconstruction's contribution to the issue of philosophy and criticism, the positions of de Man and Derrida are not to be equated. Although the ramifications of this distinction extend beyond the limits of the present volume, the originality of de Man vis-à-vis Derrida is evident here.

G. E. A.

7

The *Différance* Between
Derrida and de Man

Irene E. Harvey

Before investigating the 'defensibility' of deconstruction in literary criticism, I wish to examine the nature of the question itself. The issue is framed here, *as if* deconstruction entailed the following: (1) a methodology, as such detachable from its 'object' of analysis and the 'subject' analyzing; (2) a unitary object; as if a 'proper name' with the 'proper' inscribed (as essence of zone of being), demarcated or circumscribed according to metaphysics' founding opposition of inside and outside, therein making deconstruction in a certain sense *context-free* or infinitely transferable (from text to text and context to context; and (3) something therefore distinct from the nature of textuality itself.

Contrary to these assumptions, I suggest that none of these traits defining deconstruction are appropriate or accurate for deconstruction either for Derrida or for de Man. Further I shall attempt in this analysis to expose precisely why: (1) deconstruction has *no* essence; (2) deconstruction is not an object or a method; and (3) significant differences stand between deconstruction (in theory and practice) for Derrida and for de Man. This latter issue shall provide the lens through which the more general concerns above shall be examined or illuminated (in metaphysical terms) or (to borrow from Derrida) remarked or reinscribed in my analysis here.

Finally in returning to the issue of *defensibility*—as if deconstruction is under attack (which indeed it is)—I will suggest that textuality itself for de Man is intrinsically 'self-deconstructive' and hence literary criticism is not in a position to either adopt or deny this trait, which *constitutes* its object of analysis as such. On the other hand, for Derrida, deconstruction is "applied to the text," but only insofar as 'text' is reducible to 'book,' which after deconstruction is not only no longer possible but revealed to have, *never* been possible in the first place.

Let us now turn, therefore, to the *différance* within the notion of deconstruction itself and thus to the irreducibility of its (their) plurality.

De Man claims: "The *deconstruction* is not something we have added to the text but it *constituted* the text in the first place. A literary text simultaneously asserts and denies the authority of its own rhetorical mode."

Furthermore: "*Poetic writing* is the most advanced and refined mode of deconstruction."[1]

Whereas for Derrida, deconstruction "aims at a certain relationship, unperceived by the writer, between what he commands and what he does not command of the patterns of language that he uses." In addition, Derrida aims "to reveal the economy of a written text" and "to undo onto-theology."[2] At first sight these two explanations of deconstruction may indeed seem to be the same, or at least complimentary aspects of the same project, but, I suggest, this is not the case. In fact, for de Man 'deconstruction' is a textual structure that is always already there and, as he says, 'constitutes' the text. For Derrida, however, deconstruction is a strategy applied to the text and its results entail the revelation of what he terms "the play of the supplement" or *différance*. This 'play,' albeit not a structural feature as such, is intrinsic to the constitution of textuality.

Returning to de Man I find the results of 'deconstructive discourse' to be a certain mechanical grammar that "repeats the very errors it denounces" in metaphysics. In addition, deconstruction as an ironic event entails a certain reversal of the 'dialectic movement,' which "produces the text."[3] Thus he insists upon a certain interminable oscillation between 'deconstruction' and dialectics as the intrinsic nature of textuality.

For Derrida, however, the aim of deconstruction is to destroy the *Aufhebung*, which allows for the dialectical movement itself.[4] Rather than being implicated in a reversing economy with dialectics, deconstruction "leaves a track in the text it analyzes,"[5] preventing a repetition of the same and, a fortiori, an eternal recurrence of the dialectic.

De Man acknowledges "having first seen the term deconstruction in the work of Derrida" yet insists that the process therein described originated with Nietzsche. This lack of distinction between Derrida's usage and formulation of deconstruction and "the same process" in Nietzsche seems to be symptomatic of several other unacknowledged distinctions that should be made. The first is between Derrida and Nietzsche with respect to their objections and treatments of metaphysics, and also Derrida's claims concerning the 'failure' in Nietzsche's attempt to overcome the metaphysical tradition. This failure is a function of Nietszche's simple oppositional stance (in particular concerning the death of God), which paradoxically, according to Derrida, sustains Nietzsche's membership squarely within the tradition. I shall show therefore that de Man's adherence to Nietzsche, in this respect, subjects his own position to Derrida's criticism of this 'oppositional' stance.

De Man's usage of the term 'deconstruction' is ambiguous in itself in the following respect. On the one hand, he portrays deconstruction as a process that is applied to the text (from without, in a certain sense), but on the other hand he insists that discourse itself and hence textuality as such is intrinsically 'self-deconstructive.' He therefore uses deconstruction as both a means and an end in the act of reading. For example, he says:

> It remains for the *commentator* to undo, with some violence, the historically established pattern or, as Derrida puts it, the 'orbit' of significant misinterpretation—a pattern of which the first example is to be found in Rousseau's own writings—and thus, by a *process of 'deconstruction,'* to bring to light what had remained unperceived by the author and his followers.[6]

Thus the systematic blindness of reading traditions can be transformed into insight, de Man insists. On the other hand, he also states the following:

> This complication is characteristic for all *deconstructive discourse:* the deconstruction states the fallacy of reference in a necessarily referential mode. There is no escape from this, for the text also establishes that *deconstruction* is not something we can decide to do or not to do at will. It is *co-extensive with any use of language* and this use is *compulsive,* or as Nietzsche formulates it, imperative.[7]

In this formulation it seems that de Man is establishing 'deconstruction' as an inevitable and essential textual structure. Indeed, as he says, it is "co-extensive with any use of language." If these two above claims can be understood as not 'self-deconstructive' in themselves, we might consider the implications of de Man's claims as a whole here. In a certain sense, he violates or transcends the metaphysical distinction of inside/outside, activity/passivity, such that deconstruction is neither a subjective activity nor an object as such. It is a process. Indeed it is the act of commentary or interpretation on the one hand and it is this act that is "co-extensive with any use of language," on the other. This is to say, then, that 'deconstruction' as judgment is unavoidable and the necessarily inadequate structure of interpretation.

De Man himself is not unaware of this transcendence of 'deconstruction' beyond metaphysical determinations as such. He also says (with respect to Rousseau in particular, but as an example of something that extends beyond this particularity):

Any Rousseau text that puts such polarities into play will therefore have to set up the fiction of a natural process that functions both as a *deconstructive instrument* and as the outcome of the deconstruction.[8]

He thus states explicitly the problem and the solution (which is never adequate) with regard to the 'locus' of deconstruction. It is quite simply the means (as instrument) yet also the result (as the end or target). What this means, however, is that deconstruction, for de Man, aims toward its own self-realization.

The process or act of deconstruction (synonymous with reading itself, for de Man, is essentially a teleological one, which, far from being oriented toward the "meaning of the text" in a hermeneutic sense, is directed toward the revelation of its own structure as such *within* the text under analysis. Is this collapse of means and end not precisely the problem that Hegel revealed in Kant? Is the deconstruction that aims toward nothing but its own 'self-consciousness' not, on the one hand, a replay of the Kantian application of categories of the understanding to the world, which in the end find nothing of the world but promote a self-conscious awareness of the categories? On the other hand, if deconstruction aims toward itself as the realization of the subject in the object, which in turn objectifies the subject and subjectivizes the object, is this process not precisely Hegel's own strategy in the *Phenomenology of Spirit* with regard to the attainment of self-consciousness of *Geist*?

If the Hegelian critique of Kant can be applied to de Man's usage of deconstruction here, then we are left with nothing but a reification of the process, on the one hand, and a text that is always essentially absent, on the other. Deconstruction is all that is found—always and everywhere—for it is "co-extensive with our use of language." If, however, de Man's usage of deconstruction is more analogous to Hegel's proceedings for the realization of *Geist*, then we have a paradox to consider with regard to the self-conscious aspects of *Geist* and deconstruction.

For de Man the will has nothing to do with the deconstructive process. "It is not something we can decide to do or to not do" it is instead a 'compulsion.' Perhaps the attainment of self-consciousness of Spirit for Hegel could also be summed up in this form, but it would become somewhat ironic if *Geist* achieved such a feat in spite of itself. In applying de Man to Hegel, de Man's analysis illustrates a certain truth of deconstructive discourse in that all texts become essentially ironic—including Hegel's.

For the moment, however, I shall leave the above aporia open and not decide who should be applied to whom. I have sought to point out several possibilities that would result in confirmations and disconfirmations of claims made by each thinker. Perhaps these are the antinomies of deconstruction.

Derrida claims that deconstruction is not neutral in any sense but rather that it intervenes.[9] He also insists, as with de Man, that deconstruction in the end always becomes (to a certain extent) a victim of its own work. Thus deconstruction, implicated in its own findings, is a result of its praxis. This implication and complicity, however, is not due to deconstruction. It is the *product* of its own work and due to the structure or strategy of its intervention as such. Derrida explains:

> The movements of deconstruction do not destroy structures from the outside. They are not possible nor can they take accurate aim except by *inhabiting those structures*. Inhabiting them in a certain way . . . operating necessarily from the inside, borrowing all the strategic and economic resources of subversion from the old structure, borrowing them structurally. That is to say without being able to isolate their elements and atoms, the enterprise of deconstruction always and in a certain way falls prey to its own work.[10]

As distinct from de Man's notion of deconstruction, it seems that Derrida's deconstruction is not a textual structure but rather 'borrows' from the structure under analysis in order to reveal the latter's presuppositions and essentially metaphysical assumptions.

Derrida also claims that deconstruction, as a process applied to the text "leaves a track in the text," opens up the dialectics of closure, and results in the placing or revealing of a 'fold' in the *Aufhebung* of the concept itself. Rather than aiming toward its own realization, or 'self-consciousness,' as de Man's portrayal seems to indicate, deconstruction for Derrida destroys itself in its very accomplishment. That is, deconstruction is a finite intervention that disrupts the closure of the 'book' and transforms it into a 'text.' In this sense, then, Derrida's deconstruction does not aim toward itself but toward "the undoing of ontotheology" and ultimately, the destruction of the *Aufhebung*. Deconstruction for Derrida therefore essentially aims to reveal that which allows for the conditions of the possibility of textuality itself and a *fortiori* metaphysics as such. This is certainly not deconstruction but rather the movement of *différance*, as I shall explain in greater detail shortly.

Concerning the relation of deconstruction, for Derrida, to the text and to its aims, he says the following:

> As the primordial and indisposable phase, in fact and in principle, of the development of this problematic (*différance*), consists in questioning the *internal structure* of these texts as *symptoms*; as that is the only condition for determining these symptoms themselves in the totality of their metaphysical appurtenance. I draw my argument from them in order to isolate, in Rousseau (for example) and in Rousseauism, the theory of writing.[11]

The "theory of writing," or what will later be called *différance* by Derrida, is therefore not reducible to the process that allows for its revelation or deconstruction as such. In fact, deconstruction "consists in the questioning of the internal structure of these texts as symptoms." It is not *à la fois* the symptom and the disease, as it seems to be for de Man. In addition, Derrida insists that deconstruction as a preliminary phase in the process of revealing the play of *différance* must be overcome by an analysis of these symptoms themselves in the "totality of their metaphysical appurtenance." This process is not reducible to deconstruction but rather provides the basis for the understanding of *différance* as a "logic of the supplement." Indeed for Derrida this 'result' of deconstruction is not radically severed or severable from metaphysics, but it also does not lead to a "return to the dialectic."

The results of deconstruction, for de Man, entail a two-fold pattern. On the one hand, deconstruction reveals a certain inadequation of form and content, theory and praxis, in the manifestation of the text itself the difference lies between "metalinguistic statements about the rhetorical nature of language and . . . a rhetorical praxis that puts these statements in question." This "semantic dissonance" allows the text to be opened up in the process of deconstruction and is also the very essence of "deconstructive discourse" itself for de Man. Thus deconstruction deauthorizes the claims of metaphysics in its portrayal of a certain essential overdetermination inherent in textuality and language as such, which has the tendancy to invert and therein subvert its own claims (theory) in its manner (praxis) of exposition.

On the other hand, deconstruction's second result, no less significant than the first, entails the exposure of an inevitability and endlessness in the process of deconstruction itself is a process that is interminable (for de Man):

> The epistème has hardly been restored in fact to its former glory, but it has not been eliminated either. The difference between performative and constative language is *undecidable*; the deconstruction leading from one model to the other is irreversible but it always remains suspended, regardless of how often it is repeated.[12]

Thus the product of deconstruction is a certain awareness of *différance*, the inadequation mentioned earlier, which ultimately cannot be overcome by synthesis nor reduced to a choice. This paralysis involves the undecidability of choice between deconstruction and dialectics—both of which are 'text-productive.'

De Man claims that the revelation of 'contradictions,' or a certain inadequation of form to content in textuality as revealed by deconstruction (1), "never reaches the symmetrical counterpart of what it denies,"[13] yet also (2) "the discourse by which the figural structure of the self (for example) is asserted fails to escape from the categories it claims to deconstruct."[14] Thus he exposes a certain asymmetry within deconstruction itself; indeed the same asymmetry or inadequation exposed by deconstruction in textuality in general. We therefore have the same structure appearing in the 'solution' as in the 'problem.' Perhaps this is simply an "essential structure of textuality," and because deconstruction, in exposing its results, therein textualizes them and hence participates necessarily in the very problem it sought to reveal. But why is this a "greater darkness" than ever for de Man? He explains the situation in the following way:

> *Deconstruction* of figural texts engender lucid narratives which produce, in their turn and as it were within their own texture, a darkness more redoubtable than the error they dispell.

For instance: "in this text [*Julie*] . . . *darkness* falls when it becomes evident that Julie's language at once *repeats* the notions she has just denounced as errors." Further: "She construes the new world into which she is moving as an *exact repetition* of the one she claims to have left behind." And finally: *The repetition differs from its earlier version, not in structure, but by a thematic shift."*[15]

Thus de Man portrays deconstruction as an intrinsically tragic phenomenon but no less avoidable or reducible because of this. The "darkness of the repetition of the errors just denounced" is the eternal recurrence of the same, for Nietzsche and for de Man, evidently. The ironic *structure* of deconstruction differs from that which it 'deconstructs' (which can only ultimately be itself in de Man's analysis, for the discourse itself is deconstructive, he says) only by a thematic shift, but not 'in structure.' Deconstruction's blind spot is precisely its form. Although its content is profound and enlightening its manner or praxis is indistinguishable from that which it aims to deconstruct.

What is produced is a certain interminable oscillation between deconstruction, which unravels, therein revealing discontinuities and inadequations—in short, differences—and the "dialectic movement which produces the text" as a continuous unity with the apparent synthesis of differences into totalities. There seems to be a paradox here, however, for deconstruction, on the one hand, exhibits itself as having the same structure as "the dialectical movement," yet, on the other hand, sustains a certain asymmetrical relation with that which it aims to deconstruct; namely this same dialectic. For de Man, the asymmetrical exchange allows for the appearance of either. Their existence in time as such are *moments* of a more general process. Indeed, this more general process could be called irony per se, establishing the synthesis (albeit an uneasy one) of the opposition of 'deconstruction' and 'dialectics.' His pathway to such a conclusion is of some interest here:

1. There can be no escape from the *dialectical movement* that produces texts.
2. The *deconstruction* of metaphorical figures remains a *necessary moment* in their production.
3. Contrary to received opinion, *deconstructive* discourses are suspiciously text-productive.[16]

Thus he posits the irreducible complicity of dialectics and textuality, introducing deconstruction as a moment (also irreducible in the production of metaphorical figures, which as we know are essential to texts), and finally returning to synthesize deconstruction and dialectics in a 'suspicious' recognition of their collaboration in the process of textual production. The conditions of the possibility of this exchange, which is in essence not an exchange at all, must now be examined in some detail. The text for de Man is ultimately a "grammatical machine" and yet also "a serpent that bites its own tail."[17]

According to de Man, the lesson of deconstruction entails the following displacement:

> The text as body . . . is displaced by the text as *machine* and in the process, it suffers the loss of the illusion of meaning. The *deconstruction* of the figural dimension is a process that takes place *independently of any desire*; as such it is not unconscious but *mechanical*, systematic in its performance but arbitrary in its principle, like a *grammar.*[18]

We should recall that deconstruction earlier was not something one decided to do or not do, but rather was a compulsion and coextensive with any use of language. We can now realize more precisely what "the use of language" means for de Man. "Independently of any desire" the machine of textuality ironizes the very desire that puts it into play. If irony is the (albeit effaced) third term or structure of the structure for de Man, it is nevertheless the ultimate grammar of textuality and in turn takes on a mechanical and arbitrary character. Irony is beyond humanism and beyond control. It is a structure that is all-encompassing by its (only apparent) 'weakness.' The oscillation set up between dialectics is essentially a dialectical process itself. Deconstruction for de Man is but a 'moment' of the process. Indeed it is the middle term that plays nothing but a 'negative' role. It reverses the dialectical totality and is itself in turn reversed. The overall process being irony or tragedy, as per Hegel, and yet ultimately the radical denial of consciousness, unconscious, and the will in general. De Man is explicit on this point:

> The *deconstruction* of metaphor and of all rhetorical patterns such as mimesis, paranomasi, or personification that use resemblance as a way to disguise differences, takes us back to the *impersonal precision of grammar* and a semiology derived from grammatical patterns.[19]

Far from being released from the totalization intrinsic to dialectics, de Man situates textuality within an essential and general grammar—precise and mechanical in essence. Have we not therein returned to Leibniz and his contemporary representative, Chomsky, and the presupposition of a potentially mathematical language and ultimately a mathematical universe? All textuality seems to be reducible to this one "impersonal precision of grammar," and thus to a certain set of rules, as finite and definitive: the *code* for all other codes. Indeed the code for de Man is paradoxically the very structure of deconstruction itself. Its ironic means and mode of production situate it at once in the middle (as the mediating term in the dialectic) and yet also, as Hegel has amply illustrated, as the center. It is the model, on the one hand, for the dialectical process, but is, however, structurally identical to that process. Thus de Man situates deconstruction explicitly 'outside' dialectic, yet implicitly and essentially reducible to the same. Thus deconstruction becomes "suspiciously text-productive."

Ultimately, for de Man, what is at stake here is the nature of language, and indeed it does have a nature:

> A totally enlightened language, regardless of whether it conceives of itself as a consciousness or not, is *unable to control* the recurrence, in its readers as well as in it, the errors it exposes.[20]

Thus language indicts itself, in its very potency and impotence. The knowledge of this structure as the grammar of textuality itself makes no difference whatsoever. Knowing that irony, if indeed this is the case, is the essence of textual production, one is still "out of control" or more precisely, totally *controlled* by it. The eternal recurrence of the same is undaunted by the difference between what de Man has so appropriately named 'blindness' or 'insight.' Indeed his third term, which allows for the emergence of this duplicity, is that "even greater darkness" that an apparent insight produces. Ultimately, then, insight is an even greater illusion than blindness.

One of Derrida's principal aims for deconstruction, we should recall, is to "reveal the economy of the written text." Furthermore, he insists, *différance* is the most general concept of economy itself. Thus it would

seem that *différance* as the economy of the written text must be the product or result of deconstruction. It is therefore toward the difference
between deconstruction and *différance*, on the one hand, and between
dialectics or metaphysics and *différance* on the other that we must turn
our attention here. Unlike de Man, Derrida does not speak of irony, nor
of a "reversal" or "exchange of attributes" as the results of deconstruction. However, the difference between the economy of *différance* or
différance as economy and the "exchange (or reversal) of attributes" must
also be clarified here. Finally, for Derrida, there is no possibility of a
"return" to dialectics or to a 'predeconstructive' stage *after* the process of
deconstruction. The results are, contrary to de Man's approach, irreversi-
ble. We must now direct our attention to these differences, that are a
result of *différance*.

Deconstruction, for Derrida, reveals the *movement* that is constitutive for textuality itself but which at the same time is both the condition
of the possibility and the impossibility of metaphysics. This movement is
"strategically nick-named" *différance* by him, for it is neither a 'word,'
'name,' or 'concept.' *Différance* appropriates nothing and thus escapes
absolute delimitation and determination, yet allows for the same. As
Derrida says:

> *différance* is not a process of propriation in any sense whatever. It is neither
> position (appropriation) nor negation (expropriation), but rather other.
> Hence it seems—but here, rather, we are marking the necessity of a future
> itinerary—that *différance* would be no more a species of the genus *Ereignis*
> than Being.[21]

Thus *différance* as a movement and as a 'structure' is not reducible
to a process of experience and a fortiori not capturable within what we
might term a phenomenology of writing. As Derrida says: '*différance*
n'est pas,' that is it escapes the replacement of an object for a subject; as
an entity, it does not exist.

So far we find little difference between Derrida and de Man concerning the notion of 'movement' in the text. However, the structure of this
movement in Derrida does not take the form of either an exchange of
attributes or a reversal of properties.

Derrida claims that the movement of *différance* entails a twofold
process of timing and spacing, which continually opens the space of repetition and representation yet also makes repetition and representation,
properly speaking, impossible. This shifting ground of textuality is revealed by deconstruction in the 'découpage' of the 'same' from context to
context, and in their juxtaposition, which reveals the differences essential
to the result of this process of *différance*. Far from being a reversal, dif-

ferences—as a result of context-specific determinations—reveal simply the myth imbedded in, yet denied by metaphysics. The essence of essence, or the identity of identity, is simply a function of an irreducible yet repressed or effaced difference. This difference is a result of the time and space of textuality itself; an irreducible movement Derrida names *différance*.

Thus deconstruction opens up the text in such a way as to reveal the "effects of *différance*." As I have shown, this is not an "exchange of attributes" but rather the play of presence and absence with respect to the constitution of identity as the same in its reduction and effacement of differences. But the effacement, Derrida insists, always leaves a trace; it is never a perfect crime. And such is the place, marked in the text perhaps by a footnote, perhaps by a *necessary* ambiguity, where deconstruction begins its work. Thus the "signs of *différance*" are followed in order to produce or reveal this movement.

Derrida's relation to Hegel is significant, for Derrida "aims to destroy" (Hegel's notion of dialectics) by process of deconstruction, therein revealing *différance* and in turn 'absence' at the heart of 'presence' and metaphysics itself. Derrida insists that the 'economy' of the dialectic in Hegel's system must be reinscribed within a "more general economy," which has been effaced in the production of 'Absolute Knowledge' as such. As he says:

> Through such a relating of a restricted and a general economy the very project of philosophy, under the privileged heading of Hegelianism, is displaced and reinscribed. The *Aufhebung—la relève—*is constrained into writing itself otherwise. Or perhaps simply into writing itself. Or, better, into taking account of its consumption of writing.[22]

This consumation of writing is precisely the effacement of the sign that Hegel insists is required and actually possible in the progress toward Absolute Knowledge. The history of history is thus the detour via the sign from one full presence to another, yet same, full presence. Thus the 'nonconscious' becomes, in the end, totally conscious for Hegel; and the means, history and the sign, are overcome at the summit of truth and self-conscious Absolute Knowledge. For Derrida, however, the sign as a means, as the detour, the passage, the 'way,' is irreducible. Indeed the sign is the scaffolding upon which Absolute Knowledge hangs and therein ultimately is the latter's downfall or undoing. The effacement of the sign is also an effacement of the process and yet as we know from Hegel himself the process is all. The road to science is science itself and the difference between them is nonexistant. Yet, once reached, the realization of the telos erases its own pathway to itself.

Paradoxically Hegel wrote the text of Absolute Knowledge with the hope of assisting history by bringing it into the world in manifest form.

Thus even at this stage the 'text' is used as a sign for what is not yet present—although already presented in theory. Hegel as well knew that the manifestation by 'sign,' by text, was not sufficient, despite its necessity as a stage in the process of the dialectical movement of history.

Derrida, however, insists that Hegel denies the ground for his own project and this denial itself makes the project possible. The "wager for reason"[23] is made so that a totally reasonable articulation of the world *could* be considered Absolute Knowledge. This wager of course is unexamined and unadmitted by Hegel. It is a given, yet pregiven. Just as the sign is the 'detour' so too the ultimate valorization of reason is a radically dogmatic assumption—both true and false in terms of the tradition and history of metaphysics of which Hegel is without doubt the highest, most complete, expression. Thus Hegel is correct yet nonetheless remains trapped within a more general economy, beyond metaphysics, which *allows* for his system yet which by necessity can have no place inside it. The irreducibility of the sign, both recognized and in turn effaced by Hegel, is the place where Derrida aims to mark a 'fold' in the *Aufhebung*; a fourth term in the system that cannot admit to more than three. Thus far from being an 'other' for metaphysics or Hegelian dialectics the notion of *différance* for Derrida entails a shift in levels of interpretation and understanding—a ground for that which is said to ground itself; the origin of the origin, as Derrida says, which by necessity can no longer be called an origin.

Also, as distinct from de Man, *différance* does not allow for the 'return' of metaphysics or for its maintenance, albeit in a relation of oscillation. Rather, for Derrida, there is no economy between dialectics and *différance*. Instead *différance* when recognized can reinscribe dialectics in a "more general economy" beyond the light of reason itself. Deconstruction, however, might be said to entail a certain economic relation to metaphysics on the one hand and *différance* on the other. However there is no ultimate synthesis, for neither can be the third term and no two terms can be considered in opposition. The excesses of each 'process' flow out and over into the others, systematically indeed, but not without desire. Thus in referring to dialectics we find a certain irreducible "human hand" behind or beneath the process or structure that seems to exist in and for itself. It is this attribute of the *"force de la faiblesse"* that nevertheless forces force, to which we must turn now. As distinct from de Man, Derrida's "economy of *différance*" as the astructural structure of textuality is not a code, a grammar, or a mechanical operation.

For Derrida, the interpretation of a text in a non-dialectical, non-metaphysical manner is analogous to the opening up of a flower as it blossoms.[24] The petals, although joined at the center, that "invisible point of orientation," overlap but do not interrelate in a dialectical or dominating fashion. Together they form a whole but as multi-dimensional, non-linear, non-geometric gathering—not as a mathematical structure or as a mechanical ordering of the parts. For de Man, we should recall that the "metaphor of the text as body must be overcome by that of the text as machine," for it entails an "impersonal grammar" that is more powerful and more extensive than any desire of either writer or reader. This is the grammar of irony or reversal and repetition.

For Derrida, however, repetition is never possible in a strict sense. Rereading is intrinsically other, just as rewriting is, and thus the text, as a finite system of propositions with a fixed code or structure, is a myth— and a metaphysical one at that. Nevertheless, as I have shown, for Derrida *différance* has been revealed as the *animating factor in* in all textuality. The difference from de Man is that *différance* is *not* a grammar and, properly speaking, not a structure. It is a movement of play, not a calculus; a shaping and shifting of textual production that never rests inertly within the constitution of the same. Nevertheless, Derrida concedes that *différance* as having no force of its own is indeed forced and expropriated by metaphysics. Indeed deconstruction aims precisely to reveal this expropriation as appropriation, therein tracing the steps in the constitution of metaphysics itself as it attempts to eradicate *différance* from the "house of Being." Because of this very "weakness" of *différance* the flowering of the text can always become a dead flower dried within the pages of the book.[25] It *can*, he says, but must or need not. This is, therefore, the danger and the power of the usurpation of metaphysics and not an essentially unavoidable or intrinsic reversal, repetition, or eternal recurrence of the same. The transformation of the possibility of metaphysics' reappropriation of *différance* has thus become the tragic and indeed ironic necessity of the same for de Man.

I suggest finally that rather than valorizing Derrida's notion of deconstruction as the original and thus proper one, and also instead of returning to Nietzsche as its originator, which would ally de Man's version with the proper, it is necessary to suspend the propriety of deconstruction as such. In so doing we can see that Derrida's notion separates the deconstructive process from the revelation of *différance* within metaphysics only by a recognition of a certain economy entailed therein. De Man's notion of deconstruction, on the other hand, seems to entail *différance* within its very practice and thus appears to be the 'other' as opposed to metaphysics, or textual totalizations, as de Man would perhaps prefer to call the 'problem.' It therefore remains to be analyzed in greater depth whether or not these two versions of deconstruction have essentially the same relationship to metaphysics after all, or whether the oscillation that de Man seems to end up with is parallel or perhaps even the key to understanding Derrida's as yet still implicit "more general economy." In view of this future and necessary project, I shall suspend judgment at this point, leaving the two deconstructions distinct and yet perhaps not so radically different as one may have been led to believe.

Returning to the initial question, I can now suggest that, for de Man, literary criticism and deconstruction are intrinsically inseparable (in that both are 'text-dependent'), while for Derrida deconstruction is also a 'philosophical' enterprise, which—as in the Kantian notion of critique—aims to reveal the conditions of the possibility of textuality itself. One might well conclude, however, that this enterprise is inseparable from what is today called literary criticism. And finally, concerning the issue of the "defensibility of deconstruction," not only is there a transformation of deconstruction as concept to deconstruction as essentially plural, but there is also serious question as to the "defensibility of literary criticism for deconstruction." In the end, it may well be that, for the sake of literary criticism, 'defensibility' itself is in need of deconstruction, or more precisely, deconstructions.

8

Phenomenality and Materiality
in Kant

Paul de Man

The possibility of juxtaposing ideology and critical philosophy, which is the persistent burden of contemporary thought, is pointed out, as a mere historical fact, by Michel Foucault in *Les mots et les choses*. At the same time that French ideologues such as Destutt de Tracy are trying to map out the entire field of human ideas and representations, Kant undertakes the critical project of a transcendental philosophy, which, says Foucault, marks the "retreat of cognition and of knowledge out of the space of representation" (p. 255).[1] Foucault's ensuing historical diagnosis, in which ideology appears as a belated manifestation of the classical spirit and Kant as the onset of modernity, interests us less than the interplay between the three notions: ideology, critical philosophy, and transcendental philosophy. The first term of this triad—ideology— is the most difficult to control and one may hope that the interrelationship with the two others might be of some assistance.

A possible starting point can be found in the introduction to the *Third Critique* in a difficult but important differentiation between transcendental and metaphysical principles. Kant writes as follows:

> A transcendental principle is one by means of which is represented, a priori, the universal condition under which alone things can be objects of our cognition. On the other hand, a principle is called metaphysical if it represents the a priori condition under which alone objects, whose concept must be given empirically, can a priori be further determined. Thus the principle of the cognition of bodies as substances and as changeable substances is transcendental if thereby it is asserted that their changes must have a cause; it is metaphysical if it asserts that their changes must have an *external* cause. For in the former case, bodies need only be thought by means of ontological

predicates (pure concepts of understanding)—for example, as substance—in order to permit the a priori cognition of the proposition; but in the latter case the empirical concept of a body (as a movable thing in space) must lie at the base of the proposition, although once this basis has been laid down, it can be seen completely a priori that the other predicate (motion by external causes) belongs to the body.[2]

The difference between transcendental and metaphysical concepts that concerns us is that the latter imply an empirical moment that necessarily remains *external* to the concept whereas the former remain entirely interconceptual. Metaphysical principles lead to the identification and definition, to the knowledge, of a natural principle that is not itself a concept; transcendental principles lead to the definition of a conceptual principle of possible existence. Metaphysical principles state why and how things occur; to say that bodies move because of gravity is to reach a conclusion in the realm of metaphysics. Transcendental principles state the conditions that make occurrence in general possible at all: the first condition for bodies to be able to change is that such a thing as bodies and motion exist or occur. The condition of existence of bodies is called substance; to state that substance is the cause of the motion of bodies (as Kant does in the passage quoted) is to examine critically the possibility of their existence.

Metaphysical principles, on the other hand, take the existence of their object for granted as empirical fact. They contain knowledge of the world, but this knowledge is precritical. Transcendental principles contain no knowledge of the world or anything else, except for the knowledge that metaphysical principles that take them for their object are themselves in need of critical analysis, for they take for granted an objectivity that, for transcendental principles, is not available a priori. Thus the objects of transcendental principles are always critical judgments that take metaphysical knowledge for their target. Transcendental philosophy is always the critical philosophy of metaphysics.

Ideologies, to the extent that they necessarily contain empirical moments and are directed toward what lies outside the realm of pure concepts, are on the side of metaphysics rather than critical philosophy. The conditions and modalities of their occurrence are determined by critical analyses to which they have no access. The object of these analyses, on the other hand, can only be ideologies. Ideological and critical thought are interdependent and any attempt to separate them collapses ideology into mere error and critical thought into idealism. The possibility of maintaining a causal link between them is the controling principle of rigorous philosophical discourse: philosophies that succumb to ideology lose their epistemological sense, whereas philosophies that try to bypass or repress ideology lose all critical thrust and risk being repossessed by what they foreclose.

The Kant passage establishes two other points. By speaking of a *causal* link between ideology and transcendental philosophy, one is reminded of the prominence of causality in Kant's example, the focus on the internal or external *cause* of the motion of bodies. The example of bodies in motion is indeed more than a mere example that could be replaced by any other; it is another version of definition of transcendental cognition. If critical philosophy and metaphysics (including ideologies) are causally linked to each other, their relationship is similar to the relationship, made explicit in the example, between bodies and their transformations or motions. Critical philosophy and ideology then become each other's motion: if an ideology is considered to be a stable entity (body, corpus, or canon), the critical discourse it generates will be that of a transcendental motion, of a motion whose cause resides, so to speak, within itself, within the substance of its own being. And if the critical system is considered stable in its principles, the corresponding ideology will acquire a mobility caused by a principle that lies outside itself; this principle, within the confines of the system thus constituted, can only be the principle of constitution, the architectonics of the transcendental system, which functions as the cause of the ideological motions. In both cases, it is the transcendental system, as substance or as structure, that determines the ideology and not the reverse. The question then becomes what the substance of a transcendental discourse would have to be. To try to answer this question from the inside of the Kantian text is the tentative purpose of this still introductory and expository paper.

The second point to be gained from the same passage has to do with the aesthetic. Immediately after distinguishing between transcendental and metaphysical principles, Kant goes on to distinguish between "the pure concept of objects of possible subjective cognition (*der reine Begriff von Gegenständen des möglichen Erfahrungserkenntnisses überhaupt*)" and "the principle of practical purposiveness, which must be thought as the idea of the determination of a free will"; the distinction is a correlate of the prior, more general, distinction between transcendental and metaphysical principles. The distinction directly alludes to the division between pure and practical reason, and corresponds to the major division in the corpus of Kant's works. One sees again how the *Third Critique* corresponds to the necessity of establishing the causal link between critical philosophy and ideology, between a purely conceptual and an empirically determined discourse. Hence the need for a phenomenalized, empirically manifest principle of cognition on whose existence the possibility of such an articulation depends. This phenomenalized principle is what Kant calls the aesthetic. The investment in the aesthetic is therefore considerable, for the possibility of philosophy itself, as the articulation of a transcendental with a metaphysical discourse, depends on it. And the place in the *Third Critique* where this articulation occurs is the section on the sublime; in the section on the beautiful the articulation is said to be between understanding (*Verstand*) and judgment. In both cases, one meets with great difficulties; the motives for this are perhaps easier to perceive in the case of the sublime, possibly because reason is explicitly involved.

The complexity and possible incongruity of the notion of the sublime, a topic that no eighteenth-century treatise on aesthetics is ever allowed to ignore, makes the section of the *Third Critique* that deals with it one of the most difficult and unresolved passages in the entire corpus of Kant's works. Whereas, in the section on the beautiful, the difficulties at least convey the illusion of being controlled, the same can hardly be said of the sublime. It is possible to formulate with some clarity what the project, the burden, of the section might be, and equally possible to understand what is at stake in its accomplishment. But it remains very difficult to decide whether or not the enterprise fails or succeeds.

The complication is noticeable from the very start, in the introduction that distinguishes between the beautiful and the sublime. From the point of view of the main theme of the *Third Critique*, the problem of teleological judgment, or of purposiveness without purpose, the consideration of the sublime seems almost superfluous. "The concept of the sublime," says Kant, "is not nearly so important or rich in consequences as the concept of the beautiful and, in general, it displays nothing purposive in nature itself" (23; 84). "The idea of the sublime thus separates from that of a purposiveness of nature and this makes the theory of the sublime a mere appendix (*einen blossen Anhang*) to the aesthetic judging of that purposiveness" (167; 84). After that modest beginning, however, it turns out that this outer appendage is in fact of crucial importance, because instead of informing us, like the beautiful, about the teleology of nature, it informs us about the teleology of our own faculties—more specifically, about the relationship between imagination and reason. It follows, in accordance with what was said before, that whereas the beautiful is a metaphysical and ideological principle, the sublime aspires to being a transcendental one, with all that this entails.

Contrary to the beautiful, which at least appears to be all of a piece, the sublime is shot through with dialectical complication. It is, in some respects, infinitely attractive but, at the same time, thoroughly repellent; it gives a peculiar kind of pleasure (*Lust*) yet it is also consistently painful; in less subjective, more structural, terms, it is equally baffling: it knows of no limits or borders, yet it has to appear as a totality; in a philosophical sense, it is something of a monster or, rather, a ghost: it is not a property of nature (there are no such things as sublime objects in nature) but a purely inward experience of consciousness (*Gemütsbestimmung*), yet Kant insists, time and again, that this noumenal entity has to be phenomenally represented (*dargestellt*); this is indeed an integral part, the crux, in fact, of the analytics of the sublime.

The question becomes whether the dialectical incompatibilities will find, in the concept of the sublime, a possibility of resolution. A first symptom that this may not simply and unambiguously be the case appears in an additional complication that makes the schema of the sublime distinct from that of the beautiful. One can grant that it is methodologically as legitimate to evaluate the impact on us of the sublime, as pleasure or as pain, in terms of quantity instead of, as is the case with the beautiful, in terms of quality. But, if this is indeed the case, why then can the analytics of the sublime not be closed off with the section on the mathematical sublime, centered on quantity and on number? Why the need for another section, nonexistent in the area of the beautiful, which Kant calls the *dynamic* sublime, and of which it will be difficult to say whether it still belongs to the order of quantity or of quality? Kant gives *some* explanation of why this is needed, but this explanation raises more questions than it answers (§24). The sublime produces an emotional, agitated response in the beholder; this response can be referred back to the needs of knowledge (in the mathematical sublime) as well as to the needs of desire (*Begehrungsvermögen*) in the dynamic sublime. In the realm of aesthetic judgment, both have to be considered regardless of purpose or interest, a requirement that can conceivably be met in the realm of knowledge but that is much less easy to fulfill in the realm of desire, all the more so because it is clearly understood that this desire has to be considered in itself, as subjective manifestation, and not as an objectified knowledge of desire. And indeed, when we reach the section on the dynamic sublime, we find something quite different from desire. The need for the additional subdivision, as well as the transition from the one to the other (from mathematical quantity to the dynamic) is by no means easy to account for and will demand an avowedly speculative effort of interpretation, of which it is not certain that it will succeed.

The antinomies at play in the mathematical sublime are clearly defined as are the reasons of their relevance for aesthetic judgment. The mathematical sublime starts out from the concept of number. Its burden is that of calculus, as one would expect in a philosopher whose master's thesis dealt with Leibniz: it is the burden of realizing that finite and infinite entities are not susceptible of comparison and cannot both be inscribed within a common system of knowledge. As calculus, as computation based on number, the proposition is self-evident and, in the infinitesimal realm of number (the powers of number, says Kant, reach the infinite

[173; 89]), it creates no difficulties: the infinitely large (or, for that matter, the infinitely small) can be conceptualized by means of number. But such a conceptualization is entirely devoid of phenomenal equivalences; in terms of the faculties, it is strictly speaking unimaginable.

This is not, however, how the sublime has been defined. The sublime, in quantitative terms, is not mere quantity or number, still less the notion of quantity as such (*Quantum*). Quantity thus conceived, and expressed by number, is always a relative concept that refers back to a conventional unity of measurement, pure number is neither large nor small, and the infinitely large is also the infinitely small: the telescope and the microscope, as instruments of measurement, are the same instrument. The sublime, however, is not "the large" but "the largest" as such, it is that "compared to which everything else is small." As such, it can never be accessible to the senses. But it is not pure number either, for there is no such thing as a "greatest" in the realm of number. It belongs to a different order of experience, closer to extension than to number. It is, in Kant's words, "absolute magnitude (*die Grösse*—or better, *das Grösste schlechthin*), as far as consciousness can grasp it in an intuition (*so weit das Gemüt sie in einer Anschauung fassen kann*) (173; 90). This phenomenalization cannot stem from number, only from extension.

The sentence is another version of the original statement that the sublime is to be borderless (*unbegrenzt*) yet a totality: number is without limit, but extension implies the possibility of a totalization, of a contour. The mathematical sublime has to articulate number with extension and it faces a classic problem of natural philosophy. The fact that it is a recurrent philosophical theme does not make it any easier to solve, nor does it allow one to overlook the intricacies of the arguments by which the solution is attempted just because the burden of argument turns out to be familiar.

Kant tries to articulate number with extension by ways of two demonstrations, the first epistemological, the second in terms of pleasure and pain. Neither of these arguments is truly conclusive. On the level of understanding, the infinity of number can be conceived as a purely logical progression, which is not in need of any spatial concretization. But, on the level of reason, this *comprehensio logica* is no longer sufficient. Another mode of understanding called *comprehensio aesthetica* is needed, which requires constant totalization or condensation in a single intuition; even the infinite "must be thought as entirely given, according to its totality" (177; 93). But because the infinite is not comparable to any finite magnitude, the articulation cannot occur. It does not, in fact, ever occur and the *failure* of the articulation becomes the distinguishing characteristic of the sublime: it transposes or elevates the natural to the level of the supernatural, perception to imagination, understanding to reason. This transposition, however, never allows for the condition of totality that is constitutive of the sublime, and it can therefore not supercede the failure by becoming, as in a dialectic, the knowledge of this failure. The sublime cannot be defined as the failure of the sublime, for this failure deprives it of its identifying principle. Neither could one say that, at this point, the sublime fulfills itself as desire for what it fails to be, for what it desires— totality—is not other than itself.

The same pattern returns with regard to pleasure and pain. It is clear that what the sublime achieves is not the task required by its own position (articulation of number and extension by ways of the infinite). What it achieves is the awareness of another faculty besides understanding and reason—namely, the imagination. Out of the pain of the failure to constitute the sublime by making the infinite apparent (*anschaulich*) is born the pleasure of the imagination, which discovers, in this very failure, the congruity of its law (which is a law of failure) with the law of our own suprasensory being. Its failure to connect with the sensory would also elevate it above the sensory. This law does not reside in nature but defines man in opposition to nature; it is only by an act of what Kant calls subreption (180; 96) that this law is fallaciously attributed to nature.

But is not this subreption a mirror image of another, previous subreption by which the sublime subreptitiously posits itself by claiming to exist by dint of the impossibility of its own existence? The transcendental judgment that is to decide on the possibility of existence of the sublime (as the spatial articulation of the infinite) functions metaphorically, or ideologically, when it subreptitiously defines itself in terms of its other— namely, of extension and totality. If space lies outside the sublime and remains there, and if space is nevertheless a necessary condition (or cause) for the sublime to come into being, then the principle of the sublime is a metaphysical principle that mistakes itself for a transcendental one. If imagination, the faculty of the sublime, comes into being at the expense of the totalizing power of the mind, how can it then, as the text requires, be in contrastive harmony (182; 97) with the faculty of reason, which delimits the contour of this totality? What the imagination undoes is the very labor of reason and such a relationship cannot without difficulty be said to unite both of them, imagination and reason, in a common task or law of being. Kant's definition of aesthetic judgment as what represents the subjective play of the faculties (imagination and reason) as harmonious through their very contrast (182; 97) remains, at this point, quite obscure. Which accounts perhaps in part for the fact that a further elaboration is needed in which the relationship between the same two powers of the mind will be somewhat less enigmatically represented; this can occur, however, only after moving from the mathematical to the dynamic sublime.

The difficulty can be summarized in a shift in terminology that occurs later in the text but that directly alludes to the difficulties we already encounter in the mathematical sublime. In §29, in the General Remark upon the exposition of the aesthetic judgment, appears the most concise but also the most suggestive definition of the sublime as "an object (of nature) the representation (*Vorstellung*) of which determines consciousness (*Gemüt*) to *think* the unattainability of nature as a sensory position (*Darstellung*) of ideas" (193; 108). The key word, for our present purpose, in this quotation in which every word is rich in innumerable questions, is the word *denken* in "die Unerreichbarkeit der Natur als Darstellung zu *denken*." A few lines later, Kant speaks of the necessity "to think nature itself in its totality, as the sensory representation of something that lies beyond the senses, without being able to accomplish this representation objectively" (*Die Natur selbst in ihrer Totalität, als Darstellung von etwas Uebersinnlichem, zu denken, ohne diese Darstellung objektiv zu Stande bringen zu können*) (194; 108). Still a few lines later, the word *denken* is singled out and contrasted with knowing: "*die Natur als Darstellung derselben (d.h. die Idee des Uebersinnlichen) nicht erkennen, sondern nur denken können*" (194; 108). How are we to understand the verb "to think" in these formulations, in distinction from knowing? The way of knowledge, of *Erkenntnis*, has not been able to establish the existence of the sublime as an intelligible concept. This may be possible only by ways of *denken* rather than *erkennen*. What would be an instance of such thinking that differs from knowing? *Was heisst denken?*

Still in the mathematical sublime, in §26, next to the epistemology and the endaemony of the sublime, appears another description of how an infinite quantity can become a sensory intuition in the imagination, or how, in other words, the infinity of number can be articulated with the totality of extension (173; 89). This description, which is formal rather than philosophical, is a great deal easier to follow than the subsequent arguments. In order to make the sublime appear in space, we need, says Kant, two acts of the imagination: "apprehension (*apprehensio*) and comprehension or summation (*comprehensio aesthetica*), *Auffassung* and *Zusammenfassung* (173; 90). Apprehension proceeds successively, as a syntagmatic, consecutive motion along an axis, and it can proceed ad infinitum without difficulty. Comprehension, however, which is a paradigmatic totalization of the apprehended trajectory, grows increasingly difficult as the space covered by apprehension grows larger.

The model reminds one of a simple phenomenology of reading, in which one has to make constant syntheses to comprehend the successive unfolding of the text: the eye moves horizontally in succession whereas the mind has to combine vertically the cumulative understanding of what has been apprehended. The comprehension will soon reach a point at which it is saturated and will no longer be able to take in additional apprehensions: it cannot progress beyond a certain magnitude, which marks the limit of the imagination. This ability of the imagination to achieve syntheses is a boon to the understanding, which is hardly conceivable without it, but this gain is countered by a corresponding loss. The comprehension discovers its own limitation, beyond which it cannot reach. "(The imagination) loses as much on the one side as it gains on the other" (174; 90). As the paradigmatic simultaneity substitutes for the syntagmatic succession, an economy of loss and gain is put in place, which functions with predictable efficacy, though only within certain well-defined limits. The exchange from part to whole generates wholes that turn out to be only parts. Kant gives the example of the Egyptologist Savary, who observed that, in order to perceive the magnitude of the pyramids, one could be neither too far away nor too close. One is reminded of Pascal: "*Bornés en tout genre, cet état qui tient le milieu entre deux extrêmes, se trouve en toutes nos puissances. Nos sens n'aperçoivent rien d'extrême, trop de bruit nous assourdit, trop de lumière éblouit, trop de distance et de proximité empêche la vue. Trop de longueur et trop de brièveté de discours l'obscursit, trop de vérité nous étonne.*"[3]

It is not surprising that, from considerations on vision and, in general, perception, Pascal moves to the order of discourse, for the model that is being suggested is no longer properly speaking philosophical, but linguistic. It describes, not a faculty of the mind, be it as consciousness or as cognition, but a potentiality inherent in language. For that system of substitution, set up along a paradigmatic and a syntagmatic axis, generating partial totalizations within an economy of profit and loss, is a very familiar model indeed—which also explains why the passage seems so easy to grasp in comparison with what precedes and follows. It is the model of discourse as a tropological system. The desired articulation of the sublime takes place, with suitable reservations and restrictions, within such a purely formal system. It follows, however, that it is conceivable only within the limits of such a system—that is, as pure discourse rather than as a faculty of the mind. When the sublime is translated back, so to speak, from language into cognition, from formal description into philosophical argument, it loses all inherent coherence and disappears in the aporias of intellectual and sensory appearance.

It is also established that, even within the confines of language, the sublime can occur only as a single and particular point of view, a privileged place that avoids both excessive comprehension and excessive apprehension, and that this place is only formally, and not transcendentally, determined. The sublime cannot be grounded as a philosophical (transcendental or metaphysical) but only as a linguistic principle. Consequently, the section on the mathematical sublime cannot be closed off in a satisfactory manner and another chapter on the dynamics of the sublime is needed.

According to the principles of the quadrivium, the further extension of the system number-extension should have been motion, and we could have expected a kinetic rather than a dynamic sublime. But the kinetics of the sublime are treated at once, and somewhat surprisingly, as a question of *power*: the first word of §28 (184; 99) (on the dynamics of the sublime) is *Macht*, soon followed by violence (*Gewalt*) and by the assertion that violence is the only means by which to overcome the resistance of one force to another. A classical way to have moved from number to motion would have been by way of a kinetics of physical bodies, a study, as for example in Kepler, of the motion of heavenly bodies in function of gravity as acceleration. Gravity can also be considered a force or a power, next to being a motion—as in Wordsworth's line: "no motion has she now, no force"—and the passage from a kinesis to a dynamics of the sublime could be treated in terms of mathematical and physical concepts. Kant does not pursue this line of thought and at once introduces the notion of power in a quasi-empirical sense of assault, battle, and fright. The relationship between the natural and the aesthetic sublime is treated as a scene of combat in which the faculties of the mind somehow have to overpower the forces of nature.

The necessity to extend the model of the mathematical sublime, the system of number-extension, to the model of the dynamic sublime as the system number-motion, as well as the interpretation of motion as empirical power, is not accounted for in philosophical terms in the analytics of the sublime, nor can it, especially in its latter aspect (the empiricization of force into violence and battle), be explained by purely historical reasons. The only way to account for it is as an extension of the linguistic model beyond its definition as a system of tropes. Tropes account for the occurrence of the sublime but, as we saw, in such a restrictive and partial way that the system could not be expected to remain quiescent within its narrow boundaries. From the pseudo-cognition of tropes, language has to expand to the activity of performance, something of which language has been known to be capable well before Austin reminded us of it.

The transition from the mathematical to the dynamic sublime, a transition for which the justification is conspicuously lacking in the text (§28 begins most abruptly with the word Power (*Macht*), marks the saturation of the tropological field as language frees itself of its constraints and discovers within itself a power no longer dependent on the restrictions of cognition. Hence the introduction, at this point in the text, of the concept of morality, but on the level of practical rather than pure reason. The articulation between pure and practical reason, the raison d'être of the *Third Critique*, occurs in the widening definition of language as a performative as well as a tropological system. The *Critique of Judgment* therefore has, at its center, a deep, perhaps fatal, break or discontinuity. It depends on a linguistic structure (language as a performative as well as a cognitive system) that is not itself accessible to the powers of transcendental philosophy. Nor is it accessible, one should hasten to add, to the powers of metaphysics or of ideology, which are themselves precritical stages of knowledge. Our question then becomes whether and where this disruption, this disarticulation, becomes apparent in the text, at a moment when the aporia of the sublime is no longer stated, as was the case in the mathematical sublime and in the ensuing general definitions of the concept, as an explicit paradox, but as the apparently tranquil, because entirely unreflected, juxtaposition of incompatibles. Such a moment occurs in the general remark or recapitulation (§29) that concludes the analytics of the sublime.

The chapter on the dynamics of the sublime appears as another version of the difficulties encountered in the mathematical sublime rather than as their further development, let alone their solution. Except for the introduction of the moral dimension, hard to account for in epistemological or aesthetic terms, it differs most from the preceding inquiry by concentrating on affect rather than on reason (as in the mathematical sublime) or on understanding (as in the analytics of the beautiful). The preeminence of the faculty of the imagination is maintained, as is the question of its relationship to reason, but this dialectic of reason and imagination is now mediated by affects, moods, and feelings, rather than by rational principles. The change results in a restatement and refinement rather than in a transformation of the principle of the sublime. The admirably concise definition given at the beginning of the *General Remarks* benefits from the references to mood and to affectivity but does not differ in substance from similar developments that occurred in the preceding paragraphs. Nor is it, for all its controlled concentration, in essence less obscure than the previous formulations.

The chapter also contains, somewhat abruptly, a sudden reminder that, in a transcendental aesthetic of judgment, objects in nature susceptible of producing sublime effects have to be considered in a radically non-teleological manner, completely detached from any purpose or interest that the mind may find in them. Kant adds that he had previously reminded the reader of this necessity, but it is not clear to what passage he alludes. He is rather restating a general principle that underlies the entire enterprise and that was first formulated, with all desirable clarity, at the onset of the analytics of the beautiful under the modality of quality (116; 38). This time, however, Kant relates the principle of disinterestedness specifically to objects in nature and takes for his example two landscapes:

If, then, we call the sight of the starry heaven *sublime*, we must not place at
the foundation of judgment concepts of worlds inhabited by rational beings
and regard the bright points, with which we see the space above us filled, as
their suns moving in circles purposively fixed with reference to them; but we
must regard it, just as we see it (*wie man ihn sieht*), as a distant, all-embracing
vault (*ein weites Gewölbe*). Only under such a representation can we range
that sublimity, which a pure aesthetic judgment ascribes to this object. And
in the same way, if we are to call the sight of the ocean sublime, we must not
think of it as we ordinarily do, as implying all kinds of knowledge (that are
not contained in immediate intuition). For example, we sometimes think of
the ocean as a vast kingdom of aquatic creatures, or as the great source of
those vapors that fill the air with clouds for the benefit of the land, or again
as an element which, though dividing continents from each other, yet pro-
motes the greatest communication between them; all these produce merely
teleological judgments. To call the ocean sublime we must regard it as poets
do (*wie die Dichter es tun*), merely by what the eye reveals (*was der
Augenschein zeigt*)—if it is at rest, as a clear mirror of water only bounded
by the heavens; if it is stormy, as an abyss threatening to overwhelm everything [196; 110-11].

The passage is remarkable in many respects, including its apparent
anticipation of many such passages soon to be found in the works of
romantic poets and already present, in many cases, in their eighteenth-
century predecessors. But it is just as necessary to distinguish it from
these symbolic landscapes as to point out the similarities. The predominant perception, in the Kant passage, is that of the heavens and the ocean
as an architectonic construct. The heavens are a vault that covers the
totality of earthy space as a roof covers a house. Space, in Kant as in
Aristotle, is a house in which we dwell more or less safely, or more or less
poetically, on this earth. This is also how the sea is perceived or how,
according to Kant, poets perceive it: its horizontal expanse is like a floor
bounded by the horizon, by the walls of heaven as they close off and
delimit the building.

Who, one may wonder, are the poets who thus perceive the world in
an architectonic rather than in a teleological way and how can the architectonic, then, be said to be opposed to the teleological? How are we to
understand the coinage *Augenschein* in relation to the other allusions to
sensory appearance that abound in the attempts to define or to describe
the sublime? It is easier to say what the passage excludes and how it
differs from others than to say what it is, but this may well be in accordance with Kant's insistence (195-96; 109) on the primarily *negative* mode
of the imagination. Certainly, in our tradition, the first poet we think of
as having similar intuitions, is Wordsworth who, in the nest-robbing epi-
sode in *The Prelude*, evoked the experience of dizziness and absolute
fright in the amazing lines: "The sky was not a sky/Of earth, and with

what motion moved the clouds!" Here, too, the sky is originally conceived as a roof or vault that shelters us, by anchoring us in the world, standing on a horizontal plane, *under* the sky, reassuringly stabilized by the weight of our own gravity. But if the sky suddenly separates from the earth and is no longer, in Wordsworth's terms, the sky *of* earth, we lose all feeling of stability and start to fall, so to speak, skyword, away from gravity.

Kant's passage is *not* like this, because the sky does not appear in it as associated in any way with shelter. It is not the construct under which, in Heidegger's terms, we can dwell, *wohnen*. In a lesser known passage from the *Logic* Kant speaks of "a wild man who, from a distance, sees a house of which he does not know the use. He certainly observes the same object as does another, who knows it to be definitely built and arranged to serve as a dwelling for human beings. Yet in formal terms this knowledge of the selfsame object differs in both cases. For the first it is mere intuition (*blosse Anschauung*), for the other both intuition and concept."[4] The poet who sees the heavens as a vault is clearly like this savage, and unlike Wordsworth. He does not see prior to dwelling, but merely sees. He does not see in order to shelter himself, for there is no suggestion made that he could in any way be threatened, not even by the storm—for it is pointed out that he remains safely on the shore. The link between seeing and dwelling, *sehen* and *wohnen*, is teleological and therefore absent in pure aesthetic vision.

Or, still in association with Wordsworth, one thinks of the famous passage from *Tintern Abbey*:

> And I have felt
> A presence that disturbs me with the joy
> Of elevated thoughts; a sense sublime
> Of something far more deeply interfused
> Whose dwelling is the light of setting suns,
> And the round ocean and the living air
> And the blue sky, and in the mind of man.

The sublimity of the round ocean, horizon-bound as a vast dome, is especially reminiscent of the Kant passage. But the two invocations of sublime nature soon diverge. Wordsworth's sublime is an instance of the constant exchange between mind and nature, of the chiasmic transfer of properties between the sensory and the intellectual world that characterizes his figural diction, here explicitly thematized in the "motion and spirit that impels/All thinking things, all objects of all thoughts/And rolls through all things." No mind is involved in the Kantian vision of ocean and heaven. To the extent that any mind, any judgment, is involved, it is in error—for it is not the case that heaven is a vault or that the horizon bounds the ocean like the walls of a building. That is how things are to the eye, in the redundancy of their appearance to the eye and not to the mind, as in the redundant word *Augenschein*, to be understood in opposition to Hegel's *Ideenschein*, or sensory appearance of the idea, *Augenschein*, in which the eye, tautologically, is named twice, as eye itself and as what appears to the eye.

Kant's architectonic world is not a metamorphosis of a fluid world into the solidity of stone, nor is his building a trope or a symbol that substitutes for the actual entities. Heaven and ocean as building are a priori, previous to any understanding, to any exchange and anthropomorphism that will allow Wordsworth to address, in Book V of *The Prelude*, the "speaking face of nature." There is no room for address in Kant's flat, third-person world. Kant's vision can therefore hardly be called literal, which would imply its possible figuralization or symbolization by an act of judgment. The only word that comes to mind is that of a *material* vision, but how this materiality is then to be understood in linguistic terms is not, as yet, clearly intelligible.

Not being part of trope or figuration, the purely aesthetic vision of the natural world is in no way solar. It is not the sudden discovery of a true world as an unveiling, as the *a-letheia* of Heidegger's *Lichtung*. It is not a solar world and we are explicitly told that we are not to think of the stars as "suns moving in circles." Nor are we to think of them as the constellation that survives at the apocalyptic end of Mallarmé's *Coup de Dés*. The "mirror" of the sea surface is a mirror without depth, least of all the mirror in which the constellation would be reflected. In this mode of perception, the eye is its own agent and not the specular echo of the sun. The sea is called a mirror, not because it is supposed to reflect anything, but to stress a flatness devoid of any suggestion of depth. In the same way and to the same extent that this vision is purely material, devoid of any reflexive or intellectual complication, it is also purely formal, devoid of any semantic depth and reducible to the formal mathematization or geometrization of pure optics. The critique of the aesthetic ends up, in Kant, in a formal materialism that (like the prosaism we found in Hegel) runs counter to all values and characteristics associated with aesthetic experience, including the aesthetic experience of the beautiful and of the sublime as described by Kant and Hegel themselves. The tradition of their interpretation, as it appears from near contemporaries such as Schiller onward, has seen only this one, figural, and, if you will, "romantic" aspect of their theories of the imagination, and has entirely overlooked what we call the material aspect. Neither has it understood the place and the function of formalization in this intricate process.

The vision of heaven and world entirely devoid of teleological pollution, held up here as a purely sublime and aesthetic vision, stands in direct contradiction to all preceding definitions and analyses of the sublime given in §24 on until this point in §29. Still in the condensed definition that appears in the same chapter, the stress falls on the sublime as a concrete representation of ideas (*Darstellung von Ideen*). As in the Wordsworth passage from *Tintern Abbey*, the articulation of physical motion with the movements of the affects and of practical moral judgment has to encompass natural and intellectual elements under one single unifying principle, such as the sublime. And there has been so much emphasis, from the start, on the fact that the sublime does not reside in the natural object but in the human mind (*Gemütsbestimmungen*) that the burden of the argument, much rather than emphasizing the purely inward, noumenal nature of the sublime, becomes the need to account for the fact that it nevertheless occurs as an outward, phenomenal manifestation. Can this in any way be reconciled with the radical materiality of sublime vision suddenly introduced, as if it were an afterthought, at this point in the argument? How is one to reconcile the concrete representation of ideas with pure ocular vision, *Darstellung von Ideen* with *Augenschein*?

The analytics of the sublime (like those of the beautiful) are consistently stated in terms of a theory of the faculties combined, in the dynamics of the sublime, with a theory of moral affect. "A feeling for the sublime in nature cannot well be thought without combining therewith a mental disposition which is akin to the *moral*" (194; 109). In the case of the beautiful, this moral component was also present, though in a much more subdued form. It manifested itself as the autonomy of aesthetic pleasure with regard to sensuous pleasure, a form of freedom and thus, in Kant's system where morality is always linked to liberty, at least potentially a form of moral judgment. But in the case of the sublime, the tie with morality is much more explicit, for morality is involved, not as play, but as legal or law-directed, labor (*gesetzliches Geschäft*). The only restriction that keeps the sublime from passing entirely into the camp of morality is that the faculty involved in it is not reason, or at least not an unmediated manifestation of reason, but that the sublime is represented by the imagination itself, as a tool of reason. In the laborious, businesslike world of morality, even the free and playful imagination becomes an instrument of work. Its task, its labor, is precisely to translate the abstractions of reason back into the phenomenal world of appearances and images whose presence is retained in the very word *imag*ination, *Bild* in the German *Ein*bild*ungskraft*.

Why this incarnation of the idea has to occur is accounted for in various ways. It is, first of all, a quasi-theological necessity that follows necessarily from our fallen condition. The need for aesthetic judgment and activity, although it defines man, is the expression of shortcoming, of a curse rather than of an excess of power and inventiveness. There would be no need for it "if we were creatures of pure intellect or even capable of displacing ourselves mentally in such a condition" (197; 111).

The same inherent inferiority of the aesthetic (or, more precisely, of the aesthetic as symptomatic of an inherent shortcoming in us) becomes visible with regard to moral judgment. Morality and the aesthetic are both disinterested, but this disinterestedness becomes necessarily polluted in aesthetic representation: the persuasion that, by means of their very disinterestedness, moral and aesthetic judgment are capable of achieving is necessarily linked, in the case of the aesthetic, with positively valorized sensory experiences. The moral lesson of the aesthetic has to be conveyed by seductive means, which, as we know, can reach far enough to make it necessary to read "Kant avec Sade" rather than the reverse. Instead of purely intellectual beauty we can only produce the beauty of the imagination. How this occurs is the object of a crucial and difficult paragraph (195; 109) in which the articulation of the imagination with reason, the assuredly "harmonious" relationship between reason and imagination wishfully promised at an earlier stage, is described in greater detail.

The passage introduces what will a few pages later be defined as a modulation between two moods or affects, the passage from shocked surprise (*Verwunderung*) to tranquil admiration (*Bewunderung*). The initial effect of the sublime, of a sudden encounter with colossal natural entities such as cataracts, abysses, and towering mountains, is one of shock, or says Kant, astonishment that borders upon terror (*Verwunderung, die an Schreck grenzt*). By a play, a trick of the imagination, this terror is transformed into a feeling of tranquil superiority, the admiration one expresses for something or for someone one can afford to admire peacefully, because one's own superiority is not really in question. The better one thinks of the other person, the better one has to think of oneself. How enviable a peace of mind thus achieved in the recognition of another's worth as confirmation of one's own! Moral nobility is the best ego trip available on the market—though Kant is not so blind as not to know of its cost in hidden blood and terror.

He had not always held that the serenity of admiration, the tranquility of spent emotion, is the highest of qualities. In the early, precritical essay on the sublime and the beautiful from 1764,[5] he had stated in peremptory fashion that the humor of the phlegmatic had to be rejected out of hand as having not the slightest possible relationship with beauty or sublimity, in any form or shape. It was said to be utterly devoid of any interest whatsoever. Its equivalent in terms of national stereotypes is that of the Dutch, described as a phlegmatized kind of German, interested only in the dreariest of commercial and money-making activities. I have never felt more grateful for the fifty or so kilometers that separate the Flemish city of Antwerp from the Dutch city of Rotterdam. Considerations on feminine languor and passivity, unfavorably contrasted with male energy, make for equally difficult reading in the early Kant essay. By the time of the *Critique of Judgment*, however, things have changed a great deal. "For (which seems strange) the absence of affection (*apatheia, phlegma in significatu bono*) in a mind that follows consistently its unalterable ground rules, is sublime, and in a far more outstanding way, because it is backed by the satisfaction of pure reason" (199; 113). The tranquility thus achieved receives the predicate of nobility, of a morally elevated state of mind that will then subreptiously be transferred to objects and things such as "a building, garment, literary style, bodily presence, etc." How is it, then, that the imagination can achieve the nobility of such loss of pathos, of such a serenity?

It does so by an essentially negative way, which corresponds philosophically to the elevation of the imagination from a metaphysical (and, hence, ideological) to a transcendental (and, hence, critical) principle. As long as the faculty of the imagination is considered empirically—and one is reminded that, in the late Kant, the presence of this empirical moment characterizes the metaphysical dimensions of the mind—it is free and playful, closer to what is called in English fancy rather than imagination. By sacrificing, by giving up its freedom, in a first negative moment of shocked, but pleasurable, surprise, the imagination allies itself with reason.

Why this is so is not at once clear; in affective terms, it takes on the form of a reconquered mastery, a reconquered superiority over a nature of which the direct threat is overcome. The free, empirical reaction of the imagination, when confronted with the power and might of nature, is to indulge, to enjoy the terror of this very magnitude. Taming this delectable, because imaginary, terror—the assumption always being that the person is not directly threatened, or at the very least separated from the immediate threat by a reflexive moment—and preferring to it the tranquil satisfaction of superiority, is to submit the imagination to the power of reason. For the faculty that establishes the superiority of the mind over nature is reason and reason alone; the imagination's security depends on the actual, empirical physical situation and, when this situation is threatening, it swings toward terror and toward a feeling of free submission to nature. Because, however, in the experience of the sublime, the imagination achieves tranquility, it submits to reason, achieves the highest degree of freedom by freely sacrificing its natural freedom to the higher freedom of reason. "Thereby," says Kant, "it achieves a gain in power that is larger than what it sacrifices" (195; 109). The loss of empirical freedom means the gain in critical freedom that characterizes rational and transcendental principles. Imagination substitutes for reason at the cost of its empirical nature and, by this anti- or unnatural act, it conquers nature.

This complicated and somewhat devious scenario accomplishes the aim of the sublime. The imagination overcomes suffering, becomes apathetic and sheds the pain of natural shock. It reconciles pleasure with pain and in so doing it articulates, as mediator, the movement of the affects with the legal, codified, formalized, and stable order of reason. Imagination is not nature (for, in its tranquility, it determines itself as larger and mightier than nature) but, unlike reason, it remains in contact with nature. It is not idealized to the point of becoming pure reason, for it has no knowledge of its actual predicament or of its actual strategies and remains pure affect rather than cognition. It becomes "adequate (*angemessen*) to reason on the basis of its inadequacy (*Unangemessenheit*) to this same reason in its relation to nature." In elevating this reflection of the aesthetic judgment to the point where it becomes adequate to reason (*zur Angemessenheit mit der Vernunft*), without however reaching a definite concept of reason, "the object is nevertheless represented, despite the objective inadequacy of the imagination, even in its greatest extension, to reason (*Unangemessenheit der Einbildungskraft . . . für die Vernunft*) as subjectively purposive" (195-95; 109-10), and thus, we may add, as pertaining both to reason and to practical judgment.

However complex this final formulation may sound, it is clarified and made persuasive by the road that leads up to it and is by no means unfamiliar. Even as uninspired a paraphrase as the one I have given should reveal that we are hardly dealing with a tight analytical argument (as was the case, for example, in the distinction between transcendental and metaphysical principles from which we started out). What we have here is less authoritative but a great deal more accessible. For one thing, instead of being an argument, it is a story, a dramatized scene of the mind in action. The faculties of reason and of imagination are personified, or anthropomorphized, like the five squabbling faculties hilariously staged by Diderot in the *Lettre sur les sourds et muets*,[6] and the relationship between them is stated in delusively interpersonal terms.

What could it possibly mean, in analytical terms, that the imagination sacrifices itself, like Antigone or Iphigenia—for one can only imagine this shrewd and admirable imagination as the feminine heroine of a tragedy—for the sake of reason? And what is the status of all this heroism and cunning, which allows it to reach apathia, to overcome pathos, by ways of the very pathos of sacrifice? How can faculties, themselves a heuristic hypothesis devoid of any reality—only for those who have read too much eighteenth-century psychology and philosophy might end up believing that they have an imagination, a reason, the same way they have blue eyes or a big nose—how can faculties be said to *act*, or even to act freely, as if they were conscious and complete human beings? We are clearly not dealing with mental categories but with tropes and the story

Kant tells us is an allegorical fairy tale. Nor are the contents of this tale at all unusual. It is the story of an exchange, of a negotiation, in which powers are lost and gained in an economy of sacrifice and recuperation.

It is also a story of opposite forces, nature and reason, the imagination and nature, tranquility and shock, adequacy (*Angemessenheit*) and inadequacy, that separate, fight, and then unite in a more or less stable state of harmony, achieving syntheses and totalizations that were missing at the beginning of the action. Such personified scenes of consciousness are easily identified: they are not actually descriptions of mental functions but descriptions of tropological transformations. They are not governed by the laws of the mind but by the laws of figural language.

For the second time in this text (the first time being the interplay between apprehension and comprehension in the mathematical sublime) we have come upon a passage that, under the guise of being a philosophical argument, is in fact determined by linguistic structures that are not within the author's control. What makes this intrusion of linguistic tropes particularly remarkable is that it occurs in close proximity, almost in juxtaposition, with the passage on the material architectonics of vision, in the poetic evocation of heaven and ocean, with which it is entirely incompatible.

For we are now confronted with two completely different notions of the architectonic—a word and concept I use because it appears under that name in Kant's own text. The architectonic vision of nature as a building is, in Kant, as we saw, entirely material, emphatically not tropological, entirely distinct from the cozy substitutions and exchanges between faculties or between mind and nature that make up the Wordsworthian or the romantic sublime. But the architectonic is also at times defined by Kant, though not in the *Third Critique*, in entirely different terms, much closer to the allegory of the faculties and the tale of recovered tranquility we have just been reading, much closer as well to the *Edle Einfalt* and *Stille Grösse* (noble simplicity and tranquil magnitude) of Winckelmann's neoclassicism.

Near the end of the *Critique of Pure Reason*, a chapter entitled "The Architectonics of Pure Reason," defines the architectonic as the organic unity of systems, "the unity of miscellaneous cognitions brought together under one idea" and greatly favored, by Kant, over what he calls the "rhapsody" of mere speculation devoid of *esprit de système*. That this unity is conceived in organic terms is apparent from the recurring metaphor of the body, as a totality of various limbs and parts (*Glieder*, meaning "member" in all the senses of the word, as well as, in the compound *Gliedermann*, the puppet of Kleist's *Marionettentheater*). Says Kant:

> The whole is articulated (*articulatio—gegliedert*) and not just piled on top of each other (*coacervatio—gehäuft*); it can grow from the inside out but

not from the outside in. It grows like an animal body, not by the addition of
new limbs (*Glieder*) but, without changing the proportions, by making each
individual member stronger and more efficient for its own purpose.[7]

One will want to know what becomes of this Aristotelian, zoo-
morphic architectonic when it is being considered, in the *Third Critique's*
passage on heaven and ocean, in a nonteleological, aesthetic perspective.
For one thing, it does not imply a collapse of the architectonic in the
rhapsodic, a disintegration of the building; sea and heaven, as the poets
see them, are more than ever buildings. But it is no longer at all certain
that they are still articulated, *gegliedert*.

After lingering briefly over the aesthetic vision of the heavens and
the seas, Kant turns for a moment to the human body:

> The like is to be said of the sublime and beautiful in the human body. We
> must not regard as the determining grounds of our judgment the concepts of
> the purposes which all our limbs serve (*wozu alle seine Gliedmassen da sind*)
> and we must not allow this unity of purpose to influence our aesthetic judg-
> ment (for then it would no longer be pure) [197; 111].

We must, in short, consider our limbs, our hands, our toes, our
breasts, or what Montaigne so cheerfully referred to as "*Monsieur ma
partie*," in themselves, severed from the organic unity of the body, the
way the poets look at the oceans severed from their geographical place on
earth. We must, in other words, disarticulate, mutilate, the body in a way
that is much closer to Kleist than to Winckelmann, though close enough
to the violent end that happened to befall both of them. We must consider our limbs the way the primitive considered the house, entirely
severed from any purpose or use. From the phenomenality of the aesthetic (which is always based on an adequacy of the mind to its physical
object, based on what is referred to, in the definition of the sublime, as
the concrete representation of ideas (*Darstellung der Ideen*), we have
moved to the pure materiality of *Augenschein*, of aesthetic vision. From
the organic, still asserted naively in the *Critique of Pure Reason*, to the
phenomenological, the rational cognition of incarnate ideas, which the
best part of the Kant interpretation in the nineteenth- and twentieth-
century will single out, we have reached, in the final analysis, a materialism that, in the tradition of the reception of the *Third Critique*, is seldom
or never perceived.

To appreciate the full impact of this conclusion one must remember
that the entire project of the *Third Critique*, the full investment in the
aesthetic, was to achieve the articulation that would guarantee the archi-

tectonic unity of the system. If the architectonic then appears, very near the end of the analytics of the aesthetic, at the conclusion of the section on the sublime, as the material disarticulation not only of nature but of the body, then this moment marks the undoing of the aesthetic as a valid category. The critical power of a transcendental philosophy undoes the very project of such a philosophy leaving us, certainly not with an ideology—for transcendental and ideological (metaphysical) principles are part of the same system—but with a materialism that Kant's posterity has not yet begun to face up to. This happens, not out of a lack of philosophical energy or rational power, but as a result of the very strength and consistency of this power.

What, finally, will be the equivalence of this moment in the order of language? Whenever the disruption asserted itself, in the passage in the nonteleological vision of nature and of the body and also, less openly but not less effectively, in the unexplained necessity of supplementing the consideration of the mathematical sublime with a consideration of the dynamic sublime, in the blank between §27 and §28 (as we refer to a blank between stanzas 1 and 2 of the "Lucy" poem, "A slumber did my spirit seal . . ." or between parts 1 and 2 of the *Boy of Winander* poem), whenever, then, the articulation is threatened by its undoing, we encountered a passage (the section on apprehension, the section on the sacrifice of the imagination), which could be identified as a shift from a tropological to a different mode of language. In the case of the dynamic sublime, one could speak of a shift from trope to performance.

In this case, the non-teleological apprehension of nature, a somewhat different pattern emerges. To the dismemberment of the body corresponds a dismemberment of language, as meaning-producing tropes are replaced by the fragmentation of sentences and propositions into discrete words, or the fragmentation of words into syllables or finally letters. In Kleist's text, one would isolate the dissemination of the word *Fall* and its compounds throughout the text as such a moment when the aesthetic dance turned into an aesthetic trap, as by the addition of a single mute letter that makes *Fall* (fall) into *Falle* (trap). No such artful moments seem to occur, at first sight, in Kant. But just try to translate a single somewhat complex sentence of Kant, or just consider what the efforts of entirely competent translators have produced, and you will soon notice how decisively determining the play of the letter and of the syllable, the way of saying (*Art des Sagens*) as opposed to what is being said (*das Gesagte*) —to quote Walter Benjamin—is in this most unconspicuous of stylists.

Is not the persuasiveness of the entire passage on the recovery of the imagination's tranquility after the shock of sublime surprise based, not so much on the little play acted out by the senses, but on the close proximity in sound, between the German words for "surprise" and "admiration,"

Verwunderung and *Bewunderung*? And are we not made to swallow the more than paradoxical but truly aporetic incompatibility between the failure of the imagination to grasp magnitude with what becomes, in the experience of the sublime, the success of this same imagination as an agent of reason, are we not made to swallow this because of a constant, and finally bewildering, alternation of the two terms. *Angemessen(heit)* and *Unangemessen(heit)*, to the point where one can no longer tell them apart? The bottom line, in Kant as well as in Hegel, is the prosaic materiality of the letter and no degree of obfuscation or of ideology can transform this materiality into the phenomenal cognition of aesthetic judgment.

9

On Mere Sight:
A Response to Paul de Man

Rodolphe Gasché

Although I do not intend to speculate on the various reasons why the analytics of the sublime—contrary to the analytics of the beautiful—has drawn relatively little attention from the philosopher, it may, however, be worthy of note that where this disinterest is not merely attributed to the alleged unintelligibility of the *Third Critique* as a whole, it seems to be due to a supposed excessive clarity and spotless transparency in the "Analytic of the Sublime."[1] Ernst Cassirer's treatment of the sublime in his *Kant's Life and Thought* could be evoked here as an excellent illustration of the latter reason. According to Cassirer, the chapters on the beautiful still reveal a certain foreign quality as far as the subject is concerned. And in spite of the rigor and conceptual refinement in the development of thought, Kant is said to be moving "once again on terrain that is personally and genuinely his" own—particularly when he enters upon the problematics of the sublime as the supreme synthesis between his ethical and his aesthetic principles. Therefore, Cassirer remarks that the "Analytic of the Sublime" "displays all the moments of the Kantian spirit and all those properties indicative of the man as well as the writer in genuine fulfillment and in the most felicitous mutual interpretation. Hence, the trenchancy of the analysis of pure concepts is found united with the moral sensitivity that forms the core of Kant's personality; here the eye for psychological detail, that Kant had already evidenced in the precritical *Observations on the Feeling of the Beautiful and the Sublime*, is allied with the encompassing transcendental perspectives, which he had achieved since that time over the whole domain of consciousness."[2] De Man's analysis leaves little doubt as to the nature of this hastily asserted clarity, and restores to the text of the "Analytic of the Sublime" a rather disturbing complexity.

As one of the many who are deeply indebted to Paul de Man's work, he has taught me a sense for a dimension of texts that is no longer recuperable by the conventional approaches of either thematic or formalist criticism. By bracketing, so to speak, the cognitive function of texts, and by focusing on what makes a text a text, particular texts, whether literary or philosophical, unavoidably lose their purported if not established transparency. Indeed, in centering on what has been labeled the scene of textual production the performative level of texts regain a certain unfamiliarity, and become once again uncanny and opaque. Its opaqueness, however, is due to "the prosaic materiality of language," a materiality that stares at us in the *Augenschein* of its irreducibly dismembered unity. The sort of complexity that the "Analytics of the Sublime" acquires in this manner is one that is thoroughly independent and different in nature and scope from the always still possible complications due to historical, philological, *begriffsgeschichlichen* perspectives or to intraphilosophical interpretations concerning the status of the sublime in Kant's work as a whole.

This recomplicating of texts ensues from an analysis of their performative dimension. The very possibility of retranslating the conceptual or tropological level of texts back into what de Man calls the "emphatically not tropological" materiality of language is dependent on the possibility of diagnosing not so much formal but structural breaks or discontinuities within the texts under consideration. As far as the chapter on the sublime is concerned, de Man has pointed out a whole series of such disruptions, the major ones being those between the mathematically and the dynamically sublime, as well as those between the two architectonics, or rather, between the sublime as *Darstellung von Ideen* and as *Augenschein*.

According to de Man's analysis, a certain lack in argumentation and a deficiency in the accounting creates a conceptual obscurity as to the necessity of such enigmatic juxtapositions within the text on the sublime. In the Second Book of the First Division of the First Part of the Critique of the Aesthetical Judgment, the obscurity in proceeding from the mathematically to the dynamically sublime, and in understanding the sublime as at once a presentation of ideas and an *Augenschein* is thus symptomatic of textual discrepancies that open onto the linguistic substructures of a text.

In what follows I shall take issue with this "obscurity." Without in the least questioning the validity and necessity of de Man's approach, which I hope to have summarized without too many distortions, and without questioning the legitimacy of looking for textual discrepancies in the intersection between the mathematically and the dynamically sublime, or between the two concepts of architectonics, as de Man has so convincingly done, I shall only ask whether the retranslation of the antinomies of the philosophical discourse into the formal system of language, and ultimately into the materiality of the radically untropological performative structures of language, does not require an additional intermediary step. My position, then, will be that of an *advocatus Kantii*, and of the traditional ways of philosophical mastering of intraphilosophical problems.

In general, I shall question whether or not a recourse to the canonical resources of philosophical argumentation and traditional Kant scholarship would not complicate the already quite complex operations of translation. In short, I should like to ask Paul de Man whether the discrepancies he has outlined would remain the same if one were to take into account the following four precisions: (1) Kant's transposition of the architectonics of the *First* to the *Third Critique* is very loose and inconsequential, especially in the transposing of the four judgmental functions constitutive in the table of categories to the sublime; (2) the analytics of the sublime is at the same time its deduction (As Kant has argued in §30,) and this implicit justification of the reflective moments of the faculty of the sublime (as grounded in a purposive relation of our cognitive faculties) may dissolve the contradictions in an exclusively analytic perspective; (3) Kant's essentially binary argumentative procedure, developing a logic of reflective determinations, could account for the shift from the mathematically to the dynamically sublime as a passage from, say, "idea" (the nonsensuous standard) to the "subjective faculty of ideas" (that of reason); And finally (4) Kant's own concept of dialectics could be summoned to explain the gaps in argumentation, for a Kantian dialectics —a logic of illusion (*eine Logik des Scheins*)—can never hope to effectively overcome the gulf between the faculties. And in limiting itself to a mere indication of the intelligible substratum of the antinomies, it only widens the gulf which Kant discusses in the introduction to the *Critique of Judgement*.

Invoking Kant's concept of dialectics, I do not intend to blunt the edge of the disruptions that de Man has shown to broach and breach Kant's text. Yet, if Kant is more than an epistemologist of the natural sciences (a view I share with de Man), if Kant belongs within the tradition of Spinoza and Hegel, that is, if one views Kant as a thinker of totality, then the danger in interpreting the *Third Critique* is that one either underestimates or overestimates Kant's ability to conceptualize totality. In discussing the simultaneity of the sublime as presentation of ideas and as *Augenschein*, I shall resist the temptation to Hegelianize Kant, by bridging the discrepancies, disruptions, and breaks within Kant's text. I shall attempt to illuminate, for a brief moment at least, what de Man has termed obscure.

As de Man has recalled in his most exciting analysis of the *Augenschein*, only pure aesthetical judgments concerning the sublime are in a position to achieve what Kant conceives as the task of the sublime. Whereas the beautiful achieves a conformity to the law of the judgment in its freedom in the regular and well-proportioned play of the faculties of imagination and understanding, the sublime achieves it in the relation between imagination and reason. As the examples of the sky and ocean reveal, the sublime is beheld in an intuition of mere *Augenschein*. If *Augenschein* is indeed only *material* vision, devoid of intellectual and reflective complication, the question arises as to how such a purely ocular vision could also entertain a relation to ideas, a relation required by the very definition of the sublime. If *Augenschein* is mere intuition, then it certainly cannot reconcile itself with the aesthetic judgment of the sublime's demand to present ideas.

It needs to be clarified whether one can, indeed, equate disinterested vision (a vision free of all judgment of sense, of logically determinate, and of teleological judgment) with mere vision, and whether something of the order of mere vision in de Man's sense, is at all conceivable within Kant's critical enterprise. At first, let us recall that the so-called free play of the beautiful is one of the faculties alone, and under no circumstances one of the affects or representations to which these faculties may give rise. This is all the more important in the case of the sublime, which is even more thoroughly independent of objects than is the beautiful. Therefore what the *Augenschein* shows is not itself the sublime. Sublime is rather the mood, the *Gestimmtheit*, the *Stimmung* of the mind in the contemplation of what the ocular vision reveals. Sublime is the poet's *act of* finding the ocean sublime. Instead of an unmediated vision, we already have a reflective, that is, aesthetic judgment at the basis of the poet's glance. Ultimately, it would be important to determine the precise role of the *Augenschein* in this judgment, and of course also what judgment means in this context.

Remember the famous phrase from the *Critique of Pure Reason* where Kant asserts that thoughts without content are empty, and intuitions without concepts are blind. Ultimately, intuitions without concepts are no real intuitions at all, they are mere phantoms, because the faculties do not operate alone and independently of one another. The aesthetic judgment of the beautiful is excellent proof of this essential interdependence of the faculties as it exhibits, in what is called the play of the faculties, the minimal agreement between imagination as the highest sensuous faculty and understanding as that of the concepts. In contrast, the judgment of the sublime is witness to a play that implies a minimal relation between imagination and the faculty of the ideas—namely reason. Just as the aesthetic judgment of the beautiful can be construed as the formal condition of possibility, or the minimal synthesis required for there to be cognition of nature, the aesthetical judgment of the sublime is to be understood as the minimal synthesis in order for there to be a mediation between

concepts of nature and concepts of freedom. The sublime is, by definition, this relation without which no application of reason to imagination
could be envisioned. The sublime, then, is at first a relation. Kant writes
in the *Third Critique*: "The *Sublime* consists merely in the *relation* by
which the sensible in the representation of nature is judged available for a
possible supersensible use."[3]

What sort of relation can the sublime be if one remembers that it is a
relation between a sensible faculty (however elevated) and a supersensible faculty, the "faculty expressing the independence of absolute totality?"[4]
Imagination is the faculty of *Darstellung*—that is, of the sensible presentation of the spontaneity of understanding and reason. Contrary to the
beautiful, which must be understood as the direct presentation of the
possibility of schematizing presentable concepts, the sublime takes upon
itself the presentation of what is unpresentable. Thus, the task in question is a variation of what Kant calls (in paragraph 59) "symbolic hypotyposis," a variation because, as Kant contends, there are only two sorts
of hypotyposes. Indeed, like symbolic presentation, the sublime renders
the intelligible only indirectly, and does so in what I would call a *negative*
hypotyposis. In fact, the relation established between imagination and
reason in the judgment of the sublime is not one of harmony, but of
conflict (*Widerstreit*). As a relation, however, this conflict does not exclude
totality, the severing takes place within it, and presupposes it. Let us not
forget that imagination is primarily a synthetic faculty (it represents reason on the level of the sensible). Imagination is, as Kant states, the common root for the two separate trunks (*Stämme*) of understanding and
reason, and thus closer to what Kant calls Reason in general as that of
which sensibility, understanding, and reason (in the narrow sense) are
only singularized expressions.

How does this negative presentation of the unpresentable take place
in that play of the faculties of imagination and reason that is properly
called sublime? It comes about through an extension (*Erweiterung*) of
imagination. By extending itself, imagination turns into the indirect or
negative presentation of reason. The extension corresponds to the establishing of a relation, between imagination and reason. Yet, how are we to
understand "extension" here? How are we to think this synthesis, for, in
Kant's language, extension is clearly a synthetic act? Imagination is extended when it gives up its bias toward sensibility, when it interrupts
its function as an agency of rendering sensible—in short, as soon as it
stops its presenting function. This extension takes place through an act
of freedom, in an act of self-determination. Kant makes it quite clear, as
de Man points out, that the extension of imagination is the result of a
self-violation and self-dispossession of imagination by which it sacrifices
its sensible nature—that is, its destiny as a faculty of mere presentation.

By this dominion, exercised by imagination itself, against itself, imagination submits to the rule of reason or, what is the same, to the law of freedom as the law of absolute totality. By this act of freedom as the greatest extension of which imagination is capable, imagination turns into the subjective-purposive presentation of the unpresentable, a presentation it achieves, precisely, in sacrificing its sensible destiny as a power of presentation.

In the context of Kant's treatment of the sublime, the reference to the Jewish command, "Thou shalt not make thyself any graven image, nor the likeness of anything which is in heaven or in the earth or under the earth," as a command of reason, and as the most sublime passage in the Jewish law, leaves no doubt that the relation between imagination and reason presupposes that the first gives up its attempt to visualize reason, to make an image of it, achieving in this manner a likeness without an image of what is unpresentable.[5] In short, then, the sublime is witness to a minimal (negative) presentation of the ideas, or rather of the faculty of ideas, namely, reason, and which itself, in its negativity, is the matrix of all sensible actualization of these ideas in the ethical realm.

Let us now circle back to the problematics of the *Augenschein*. For reasons already mentioned, it is difficult to imagine that Kant could think of it as mere, unmediated ocular vision. Inasmuch as there is no intuition without reference to concepts, there is also no intuiting without at least a negative relation to reason. Before returning to this minimal relation to reason, let us first note that there is a strong link in the philosophy immediately preceding Kant (from Wolff to Baumgarten) between the sensible faculty of imagination and eyesight. Apart from their reproductive function, the specificity of the images of imagination consists of conferring a sensible unity (individuality) upon appearances. What Kant calls "immediate intuition," or the "mere sight," or "what merely strikes the eye," is akin to Baumgarten's *dispositio naturalis ad perspiciam* through which nature is perceived in its totality, — not in a conceptual mode, but according to a mode immanent to its being.[6]

The *Augenschein* is a sensuous synthesis of phenomenality in a phenomenal manner. In Kant, this synthesis is made possible by the fact that the *Augenschein*, as soon as it enters into the service of the sublime, no longer sees anything determinate but the unseeable itself. What does the *Augenschein* reveal if not nature as a whole? The sky is "a distant, all-embracing, vault" (an example of the mathematically sublime) and the ocean is a totality. Or the *Augenschein* is a negative presentation of our incommensurable faculty of reason in the image of the "abyss threatening to overwhelm everything" natural (and, hence, an example of the dynamically sublime). Thus, in seeing nothing determinate, but the unseeable par excellence, the *Augenschein* yields to the law of freedom and reason.

In being free from concepts of understanding, the *Augenschein* resembles reason.

But, ultimately, the unseeable revealed by the *Augenschein*, as the *one* glance that embraces at once center and periphery, fails to show what it shows. For Kant the endeavor to present the intelligible totality as the totality of nature is impossible, not only because that totality is unpresentable, but also because no totalization of nature can be achieved. The *Augenschein*, however, though failing to present the intelligible, offers it to thought. Though the synthesis by imagination of the whole of nature has failed, the *Augenschein* is sublime because it reveals "imagination in its greatest extension"—that is, imagination as yielding to "the principles of the schematism of the judgment (being so far, therefore, ranked under freedom).''[7] Thus, the *Augenschein*, shows imagination to yield to reason. It is witness to a minimal relation of imagination to that faculty.

This conclusion springs forth from Kant's rather intricate statement that, despite what the *Augenschein* shows, the ocean must (nonetheless) be judged sublime (*man muss den Ozean bloss, wie die Dichter es tun, nach dem, was der Augenschein zeugt . . . dennoch erhaben finden können*). Rather than being mere ocular vision, the "immediate intuition" of the *Augenschein* is immediate in its negative presentation of the faculty of the ideas. Instead of being an obstacle to the presentation of ideas, the *Augenschein* seems to be another name for the extended imagination itself, and, consequently, the very presentation, however negative, of the faculty of absolute totalization.[8]

Part IV

*The Rhetoric and Practice
of Deconstruction:
Reading de Man*

PRELIMINARY REMARKS

This part is devoted exclusively to the work of Paul de Man and the impact it has made upon the world of letters, particularly in the Anglophone countries. Given this focus, the essays presented here constitute an extension of several discussions carried out in part III. Each contributor pursues a specific inquiry into the predicament of de Manean deconstruction: the deconstructive reading is self-implicating, for its form ironically duplicates the aporias it thematizes in the text. This predicament is reflected in de Man's deconstruction of the problem of literary history, his appropriation of the terms "constative" and "performative" from J.L. Austin, and in the dilemma of deconstruction in relation to the academic institution. Our contributors examine each of these instances in turn.

In "Paul de Man and the Subject of Literary History," Gregory Jay discusses de Man's criticism of the desire for a genetic narrative that would articulate a history of literature, and of the "subject" that would speak such a narrative. For de Man, the history of literature becomes a problem with the advent of romanticism, which he understands as "the passage from a mimetic to a genetic concept of art and literature, from a Platonic to a Hegelian model of the universe." In *Allegories of Reading* de Man deconstructs the history of romanticism itself, a history that doubles the problematic of genesis back upon its own "origin." For de Man, the strategic effect of this doubling is the textualization of concepts such as "history," "romanticism," "literature," and so forth. In other words, the paradox of the romantic desire for a literary history, which is a desire for its own history and its own origin, becomes a textual aporia. Any articulation of this history would be, at the same time, an articulation of its impossibility. As Jay points out, literary history occurs in the dynamics of the text, specifically in its allegories and aporias, and he takes this to be the primary concern of *Allegories of Reading*.

Citing the essay entitled "Genesis and Genealogy," Jay reviews de Man's reading of Nietzsche's "post-romantic" text, *The Birth of Tragedy*. Here, de Man shows that Nietzsche imposes his own genetic methodology upon the problematic of origins so central to romantic theory and criticism. Nietzsche's narrative repeats the very paradigms of origin (such as memory, perception, imaginary consciousness, etc.) that it deconstructs in recounting the history of tragedy, from the ancient goat-dance to Wagnerian opera. Furthermore, Jay suggests that de Man's reading of Nietzsche reflects a concern for the "subject" or "self" of historical narration.

De Man reduces this self to the tropological function of *prosopopeia*, which is an apostrophe to an absent or voiceless entity, which posits the possibility of a reply, and therefore endows what is absent or voiceless with the power of speech. De Man characterizes *prosopopeia* as a master trope; it is the very figure of the reader and reading. Jay points out that the absent voice of Nietzsche's text is Dionysus, and that de Man repeats this trope in his reading of Nietzsche. For in his deconstruction of Nietzsche's "melocentrism," the fictionalized presence of Dionysus, de Man himself appeals to an absent subject for whom the mechanism of language can be seen as prior to anything like an expression of will or psychic energy. Hence, Jay argues, Paul de Man's rhetoric would seduce us into an identification, which it also forbids. De Man's reading re-inscribes, via *prosopopeia*, the aporia of Nietzsche's text, confirming de Man's claim that deconstruction is text-productive and self-implicating. Thus Jay's essay serves as a caveat to any lector who is tempted to find in de Man the security of an extratextual identity or referent. As Jay points out, de Man's own voice is as fictional as that of Dionysus.

In "Recovering the Figure of J.L. Austin in Paul de Man's *Allegories of Reading*," Brian Caraher continues in the same vein. He suggests that J.L. Austin functions as a rhetorical figure in de Man's text, where de Man employs the Austinian terms "constative" and "performative," particularly in his readings of Nietzsche. In certain aphorisms, Nietzsche speculates that the laws of logic are normative insofar as they are "imperative." That is to say, the laws of logic are carried out via propositional speech acts, mandating that language must first posit entities in order to know them. De Man shows that Nietzsche's claim, which wants to be understood prepositionally, must by its own mandate posit *itself* as knowledge. As de Man says, "the deconstruction states the fallacy of reference in a necessarily referential mode." Caraher follows up on this point vis-à-vis de Man's deconstruction of the constative and performative functions of language *à la mode d'Austin*.

Caraher notes that in *How to Do Things with Words* Austin would show that the performative function of language deconstructs and supercedes the constative function. De Man, however, plays these terms off against one another, not allowing the referential (constative) function to dissolve by force of the performative function—as his reading of Nietzsche would attest. Caraher characterizes Austin's text as a "phenomenalist" and "pragmatic" reading of rhetoric, which performs its own valorization of the "performative" over the "constative." Furthermore, Caraher understands this as an attempt to undermine the positivist and atomist theories of language that have dominated Anglo-American philosophy. De Man's defense of the "constative" would therefore reinstate the positivist paradigm as inescapable, though not completable. In this regard, Caraher concludes that de Man's figuralization of Austin constitutes a reversal of the Austinian text. Where Austin seeks to perform the impossibility of the constative function, de Man sets constatization and performance against each other—"a gesture," notes Caraher, "which merely re-positions and makes impossible the notion of the 'performative.' " However, as de Man would insist, and as Caraher's appeal to "gesture" would suggest, the deconstruction states the fallacy of performance in a necessarily performative mode.

Howard Fleperin's essay, "The Anxiety of American Deconstruction," considers the dilemma that deconstruction poses for academic institutions, as well as the dilemma presented to deconstruction by its own institutionalization. As Felperin points out, the relationships between deconstruction and the academy are themselves deconstructive. This holds especially for "American" or "Yale" deconstruction and its leading practitioner, Paul de Man. Felperin remarks that although Derrida operates within a philosophical context, and appeals to *différance* as a dissolution of the categorical distinctions between "literary" and "ordinary" language, American deconstruction, following de Man, still considers literariness to be a privileged moment. This is so, he says, even if "its enlightenment consists precisely in its disclaimer of what is normally claimed for it. . . . The revelation literature offers is that it can never be what the institution of its study blindingly takes it to be." Hence the anxiety of American deconstruction: it would maintain the privileged status of literature while denying as arbitrary the institution of letters, and while its practitioners enjoy influential positions within that institution.

In addition, Felperin surmises that because Derrida maintains close ties with philosophy, he is perhaps less anxious and less anxiety-provoking relative to the Anglo-American world, where philosophy tends to confine itself within narrowly defined professional interests, and is of little consequence for society at large. The literary tradition, on the other hand, persists in claiming a central and universal role in Anglophone societies, and so de Man's literary orientation would give deconstructive practice a sharper edge in the English-speaking world. In New Haven, in particular, the literary tradition and the academic institution are also historically linked to a puritanical "work ethic." Felperin suggests that the seriousness of Yale deconstruction, in contrast to the laissez-faire playfulness of its French counterpart, is explicable in terms of its valorization of the *work* of criticism for the sake of work itself. In this respect, deconstruction seems not to have attained critical distance from a tradition that it would otherwise regard as arbitrary and groundless.

In focusing upon the institutional import of deconstruction, Felperin's essay reiterates many of the points at issue in the first section. Indeed, it shows the scope of a problematic that is crucial for virtually all the pieces presented in this volume: the relation of deconstruction to its "other." As noted in the introduction to part I, this problematic includes other strategies of criticism within the relation between a deconstructive reading and its text. It also includes the relation of difference between specific deconstructive practices (Derrida and de Man), between the "faculties" of criticism and philosophy, and between deconstruction and the larger texts of social and cultural institutions. Consistently, a pattern emerges from the discussions presented thus far: the relation between deconstruction and its other(s) is itself deconstructive. In lieu of an objective or methodological essence, this pattern indicates a principle of rigor for deconstructive practice. It serves, as well, as an organizing principle for the treatment of deconstruction and its differences.

G.E.A.

10

Paul de Man and the
Subject of Literary History

Gregory S. Jay

What direction can the writing of literary history take in the aftermath of deconstruction? In 1949, Wellek and Warren were impelled to ask a similar question in the wake of the New Criticism: "Is it *possible* to write literary history, that is, to write that which will be both literary and a history?" (252).[1] Their emphasis on the study of literature as an intrinsic, formalist enterprise led Wellek and Warren to call for a literary history written in accordance with such principles: "Why has there been no attempt, on a large scale, to trace the evolution of literature as art" rather than "as mere document for the illustration of national or social history" (252-53)? Critical theory today, with its emphasis on textuality, discourse, and rhetoric, has once more forced us to ask what relation—if any—links literature to history, politics, psychoanalysis, and the other human sciences. How we conceive of that relationship will largely determine how we will construct our versions of literary history, if indeed we do not abandon the project altogether.

Paul de Man's approach to the question of literary history turns, like that of Wellek and Warren, on the question: "What is literature?" Throughout his career, however, from "Form and Intent in the American New Criticism" to "Resistance to Theory," de Man rejected any literary theory based on aesthetics (this lesson seems to have escaped many of those who have blindly accused de Man of aestheticism). The antiaesthetic character of de Man's deconstructive enterprise comprises part of his general philosophical position in the wake of Heidegger, and entails rethinking the subjects of consciousness, language, and history. Deconstruction, whether de Man's or Derrida's, dis-closes these terms and short-circuits the interpretive narratives they often serve to center. Literary history, as one of these stories, will be subjected by de Man to a more than rigorous critical exposure.

For the New Critics, literary ontology centered itself in those "ambiguities" or "paradoxes" that Cleanth Brooks named as constituting literary language as such.[2] De Man tropes "paradox" with "aporia," a term for textual impasses, which resist the unifying hermeneutics of formalism, aestheticism, ideology, and onto-theology. In "The Dead-End of Formalist Criticism," de Man argues that the delusory ontological unity ascribed to the poetic artifact is an effect of reading as it defends against aporia. In a formulation he will never veer from, de Man declares: "The text does not resolve the conflict, it *names* it."[3] Relying unabashedly on his reading of Heidegger, de Man reinscribes the Marxist and Sartrean explanations for contradiction, alienation, and difference: "The problem of separation inheres in Being, which means that social forms of separation derive from ontological and metaphysical attitudes. For poetry, the divide exists forever" (BI, 240).

The consequences of this poetic ontology for the writing of literary history are spelled out at the end of "Literary History and Literary Modernity," as De Man wonders:

> Whether a history of an entity as self-contradictory as literature is conceivable. . . . It is generally admitted that a positivistic history of literature, treating it as if it were a collection of empirical data, can only be a history of what literature is not . . . On the other hand, the intrinsic interpretation of literature claims to be anti- or a-historical, but often presupposes a notion of history of which the critic is not himself aware [BI, 163].

De Man's allusion to Wellek and Warren echoes the division of *Theory of Literature* into sections on "extrinsic" and "intrinsic" studies of literature, and recalls the dilemma of their book's concluding chapter, "Literary History." Its placement at book's end implies the achievement of a totalization that the chapter's own argument fails to establish, except in such tautologies as "our starting point must be the development of literature as literature" (264). Wellek and Warren's final paragraph collapses into a series of qualifications, self-doubts, apologies, and prophesies that betray the cost of their paradigmatic opposition between referential and artistic discourses. De Man departs from their premises in radicalizing paradox into aporia, and suggests a new way of reading that would resist the parallel temptations to the mimetic and aesthetic fallacies:

> Could we conceive of a literary history that would not truncate literature by putting us misleadingly *into* or *outside* it, that would be able to maintain the literary aporia throughout, account at the same time for the truth and the

falsehood of the knowledge literature conveys about itself, distinguish rigorously between metaphorical and historical language, and account for literary modernity as well as for its historicity? [BI, 165].

As we shall see, this forecasts de Man's reading of romanticism as a case study in the blindness and insight of attempts to write literary history.

De Man's antipathy to formalism pervades "The Resistance to Theory," where he assaults the error made in assimilating "literariness" to "aesthetic response," and warns against the "strong illusion of aesthetic seduction."[4] But he similarly mocks how, as he put it in "Semiology and Rhetoric," "critics cry out for the fresh air of referential meaning."[5] De Man muses upon the anxiety of reference that haunts so many of his humanist or Marxist antagonists, and he resolutely maintains his position that the study of texts cannot be reduced to the referents, which are one of their effects: "In a genuine semiology as well as in other linguistically oriented theories, the referential function of language is not being denied— far from it; what is in question is its authority as a model for natural or phenomenal cognition."

Reinscribing Marx, de Man deftly observes that what "we call ideology is precisely the confusion of linguistic with natural reality," so that "more than any other mode of inquiry, including economics, the linguistics of literariness is a powerful and indispensable tool in the unmasking of ideological aberrations, as well as a determining factor in accounting for their occurrence" (11). In pointed contrast to Frederic Jameson, for instance, who attempts to write a kind of literary history that would accommodate textuality and deconstruction to dialetical materialism through a theory of the "political unconscious" and its symbolic *resolutions* of social contradictions, de Man appears implacable in his subordination of all other interests to the study of the irreconcilability distinguishing textual economies.

We cannot, then, canonize de Man as the heir apparent in the genealogy of formalist criticism. This would be, first, to completely ignore his repeated injuctions against formalism, which are based on his career-long concern with *signification*, a process of temporality that formalism submits to closure and reification.[6] If one has not understood the displacement of formalism by deconstructive semiology in de Man's work, then one has not read de Man. Secondly, we cannot ignore de Man's insistent and ironic troping of terms from the human sciences and their referential discourses. Stylistically, de Man's irony includes a mode of repetition, wherein the concepts of aesthetics or psychoanalysis or phenomenology or speech act theory or classical rhetoric are reinscribed, and often mixed together, as in the following excerpt from *Allegories of Reading:*

The very pathos of desire (regardless of whether it is valorized positively or negatively) indicates that the presence of desire replaces the absence of identity and that, the more the text denies the actual referent, real or ideal, and the more fantastically fictional it becomes, the more it becomes the representation of its own pathos. Pathos is hypostatized as a blind power or mere "puissance de vouloir," but it stabilizes the semantics of the figure by making it "mean" the pathos of its undoing [AR, 198-99].

The pathos of *our* undoing lies in calculating the effect of this Babylonish dialect. We may even read it self-reflexively: "the more fantastically fictional it becomes, the more it becomes the representation of its own pathos." In any case the effect is not to destroy reference or annihilate form; it is rather to disseminate them. "Contrary to received opinion," writes de Man, "deconstructive discourses are suspiciously text-productive" (AR, 200).

Perhaps the most frequently reinscribed concept in the texts of de Man is that of the "self," which suffers an extreme identity crisis under the pressures of a post-Freudian, post-phenomenological, and post-Saussurean critique. In de Man's rhetorical injunctions against literary conceptions of selfhood, however, one reads the traces of an authorial desire, and the continued return of phenomenological and psychoanalytic tropologies. This ironic re-voicing will, in turn, bear quite crucially on the narration of literary history. As de Man inherits it, the self stands as the conjunction between synchrony and diachrony, or consciousness and history: a purely "literary" history would entail the erasure of the author, whose self does not belong to the history of literature; and a history of literature as the history of consciousness would once more repress writing. If literature is to have a history, it must consist of heterogeneous moments, of temporal differences and delays, of punctuations and articulations, which by definition are not identical and do not occur at the "same time." The "self" appears as the name and instance grounding such events of difference. Of the referent-effects that function as such articulations and identities, the self has occupied a valorized position, especially insofar as it offers its voice as the origin of meaning.

An allegory of de Man's readings, then, detects him opening up the otherwise closed systems of criticism through a syncronic account of the ever "present" aporia inhabiting all signification; yet the aporia is not a form in any conventional sense, but a name for the temporality and difference energizing any production of meaning. A re-turn of diachrony, history, genealogy, and even subjectivity occurs, methodologically and thematically, whenever de Man sets out upon their deconstruction, for it is not their absence, but their ironic ontology, that fascinates him. De Man's deconstruction of the literary self appears highlighted in the rhetorical figure of *prosopopeia*, which he calls "the master trope of poetic discourse."⁷ The "figure of prosopopeia," says de Man, is "the fiction of an apostrophe to an absent, deceased, ot voiceless entity, which posits the possibility of the latter's reply and confers upon it the power of speech." Prosopopeia provides "a mask or a face" along with a voice, and is thus the "trope of autobiography" as well.⁸ The rhetorical double play of de Manian prosopopeia parallels that of Derrida's supplement: "*prosopon-poiein* means to *give* a face and therefore implies that the original face can be missing or nonexistent" (HI, 30). Thus de Man nominates proso-popeia as his master trope (or as the trope of mastery) because its supple-mentary work dismembers or disfigures the order of meaning set down by myths of authorship, grammar, and reference:

> As soon as we understand the rhetorical function of prosopopeia as positing voice or face by means of language, we also understand that what we are deprived of is not life but the shape and sense of a world accessible only in the privative way of understanding [RR, 80-81].

Consciousness *is* prosopopeia.⁹

De Man's interest in prosopopeia, I suspect, stems in part from its tropological mixture of vocal and visionary phenomena: prosopopeia gives voice to invisible, often quite dead, subjects—like consciousness of literary history. We should not be surprised, then, to find de Man declar-ing that prosopopeia, "as the trope of address, is the very figure of the reader and of reading" (HI, 31). Reading de Man's grammatically explicit statements or rhetorically inflected doubts about the relation of language to other domains, one thus must give voice to the figures his rhetoric contains: those of history, politics, phenomenology, semiotics, psychoa-nalysis, and of the author himself.

Barbara Johnson quite cleverly discovers that, in a crucial passage on the "eclipse of the subject" in language, de Man's own sentence con-tains a "grammatical anacoluthon," for he has left out the grammatical subje⸱⸱ itself, so that his text "*enacts* the eclipse of the interpreting subject that it describes."¹⁰ Unfortunately, this example lapses into formalism, for now form and meaning unite in the art of de Man's grammatical lapse.¹¹ Elsewhere de Man's prosopopeia turns literary history into a kind of overdetermined ventriloquism or deconstructive vaudeville. De Man gives voice and face to what a previous grammar would call nonexistent or unheard-of figures.

What could critical prosopopeia give voice to in an analysis of de Man's *Allegories of Reading*? One may overhear how his own rhetoric supplements, not an absence, but prior figures of reading and of literary history (including his own earlier work). The "Preface" imposes a retro-spective coherence on this collection of essays when it states that "*Alle-*

gories of Reading started out as a historical study and ended up as a theory of reading." Figured here is a critic whose intended "historical reflection on romanticism" is thwarted by "local difficulties of interpretation." De Man finds this "shift" "typical of my generation." "It could, in principle," he writes, "lead to a rhetoric of reading reaching beyond the canonical principles of literary history which will still serve, in this book, as the starting point of their own displacement" (AR, ix). These "canonical principles" will include theme, authorial origin, chonology, reference, and historical context. The displacement of each of these devices for constructing literary history is the most salient feature of de Man's chapters. Yet we note that the canonical principle of the aporia between history and literature, inherited from Wellek and Warren as well as from the debate between E.R. Curtius's historical tropology and Erich Auerbach's figural historicism, reappears as the very fate of de Man's own readings. The attempt to write literary history has once more ended in a meditation on the impossibility of the task.[12]

The displacement of canonical literary history, however, is itself narrated as a historical event, "typical" of a specific "generation," and thus represented by de Man in terms that seem to contradict his explanation that "local difficulties of interpretation" were the ahistorical determinants of his readings. Within the history of de Man's own career, the itinerary stated here follows the program outlined at the end of "Literary History and Literary Modernity." There de Man argued that though the "need to revise the foundations of literary history may seem like a desperately vast undertaking," especially "if we contend that literary history could in fact be paradigmatic for history in general," solace is found in the recognition that "all the directives we have formulated as guidelines for a literary history are more or less taken for granted when we are engaged in the much more humble task of reading and understanding a literary text" (BI, 165).

Literary history takes place in the figural dynamics of the text, particularly in the tropes and allegories of its aporias, so that attention to the aporias becomes the most authentic approach to how suspension, bridging, meaning, and narration come into being, bringing history and the subject along with them. This process will in fact be the chief concern of *Allegories of Reading*, as it is of de Man's reading of romanticism. One must then take quite ironically, if still seriously, the announcement in the "Preface" to *The Rhetoric of Romanticism* that "Except for some passing allusions, *Allegories of Reading* is in no way a book about romanticism or its heritage" (RR, vii). At least one chapter, "Genesis and Genealogy (Nietzsche)," explicitly addresses the problem of literary history in the case of romanticism.

De Man's admission of a genealogical imperative in the history of his own book comes as a surprise in light of his recurrent critique of the genetic fallacy. De Man takes indirect aim at Harold Bloom in attacking critics who see romanticism as a Hegelian narrative of "the emergence of a true Subject" (AR, 80). In contrast, de Man undertakes to read Nietzsche's *Birth of a Tragedy* in "the clarity of a new ironic light" that will expose the "hollow" at geneticism's core, and undo the biological and familial models used by Bloom and others to conceive literary history. This chapter bears close scrutiny, for its investigation of Nietzsche's historiography and Nietzsche's voice often functions self-reflexively in the unfolding of de Man's own text. The displacement of articulate authorial consciousness by a figure of rhetorical prosopopeia in Nietzsche's (and de Man's) text will cause great difficulties for the subject of literary history.

"Genesis and Genealogy" challenges "the genetic pattern of literary history and of literary texts" used in most descriptions of romanticism. Repeating his now familiar criticism of the "detour or flight from language" by scholars who "feel more at home with problems of psychology or historiography," de Man charges that the recourse to the "nonlinguistic referential models used in literary history" is motivated by the analyst's anxiety before the "very semiological properties" of the text—especially its aporias. "Romanticism," de Man notes, "is itself generally understood as the passage from a mimetic to a genetic concept of art and literature, from a Platonic to a Hegelian model of the universe" (AR, 79).

Theorists of romanticism or post-Romanticism, in other words, project their own genetic methodology onto the textual structures and literary history of romanticism, resolving its aporias into certain reassuring narratives. For de Man, the genetic model recalls and totalizes temporality into a presence of meaning, and is inseparable from the paradigms of memory, perception, imagination, and consciousness so frequently thematized in romantic texts and criticism. Consciousness is the agency (and agon) of genealogy. The traditional portrayal of romanticism as an onto-theology of recollected presence united in a genetic whole "is caught in a nondialectical notion of a subject-object dichotomy, revealing a more or less deliberate avoidance of the moment of negation that coincides, for Hegel, with the emergence of a true Subject." Ironically, the pursuit of Hegelian negation may end up "with an altogether un-Hegelian concept of the subject as an irrational, unmediated experience of particular selfhood (or loss of selfhood)." The "true Subject" returns, however negatively, in the narrative of this loss—this alienation and end of man—which (even in the work of Foucault) invokes the metaphorics of genealogy: "The allegorization and ironization of the organic model," concludes de Man, "leaves the genetic pattern unaffected" (AR, 80).

This structure of mere reversal holds true for literary histories that try to situate romanticism:

Within an organically determined view of literary history, Romanticism can appear as a high point, a splendor, and the subsequent century as a slow receding of the tide, a decay that can take on apocalyptic proportions. A reversed image of the same model sees Romanticism as a moment of extreme delusion from which the nineteenth century slowly recovers until it can free itself in the assertion of a new modernity. . . . The critical "deconstruction" of the organic model changes this image: it creates radical discontinuities and disrupts the linearity of the temporal process to such extent that no sequence of actual events or no particular subject could ever acquire, by itself, full historical meaning [AR, 80-81].

Here de Man repeats the argument of "Literary History and Literary Modernity," which (again using Nietzsche) had disputed the narrative granting "modernity" its teleological finality: modernity is instead the eternal recurrence of difference. Any narrative, however "deconstructive," which simply reverses the traditional poles but still arranges them as a sequence from absence to presece or vice versa is not truly historical, or literary, for it forecloses textual and temporal aporias through the imposition of an a priori paradigm.

De Man's close reading of romantic texts discloses the extent to which they themselves resist such foreclosure and geneticism:

It could be that the so-called Romantics came closer than we do to undermining the absolute authority of this system. If this were the case, one may well wonder what kind of historiography could do justice to the phenomenon of Romanticism, since Romanticism . . . would then be the movement that challenges the genetic principle which necessarily underlies all historical narrative. The ultimate test or "proof" of the fact that Romanticism puts the genetic pattern of history in question would then be the impossibility of writing a history of Romanticism [AR, 82].

This climatic "impossibility," de Man wryly observes, is confirmed by the "abundant bibliography that exists on the subject," presumably including Wellek and Warren's futile discussion of romanticism and the problems it raises for the concept of literary periods. Current enthusiasms for the differences made by "modernism" or "postmodernism" in transcending the legacy of romanticism, de Man implies, display their blindness in reading their own insights as successful supplements to the supposed grandeur or naivety of their precursors.

De Man pursues these theses through an intricate dissection of Nietzsche's *The Birth of Tragedy*, a text whose very title suggests its involvement in genealogy even as its author voices "the radical rejection of the genetic teleology associated with Romantic idealism" (AR, 82). Readers will recall Nietzsche's argument that Greek tragedy descends from

Dionysian ritual, that Apollo and Socrates are reductive aesthetic declensions from Dionysian power, and that Wagner and modernity promise a rebirth of Dionysian plenitude. De Man finds, however, that "the diachronic, successive structure of *The Birth of Tragedy* is in fact an illusion," for he shows that "whenever an art form is being discussed, the three modes represented by Dionysos, Apollo, and Socrates are always simultaneously present and that it is impossible to mention one without at least implying the others" (AR, 85). This simultaneity is rewritten by geneticism, which recasts the protagonists in parental or other genealogical metaphors. Ultimately the telelogy is from the decadence of Socratic epistemology to the modern rebirth of art, which Nietzsche advocates in pronouncements of a thoroughly epistemological kind. This double writing does not bother de Man, and in his commentary we hear a rebuttal to his own critics: "One cannot hold against him the apparent contradiction of using a rational mode of discourse—which he, in fact, never abandoned—in order to prove the inadequacy of this discourse." "Nietzsche is entirely in control of this problem," says de Man, which he takes over from Kant and Schopenhauer, whom Nietzsche calls those "great men . . . able to use the devices of science itself in order to reveal the limits and relativity of all knowledge" (AR, 86).

This internal division of epistemology, however, forms only a paradox and "logical complication" that as yet remains within genealogy:

> The ambivalence of the epistemological moment, as the critical undoer of its own claim at universal veracity, is represented as a genetic development from the Alexandrian to the truly modern man, and undoubtedly owes some of its persuasiveness to the narrative, sequential mode of presentation. It does not however, in this text, put this mode explicitly or implicitly into question [AR, 86].

Critics have often pinpointed exactly this "ambivalence of the epistemological moment" in de Man's own writing, and wondered naively how logic could logically question itself, though nothing is more logical, or historically determined, than such questioning.

Ambivalence does not yield a radical critique. Something more must be considered if geneticism is to be thwarted, whether in Nietzsche's or de Man's analysis. If we seek "an underlying, deeper pattern of valorization that confers genetic coherence and continuity upon the text and that transcends the thematics of the Apollo/Dionysos or the Socrates/Dionysos dialectic," we discover that "Nietzsche [and de Man?] might be in the grip of a powerful assumption about the nature of language, bound to control his conceptual and rhetorical discourse regardless of whether the author is aware of it or not" (AR, 87). De Man will use the question of literariness as a wedge to reopen the closures imposed by the machinery of thematics and historiography. In Nietzsche's text "little is explicitly being said about the nature of literary language," and the "importance of language is consistently undercut" by a move "towards the suppression of text in favor of mime and music," or in other words from representation to presence (AR, 87).

This "dispossesion of the word in favor of music" accords, notes de Man, with Derrida's description of logocentrism in *Of Grammatology*. Nietzsche's 'melocentrism' refines "the claim that truth can be made present to man and so ironically "recovers the possibility of language to reach full and substantial meaning" (AR, 88). Contemporary readings of Nietzsche's book, in fact, agree on its "logocentric ontology," but de Man's commentary hopes to displace even these decipherments by demonstrating *their* complicity in the genetic model and the greater rigorousness of Nietzsche's text. The "new Nietzsche" of poststructuralism seems to be only a renovation of the modernist Nietzsche, still conceived genealogically, this time as the father and/or rebellious son of logocentrism (AR, 90).

Nietzsche's chief theme is the Dionysian origin, and end, of art: "the priority of the musical, nonrepresentational language of Dionysos over the representational, graphic language of Apollo seems "beyond dispute" (AR, 92). Yet this raises a question central to Heidegger and pursued by the deconstructors of phenomenology: Why must the plenitude of Being eclipse itself in the limiting, delayed, and deferred forms of representation? "Why then," asks de Man, "if all truth is on Dionysos's side, is Apollonian art not only possible but even necessary? Why the need for metaphorical appearance since the proper meaning is all that counts?" (AR, 92).

Nietzsche's answer is that "Dionysian insight is *tragic* insight," from which we are sheltered by "the protective nature of the Apollonian moment" (AR, 93).[13] But Nietzsche's own voice here does not speak the unmediated truth of Dionysos, but adopts an Apollonian mask. Notes de Man:

> It is time to start questioning the explicit, declarative statement of the text in terms of its own theatricality. The system of valorization that privileges Dionysos as the truth of the Apollonian appearance . . . reaches us through the medium of a strongly dramatized and individualized voice . . . a harangue that combines the seductive power of a genetic narrative with the rhetorical complicity of a sermon [AR, 93].

As orator, Nietzsche manipulates the "I" and "we" to convince us that he "has our best interests at heart and we are guaranteed intellectual safety as long as we remain within the sheltering reach of his voice" (AR, 94). This voice also transports the reader over the text's many digressive breaks and discontinuities. *The Birth of Tragedy* is also a drama, a spectacle of the undecidability between Dionysos and Apollo. Thus the book "is curiously ambivalent with regard to the main figures of its own discourse: the category of representation that underlies the narrative mode and the category of the subject that supports the all pervading hortatory voice" (AR, 94). As a text it cannot serve as the end, or origin, of a literary history grounded in Dionysian art or epistemological representation, for the difference between the two cannot be articulated without irony.

Nietzsche's aporia recurs structurally, as when he criticizes the use of the deus ex machina in Euripides to ground the origin and end of the drama. This recourse to a deity who guarantees "the credibility of the story" and the "reality of the mythological plot" is repeated in Nietzsche's own recourse to Dionysos and the plot of his return. *The Birth of Tragedy* is "a text based on the authority of a human voice that receives this authority from its allegiance to a quasi-divine figure" (AR, 95). It should be clear by now that de Man's attunement to Nietzsche's voice continues his concern with the trope of prosopopeia, now overheard as Nietzsche's articulation of Dionysos. And in giving voice to this prosopopeia, de Man himself repeats the structure ironically, as the authority of his own voice stems from its rigorous allegiance to the re-turn of Nietzsche, except that in place of a quasi divinity we have a figure riven by aporia.

For Nietzsche betrays himself on the subject of music. Music had been distinguished, and valorized, precisely on the basis of the difference between imitative realism and a pure art liberated from representation. But the "tragic Dionysian insight is not, as for Rousseau, an absence of all meaning, but a meaning that we are unable to face for psychological or moral reasons" (AR, 96). Referential discourses (psychology and ethics) form the knowledge of Dionysos's pure art. Only a will that represents the world to itself could arrive at such a knowledge, such a will to music, and so representation and the subject remain intrinsic to the spectacle of their deconstruction, which operates through the seductions of rhetoric: "The authority of his voice has to legitimize an act by means of which the aporia of an unmediated representation, by itself a logical absurdity, would be suspended *(aufgehoben)*" (AR, 96). Nietzsche's voice remains in the register of Hegel, though we overhear the dissonance in its sublation. De Man's voice speaks, in prosopopeia, of Rousseau, subject of his final chapters as he attempts to move his own deconstructions past the psychological and moral thematics of Nietzsche and toward the linguistics of the aporias they speak of.

Allegories of Reading tropes literary history in the double play of its own construction. The subtitle, *Figural Language in Rousseau, Nietzsche, Rilke, and Proust*, seems to promise a conventional chronological investigation of these literary figures in a narrative of tropology's increasing sophistication, perhaps reinforcing the view that sees (post)modernism as an undoing of romantic theories of language. The table of contents, however, shows that we move backward in time, from Proust to Rousseau, ironically upsetting the genetic model. More dizzyingly, de Man has arranged his chapters into a series of increasingly fecund deconstructions, each generated by aporias of grammar and rhetoric, and each emptying out yet another critical illusion, until the final chapter on Rousseau gives us the language machine as the genesis of all that we read. Historiographically, this recourse to Rousseau will parody again the return to Dionysos, as Rousseau will function as a deconstructive deus ex machina whose text discloses *l'effet machinal* of textuality.

Thus at the beginning of "romanticism" we find the end of its subjective and narrative thematics, "as soon as the text is said not to be a figural body but a machine" (AR, 294-301). *Allegories of Reading* is indeed not a history of romanticism but the demonstration of the impossibility of that history, especially when we read how much more radically Rousseau's text surpasses, in deconstructive rigor, the ambivalence of Nietzsche's: "Far from seeing language as an instrument in the service of a psychic energy, the possibility now arises that the entire construction of drives, substitutions, repressions,and representations is the aberrant, metaphorical correlative of the absolute randomness of language, prior to any figuration of meaning" (AR, 299). It is this very passage in which Johnson discovers the dangling clause and anacoluthon of the grammatical subject. Who does this "seeing," and for whom does this possibility arise, when the subject and the narrative of progressive cognition have been suspended?

For "de Man," of course, who here constructs a prosopopeia of deconstructive authority—not as the absence of the subject, but as the difference between Nietzsche and Rousseau, Nietzsche and de Man, Heidegger and de Man, Freud and Lacan and de Man. The asceticism of linguistic deconstruction before the "seduction" of psychologisms, historicisms, fictionalisms, and ontologisms is remarkable here, as elsewhere, in the severity and irony of de Man's resistance to grammatical or conceptual copulations. How allegorical, then, is the deconstruction of Nietzsche's celebration of Dionysos, god of the erotic, of union and desire? The strange cognitive and rhetorical status of de Man's prescriptions follow the methodological paradigm evolved in "Genesis and Genealogy": "the deconstruction does not occur between statements, as in a logical refutation or in a dialectic, but happens instead between, on the one hand, metalinguistic statements about the rhetorical nature of language and, on the other hand, a rhetorical praxis that puts these statements into question" (AR, 98).

De Man's own "metalinguistic statements" about the priority of the language machine form an aporia with his rhetorical praxis of willfully denouncing the weakness of those who succumb to the temptations of reference, history, psychology, theme and meaning. As in Nietzsche, this latter cognition, which is also represented as a moment of progress in the history of literary criticism, may be "translated into a statement," but "the authority of this second statement can no longer be like that of the voice in the text when it is read naively" (AR, 99). After reading de Man's analysis of Nietzsche's rhetoric, one should no longer underestimate the necessary theatricalization of de Man's own voice in his cognitive moments. De Man's careful placement of "naively" here (as elsewhere) mimics exactly, "ironically," the rhetorical recourse in Nietzsche to terms of ethical rigor and personal evaluation—to a rhetoric of subjects and their development (strength, health, will, values, etc.). To borrow de Man' question, Who would dare admit, after such a passage, to not being one of the happy few among the sophisticated critics (AR, 97)?

De Man continues by concluding that the "nonauthoritative secondary statement that results from the reading will have to be a statement about the limitations of textual authority" (AR, 99). It is this residual statement that resists totalization by the genetic model, for it cannot ground either a subject of a history of cognition. The myth of Dionysos, on the other hand, is erotic genealogy par excellence, and provides the allegory of the linguistic aporia of essence and appearance: "what we have called the genetic pattern is precisely the possibility of this bridge, of this translation . . . performed in the metaphorical narrative by which Dionysos can enter into a world of appearances and still somehow remain Dionysos" (AR, 101).

The problematic of de Man's own "textual authority" occurs self-reflexively here, for we cannot defer infinitely the sexual allegory of this textual myth. Dionysos, as is well known, participates in the genealogy of fertility gods, whose ritual dismemberment and resurrection offers yet another instance of suspension and *Aufhebung*. Almost comically, de Man suggests that Dionysos should have been more of an ascetic, should have resisted the desire to "enter into a world of appearances." Mistaking an aporia for a hymen, Dionysos puts his character into the reproductive organs of time and appearance, and so risks losing his fetishezed identity. (The play on asceticism here and elsewhere in de Man tropes the analysis of the ascetic priests in Nietzsche's *Genealogy of Morals*.)

On closer inspection, the Dionysian economy of essence and appearance, presence and representation, coincides with the *fort/da* speculation of Freud's *Beyond the Pleasure Principle*, whose castration metaphysics Derrida has playfully explicated in *La Carte postale*. In fact, de Man is entirely in control of this problem and can state it with full thematic clarity in his climactic chapter on Rousseau: "Writing always includes the moment of dispossesion in favor of the arbitrary power play of the signifier and from the point of view of the subject, this can only be experienced as a dismemberment, a beheading or a castration" (AR, 296). Only by withholding himself from representation could Dionysos keep his head, but only by risking his essence in the play of appearance could he become the truth of art and the origin of its organic genealogy. The difference between Dionysos and the priests of asceticism may not be a binary opposition, and thus one must wonder whether the asceticism of de Man's rigor is not implicated in its own rhetorical erotics. Should one listen naively to the seduction of Paul de Man?

"Contrary to common belief," writes de Man elsewhere, "literature is not the place where the unstable epistemology of metaphor is suspended by aesthetic pleasure, although the attempt is a constitutive moment of its system. It is rather the place where the possible convergence of rigor and pleasure is shown to be a delusion."[14] The "rigor" of literature lies in its incessant aporetics, which thwarts our desire to bridge or identify differences. Meaning, presence, and the self would each be the delusory products of such suspensions, and their deconstruction would interrupt the structure of historical narrative that depends upon them for its motivation and articulation. De Man's prophylactic rhetoric repeatedly cautions against succumbing to such seductions. For example, his resistance to a phenomenological criticism centered on a communion with authorial consciousness emerges in the choice of Proust and Rilke for deconstruction: "since the ostensible pathos of their tone and depth of their statement make them particularly resistant" to linguistic determinism, "one could argue that if *their* work yields to such a rhetorical scheme, the same would necessarily be true for writers whose rhetorical strategies are less hidden behind the seductive powers of identification" (AR, ix). The seduction of Paul de Man, however, entails just such an identification for, as with Nietzsche, we are continually invited to identify with the knowing prosopopeia of deconstructive authority. The narrative of *Allegories of Reading* depends upon this seductive identification, even as the grammar of its reading and the rhetoric of its injunctions forbid it.

As a theorist and practitioner of literary history, de Man reinscribes allegorically the main conceptual and methodological elements of the discipline. He opposes Bloom, considerately, whenever Bloom's system privileges the romance of the willing subject over the errancy of the trope. He opposes Frye and Jameson, insistently and indirectly, whenever such theorizing privileges the romance of symbolic resolution over the machinery of aporetic rigor. Prosopopeia allows him, however, to give voice to this aporetics with figures borrowed from the very metaphorics his own deconstructions undo, and so his allegories of reading become, like Rousseau's, narratives of desire. His literary history is a supplementary series of prosopoeitic acts whose grammars of pronouncement always carry with them the traces of their rhetorical seductions. As prosopopeia, the telling of literary history becomes a narrative of what desire and cognition give voice to in repeated conflicts whose referentiality is no less essential than its unreliability. The literary text is heard as a voice of reading supplementing what it took to be the aporia it inherits, and in deconstructing previous metaphors of understanding it generates other abysses that are in turn crossed by other epistemological romances.

Literary history would be unthinkable without the inevitable and willful seduction of the writer and the reader by the illusions of figurative language. As prosopoeitic genealogy, literary history unfolds a network of textual voices that are always read erotically, as well as rigorously, until the difference between these strategies itself becomes undecidable. The voice of the author returns: "Ego recuperation," says de Man, may be an effect "accomplished by the rigor with which the discourse deconstructs the very notion of the self. The originator of this discourse . . . remains . . . a center of authority to the extent that the very destructiveness of his ascetic reading testifies to the validity of his interpretation" (AR, 173-74). Unless we intend to take this final allusion as confirmation of de Man's identification with E.D. Hirsch, we must overhear de Man's own willingness to be seduced, as well as seducer. Even the author of *Allegories of Reading*, ascetic as he may portray himself, succumbs to the pleasures of copulative textuality as he unites Rousseau, Nietzsche, Rilke, Proust, Yeats, and Archie Bunker in a genealogy of aporias that give birth and voice to the figure we call de Man.

11

Recovering the Figure of J.L. Austin in Paul de Man's *Allegories of Reading*[1]

Brian G. Caraher

In an excellent review of Paul de Man's *Allegories of Reading*, George McFadden suggests that de Man's version of "linguistic formalism" and his sense of rhetoric as a "language of desire," which is continually opposed to "a language of needs," have as their "horizon" Sigmund Freud's "structural model" of "a closed system of relations" or "unconscious energies." As McFadden phrases it: "De Man has this Freudian unconscious for horizon: its timelessness, and the impossibility of finding in it any direct referent for the languages (and they are many) used by its desire."[2] McFadden detects this Freudian model behind the linguistic formalism that de Man supposedly derives from Ferdinand de Saussure and from the Geneva School of Linguistic Criticism, and also shares with Jacques Derrida. Nevertheless, though perhaps still within this "horizon," de Man seems more at pains to grapple with the shadowy figure of another writer, a writer who offers another and rather different sense of rhetoric. This other rhetoric, furthermore, could perhaps challenge and undermine de Man's own version of the operation of figural language. This figure is J.L. Austin, and the model of rhetoric is speech act theory.

There are numerous traces and evidences of Austin in *Allegories of Reading*, and one reviewer of the book has offered five densely-argued pages on Austin and speech act theory even before turning to de Man's appropriation and critique of Austin's terminology.[3] De Man mentions Austin by name in only three or four very brief instances, but Austin seems present in de Man's choice of his final two chapter titles: "Promises" and "Excuses"—the former perhaps due to Austin's not infrequent discussions of acts of promising in *How to Do Things with Words* and the latter to Austin's essay, "A Plea for Excuses" in his *Philosophical Papers*.

Yet the strongest and most important appropriation of Austin by de Man resides in the play of the terms "constative" and "performative" in de Man's discourse. This terminological appropriation appears most clearly in de Man's third and final chapter on Friedrich Nietzsche, "Rhetoric of Persuasion." Here de Man elaborates deconstructions of the concepts "identity" and "action" in two late fragments of Nietzsche.

The first fragment involves an attempt by Nietzsche to undermine the law of contradiction, as formulated by Aristotle. Nietzsche contends that the law of contradiction cannot be "the most certain of all principles" because at least one precondition or presupposition (*Voraussetzung*) underlies—and supposedly, therefore, undermines—it. The law of contradiction, and logic as a complete enterprise, is not "adequate to reality" as a "*criterion of truth*" because it presupposes "*our belief in things.*" Things, reality in general, *must be posited* in order for such "axioms of logic" as the law of contradiction to come into play. And this positing or supposing (*gesetzt*) of things, moreover, falls not within the logician's *assumed* indicative mood or mode but within the *imperative* mood. As Nietzsche says, the law of contradiction "means" that "opposite attributes *should* not be ascribed to" actual entities. In general, "logic would be an imperative, *not* to know the true (*erkennen*) but to posit (*setzen*) and arrange a world that *should be true for us.*" Consequently, logic has "a merely *apparent* world as its precondition" and "applies only to *fictitious truths (fingierte Wahrheiten) that we have created.*"[4] De Man remarks that his fragment of Nietzsche has to do with an "elusive" polarity "between knowing and positing *erkennen* and *setzen.*" The first part of this polarity, the "transitive function of knowing," "to the extent that it is verbal," de Man indicates "is *properly* denominative and constative" (AR, 121).

The term 'constative,' of course, is associated with J.L. Austin and integral to the rhetorical strategy of his *How to Do Things with Words.* For Austin, a "constative" utterance, or a "constative," is what is variously called a statement of fact, a statement, a denominative, or a descriptive.[5] That is, a constative purportedly describes some thing in the world and denominates the unity and coherence of its attributes. A constative would thereby allow and enable certain knowledge of entities.

The second part of Nietzsche's "elusive" polarity brings into play the operation of positing such entities. De Man terms such positing "an obligatory speech act" and not "a fact merely susceptible of being spoken" (AR, 122). The *positing* of entities is *not* "*properly* denominative and constative" but is instead "primarily a verbal process, a trope based on the substitution of a semiotic for a substantial mode of reference" (AR, 122-123). In other words, an entity cannot be denoted, indicated, or referred to and authoritatively known because language itself posits the appearance of entities; entities are presupposed by, are a precondition of, language and predication. As de Man puts it, "the positional power of language" carries with it "the radical possibility that all being, as the ground for entities, may be linguistically *gesetzt*" (AR, 123). Knowledge of entities, their attributes and identities, then, are "fictitious truths" created by language in the imperative mood or mode: "The language of identity and of logic asserts itself in the imperative mode and thus recognizes its own activity as the positing of entities. Logic consists of positional speech acts" (AR, 124). These "positional speech acts" de Man calls "performative," and their "feigned truths" are to replace the "authority" and "knowledge" of such logical truths or axioms as the law of contradiction.

Like the term 'constative,' 'performative' is closely associated with the work of Austin; de Man, however, employs the term in a markedly non-Austinian fashion. The 'performative' conception of language and linguistically-mediated knowledge, for one, does not replace the 'constative'; "the assertion that language is an act . . . cannot be taken as final":

> All *setzen* has been discredited as unable to control the epistemological rigor of its own rhetoric, and this discredit now extends to the denial of the principle of identity as well. The burden of proof shifts incessantly back and forth between incompatible propositions such as A = A, A better be equal to A or else, or A cannot be equal to A, etc. This complication is characteristic for all deconstructive discourse: the deconstruction states the fallacy of reference in a necessarily referential mode [AR, 125].

And a bit further on, in prefacing remarks on a second Nietzsche fragment, de Man claims that "the possibility of 'doing' is as manifestly being deconstructed as the identity principle": "this conception of action as a 'reality' opposed to the illusion of knowledge is, in its turn, undermined. Performative language is not the less ambivalent in its referential function than the language of constatation" (AR, 126-127).

De Man, then, seems to be playing the two conceptions of language, 'constative' and 'performative,' denominating and positing, identifying (facts, attributes of entities) and enacting (speech acts), off against one another. A characteristically de Manian 'aporia' riddles and dislodges the concepts 'identity' and 'action,' and structures the double bind of that 'elusive' polarity of constation and performance, (logically) knowing and (imperatively) positing.

De Man's employment of the terms 'constative' and 'performative,' though, yields a fairly thorough dislodging of them from the text of Austin. It would appear to be, moreover, a transumptive appropriation of them, not without certain ironic consequences for the reading of rhetoric and the rhetoric of reading. *How to Do Things with Words* deploys a quite precise rhetorical strategy, and the book's argument depends upon an attentive reading of the text as it is developed through its sequence of twelve lectures.

The first lecture does indeed counterpose 'constative' and 'performative' utterances to one another; not all utterances are statements of fact or assertions of truth or falsehood; some involve "the performing of an action" (HDTW, 6). This counterposing of 'constative' and 'performative' is assumed to be a useful and demonstrable distinction through the next three lectures as Austin generates and elaborates his "doctrine of the *Infelicities*" (pp. 14 and 12-45, in passing). The strategic purpose of this doctrine is to defend for the time being the 'performative' as a type of utterance distinct from the 'constative.' If "the appropriate circumstances" for the executing of performatives can be schematized, then the philosophical viability of the notion of the 'performative' will be considerably, and perhaps persuasively, enhanced.

One consequence of the elaboration of the "doctrine of the Infelicities," however, is that the conditions for the successful execution of performatives appear to subsume the question of true and false statements, and the very notion of the 'constative' within them (HDTW, 45-52). The 'felicity' of performatives, as the argument develops, depends upon "some important things which must be true," things which are marked by the logical relations of entailment, implication, and presupposition (HDTW, 45, 47-51). As Austin concludes the fourth lecture, he notes that "perhaps indeed there is no great distinction between statements and performative utterances" (p. 52). Indeed, quite pointedly, and as if to alert the reader from the beginning, Austin footnotes the early subdivision of "Lecture I" entitled "Preliminary Isolation of the Performative" with these words: "Everything said in these sections is provisional, and subject to revision in the light of later sections" (p. 4). By the end of the fourth lecture the revision is well underway. The next three lectures, though, compose an attempt to formulate a grammatical criterion for the notion of the 'performative'; such a criterion would purportedly allow the reduction of any performative to an "explicit performative formula" and would thereby keep performatives distinguishable from constatives and their criterion of truth and falsehood (HDTW, 53-91). The attempt is circuitous and complex, and, as Austin confesses, ends in failure (p. 91). Fairly well into the proceedings:

> It is time, then, to make a fresh start on the problem. We want to reconsider more generally the senses in which to say something may be to do something, or in saying something we do something. . . . It is time to refine upon the circumstances of "issuing an utterance" [HDTW, 91-92].

In other words, the attempt to maintain a counterposing of 'constative' and 'performative' must be discarded completely and a fuller study of the latter notion carried out in earnest.[6] The final five lectures begin this project, and "Lecture XI" even reengages Austin's preliminary distinction between constatives and performatives in order to demonstrate that the *act* of "stating is only one among very numerous speech acts" (pp. 146 and 132-46, in passing).

The attempt to appropriate and hypostatize the distinction between and counterposing of 'constative' and 'performative,' then, would appear to disrupt and occlude the rhetorical structure and temporal development of Austin's text and philosophical procedure. Austin does not play the notions of 'constative' and 'performative' off against one another as constituents of an 'elusive' polarity. His text can be said to 'deconstruct' the notion of the 'constative' while rhetorically enacting the work of construing the conditions and circumstances of linguistic performance.[7] It is a phenomenalist and pragmatic reading of rhetoric, which is also at the same time a subtle, rhetorically self-aware performance of its own temporal development as a text.[8]

Austin, it would appear, works at remedying a philosophical conundrum, which de Man seems to maintain *still riddles* logical relations and figural language alike. De Man's appropriation of Austin's terminology, though, provides a key to establishing the differences that obtain between Austin's phenomenalist reading of rhetoric and de Man's deconstructive reading of rhetoric. Austin contrives to unsettle radically, and quite ambitiously, a positivist approach to language. The ambition of this project is sounded in Austin's claim that "a revolution in philosophy" is underway; the "age-old assumption . . . that to say something . . . is always and simply to *state* something" is being put into question and demonstrated to be in error (HDTW, 3, 12). Instead, a thoroughgoing analysis of the conditions and circumstances of linguistic utterances is proposed as the work of philosophy—or at least those areas of philosophy traditionally known as logic and ontology. Rhetoric examined phenomenally, in other words, supplants the various forms of logical positivism, and philosophical and linguistic atomism which have been the inheritance, motive, and plague of much Western philosophy. The attempt to defend the notion of the "constative" is part of this positivist predilection, and the rhetorical strategy of *How to Do Things with Words* involves playing along with this predilection until it dissolves within and before the greater explanatory power and coherence of the notion of the 'performative' and a budding theory of speech acts.

De Man, however, still assumes the philosophical efficacy of the 'constative'—though it is a rather seductive and etiolated efficacy at one and the same time. It is seductive because it is a notion whose apparent efficacy seems difficult to resist. It seems reasonable to assume or to believe that language makes statements about things in the world, that it names and affirms or denies certain attributes of things. Yet this positivist framing of reference and knowledge undergoes a curious etiolation, if not vitiation: language and logical relations are themselves *posited*, and therefore our apparent certain knowledge of things is founded and founders upon an *imperative to presuppose* and believe in things. What de Man, after Nietzsche, calls "the positional power of language" problematizes the initial positivist paradigm of the relation of language to things (AR, 123). However, in order to perform this sort of deconstruction, de Man *must assume or presuppose*—indeed *posit*—the provisional efficacy or enduring allure of the positivist paradigm. His remarks on Nietzsche's fragments and his deconstructions of the concepts 'identity' and 'action' presuppose and depend upon a positivist construal of constatation, or what de Man also terms 'speech fact.' Statements, knowledge of entities, and constatives depend

> on a built-in continuity within the system that unites the entity to its attributes, the grammar that links the adjective to the noun by predication. The specifically verbal invention stems from the predication, but since the predicate is nonpositional with regard to the properties, it cannot be called a speech *act*. We could call it a speech *fact* or a fact that *can* be spoken and, consequently, known without necessarily introducing deviations. Such a fact *can*, on the one hand, be spoken (*können*) without changing the order of things but it does not, on the other hand, *have to be* (*sollen*) since the order of things does not depend on its predicative power for its existence [AR, 121-22].

Such a passage on the 'constative' seems to me akin to the work of Gottlob Frege and Bertrand Russell on the principles and relations of logical language and to the logical atomism of Ludwig Wittgenstein's *Tractatus*. A world of logical simples, speech facts, can be ordered within a grammatical system governed by rules of correspondence and syntactical relations.[9] The notion of the 'performative,' of course, then problematizes and helps deconstruct constatation for de Man. The key philosophical and rhetorical move, though, is the *presupposition* of the positivist paradigm. In presupposing such a questionable and limited paradigm for language and knowledge, de Man reveals the severe limits that circumscribe a deconstructive reading of rhetoric.

Indeed as de Man himself remarks concerning a strategic move of deconstructive practice: "this complication is characteristic for all deconstructive discourse: the deconstruction states the fallacy of reference in a necessarily referential mode" (AR, 125). The positivist paradigm necessarily marks deconstructive discourse because the deconstructive activity is itself rigorously and resolutely inscribed within that highly problematic paradigm. Deconstructive discourse depends upon, presupposes, a theory of language and knowledge, which it of course is going to find impossible to begin with. Indeed, Austin's *How to Do Things with Words* has already performed the very impossibility of the notion of the 'constative' and its attendant positivist framework and has displaced them with the possibility of a theory of speech acts. De Man's *Allegories of Reading*, though, pits constatation and performance against one another, a gesture that merely repositions and makes impossible the notion of the 'performative.'[10] As de Man concludes, "the differentiation between performative and constatative language (which Nietzsche anticipates) is undecidable" (AR, 130). He opts, in other words, for an aporia that structures the impossible logical and rhetorical relations between constatation and performance.

This pitting of the 'constative' against the 'performative' also surfaces under different terminology in de Man's first chapter, "Semiology and Rhetoric." There de Man observes "the tension between grammar and rhetoric," with particular attention to the operation of the rhetorical question (AR, 9). He chooses as a key example an ordinary language situation involving the situation-comedy character, Archie Bunker. Bunker's angry rhetorical question "What's the difference?," directed against his wife, supposedly yields a "semiological enigma" (AR, 10). Bunker is not looking for a statement of difference from his wife, but his rhetorical performance of frustration and indifference draws precisely that type of literalizing response. De Man globalizes Bunker's domestic dilemma into a semiological one: "The same grammatical pattern engenders two meanings that are mutually exclusive: the literal meaning asks for the concept [difference] whose existence is denied by the figurative meaning" (AR, 9). That is, the *coincidence* of two uses of one and the same grammatical expression ('pattern')—one 'constative' and one 'performative,' one asking for a concept and the other performing or expressing frustration— poses an impossible and irremediable dilemma.

Yet such a 'semiological enigma' obtains only because the actual conditions and circumstances of utterance are being blocked or forgotten. Archie Bunker's domestic dilemma arises, for one, because he takes no careful cognizance of his audience, his auditor or interlocutor, his wife Edith—"a reader of sublime simplicitly" (AR, 9). Seeking clarification of his wants, she has asked him a question; and he, avoiding a simple answer, responds with another sort of question apparently intended to stifle her peculiarly simple and painstaking manner and cover up his own lack of knowledge and his sense of frustration at not knowing the difference between two ways of lacing bowling shoes. Edith also takes no cognizance of her husband's embarrassed ignorance and sense of frustration.

It is a speech situation rife with infelicity and misfiring; and the viewing audience understands the *different* uses, conditions, and circumstances of both interrogatives and rhetorical questions as well as the *characters* of the two speakers and the characteristic qualities of their many interactions. Bunker may be baffled and embarrassed by his own speech acts and those of others, yet the *auditors* who laugh at the situation *understand the context*—Bunker's unending need for control and authority over the recalcitrancies of his own domestic reality. And such an audience also understands the linguistic *conditions* and *circumstances* that have *locally*, and *characteristically*, gone awry.

What is more, Bunker's blind self-positing or assertion of his own verbal authority seems always to misfire in the exigencies of actual rhetorical performances. Bathos engulfs Bunker's demands for the authority of his own rhetoric because he *posits* his own desire for unconditional assertions or statements of fact *prior to* the actual circumstances of speech situations that ironically deconstruct his rhetorical practice as well as his demand for authority. Bunker, too, is embroiled in the problematic question of counterposing the 'constative' and the 'performative.' Importantly, only a full deployment and understanding of the notion of performance, *à la* Austin and others, can perhaps debunk discursive aporias both semiological and domestic.

12

The Anxiety of
American Deconstruction

Howard Felperin

> Leopards break into the temple and drink to the
> dregs what is in the sacrificial pitchers; this is
> repeated over and over again; finally it can be
> calculated in advance, and it becomes a part of
> the ceremony.
>
> —Kafka, *Leopards in the Temple*

That deconstruction has manifested an uncanny power to arouse anxiety in the institutions of learning that house and host it will come as no surprise to students of the movement. Indeed, the present context (first a conference, then a volume) may itself be regarded as the latest, admittedly mild, attack of that continuing anxiety. Having at last been accepted as a fact of institutional life, deconstruction now presents us with the problem of how best to live with and control it, like a recently discovered disease that has proved not to be fatal, as was first feared, but merely discomforting, and for which there is still no known cure, despite continuing research. If we have not yet learned how to stop worrying altogether and love deconstruction, we have at least passed beyond the initial shock of its recognition. There are even signs that deconstruction may prove, in the course of its progress, to be self-deconstructing—that is, self-curing— so that those who come down with it may eventually find themselves diagnosed as normal once again, well and truly able to carry out the institution's business as usual. And if that turns out to be the case—so runs the argument of this chapter—it will be a new and serious occasion for anxiety.

147

In looking back at the institution's early reaction to deconstruction when it emerged in the late 1960s and early 1970s, it is not difficult to identify the source and account for the strength of the anxiety it produced. Deconstruction was—well—different. "Difference" or *différance* was, after all, its philosophical watchword and principle, and the new terminologies and methodologies with which it intervened in the institutional discourse were certainly different from those the institution, particularly the Anglo-American institution, was used to. Not only was deconstruction different from the critical and pedagogical practices in place in the sense of being alien and unfamiliar—that, after all, was true of structuralism as well—but deconstruction appeared to be disturbingly different from itself, maddeningly elusive in the unpredictable repertoire of terms and procedures then being mounted in rapid succession under its name: *"différance," "misprision," "aporia," "undecideability," "mise-en-abîme"*. . . . What would they think of next?

Not quite (or not yet) a school or a movement, its reluctance or inability to routinize itself—as distinct from structuralism's eagerness to do so—rendered it uniquely threatening to any institutional mentality. This potential enemy was doubly dangerous for being at once different and protean, not fully or clearly one thing or the other, indistinctly different. At a time when the older orthodoxies of new and practical criticism were under challenge from several theoretical quarters, deconstruction was sometimes conflated in the general alarm with other heretical movements, mistaken for a version of structuralism or confused with a kind of Marxism, as often by the heretics themselves, anxious for avant-garde reinforcement, as by the defenders of the old faith, undiscriminating in the acuteness of their sense of present danger. Only at a later stage in the ongoing triumph of theory, could it begin to be recognized that deconstruction stands against not only the old new criticism but the methodological novelties of Marxism and semiotics as well in mighty and binary opposition.

As its oxymoronic self-appellation suggested from the beginning, deconstruction was always, given its negative understanding of the differential and deferential nature of language and textuality, a practice oppositional to all philosophies of construction, the newer as well as the older, an antimethodical method. Operating from the margins, it exposed and released the anxiety of reference and representation at the only too metaphorical heart of more conventional methods, the anxiety necessarily repressed in the interest of any claim to a positive or systematic knowledge of literary texts on which our academic institutions have traditionally been based. As a form of oppositional practice, deconstruction gained considerable strategic and tactical advantage of its marginal or liminal status—comparable to that of such other liminal phenomena as ghosts, guerillas, or indeed, viruses—over its more clearly defined, predictable, indeed institutionalized, and therefore vulnerable opponents and would-be allies.

With the linguistic resourcefulness and mobility accruing from an extreme language-skepticism, deconstruction had the capacity to come in under existing or emerging critical systems at their weakest point, the linguistic bad faith on which they were built. It could thus undermine the extroverted and hypertrophied structuration of semiotics with mole-like persistence, worrying away at its linguistic underpinnings until its Babel-like towers teetered vertiginously before collapsing into the groundlessness of their own pseudo-scientific discourse. Or it could take the rhetorical "ground," the historio*graphic* soapbox as it were, out from under the solemn hectoring of Althusserian Marxism, leaving it with a lost sense of direction and the fuddlement of acute aporia. It is hardly necessary to mention in this context the deconstructive subversion, or more accurately, sublation of new criticism itself, in so far as American (as distinct from French) deconstruction carried to an unforeseen flashpoint some of New Criticism's most cherished principles. By scrutinizing the words on the page harder than New Criticism ever had, deconstruction discovered not their translucent and freestanding autonomy but, in a radical defamiliarization, their dark, even opaque, character as writing, black marks on white paper; not the organic unity that binds together irony, paradox, and ambiguity in a privileged, indeed redeemed and redeeming, language, but unrecuperable rhetorical discontinuity. Little wonder, then, that of the several schools of criticism vying for institutional dominance, deconstruction was, in its difference, the most feared, vilified, and misprized.

Nor is there need, in the present context, to document in any great detail the political and psychological conflicts that no doubt lent added piquancy, even at times acrimony, to what might have been quite amicable philosophical differences. We are dealing, after all, with recent institutional history to which most of us have borne witness, and it does not take a Michel Foucault to remind us of the will to power that inheres in any will to knowledge and its institutional discourse. Suffice it to say that considerable power was, and still is, at stake, nothing less than that latent in the pedagogical discourse and practice of literary study at all levels, from postgraduate programs down to the school curriculum—more on this shortly—so the anxiety has run high in proportion to the stakes at risk.

The agitation has so far been felt mainly at the top of the pyramid, but it is clear to all concerned that repercussions could be massive and long-term. For those critics concerned not with maintaining the continuity of institutionalized literary study in something like its present historical formalism, but with transforming it into a revolutionary political practice, deconstruction has come to be identified as an elitist cult and a reactionary force. More or less explicit in the work of such Marxist or leftward commentators as Hayden White, Frank Lentricchia, Frederic Jameson, and Terry Eagleton, is the view of deconstruction as regressive, a throwback not to the Russian formalism of the teens and twenties, as was structuralist poetics but, if anything, to the dandyist aestheticism of the eighteen-nineties, a displaced religion of art. The ultra-high formalism of deconstruction, arising from its obsession with linguistic difference and duplicity, returns criticism in such a view, to the idealist metaphysics from which it was supposed to emerge, while the practitioners of deconstruction become *capi* of a hermeneutic mafia or the high priests of a new mystery cult. The mark of such a cabal is its style, or styles—a frequent target for all opponent sides. For even after allowing that deconstruction has many styles, what they have in common is the challenge of difficulty and danger. So much so that one hears frequent charges of a deliberate obscurantism designed to exclude all but an elite—only those who already know will understand and so be saved.

But the strongest reaction to deconstruction, no less allergic but much more alarmist than that of the Marxists, has come from the upper reaches of the literary-critical establishment across the English-speaking world. This is not really surprising, for it has the most to lose. For such figures as René Wellek, M. H. Abrams, and E. D. Hirsh—to confine ourselves for the moment to America—deconstruction poses a fundamental threat to the institutional and pedagogical practices of a long dominant critical and historical humanism going back to the Renaissance. Despite their conscientious pastoral care, that orthodoxy is breaking up, and deconstruction offers no help in holding it together. Quite the opposite: as a theory of language and literary language subversive of the notion that the meanings of literary texts are determinate or determinable, much less, in M. H. Abrams' phrase, "obvious and univocal," and hence the notion that the study, not to mention the practice, of literature is a socially meaningful and valuable activity, deconstruction has been rejected as "apocalyptic irrationalism," "cognitive atheism," and "dogmatic relativism."

The fine excess of these phrases, the woundingness or woundedness of these words, should not be underestimated. The self-avowed language skepticism that deconstruction cultivates, indeed flaunts, as its philosophical program (or counterprogram), its self-proclaimed resistance to the imperialistic or totalitarian tendencies toward "positive and exploitive truth" built into any critical system—be it Marxist or semiological, historical or New Critical—obviously have grave institutional consequences. In this respect, deconstruction is a voice (or as we shall see, several distinct voices) crying out not in the desert but amid the superabundance of our overnourished institutions. Or perhaps more precisely, crying out within the desert of that superabundance. How else should the established institution react to a school that must, by its own logic, oppose institutionalization, with its tendencies toward consensus and routine, as yet another manifestation of the original philosophical sins of logocentricity, positivism, and reification? What, after all, is an "establishment" or an "institution" if not something only too pervasively and oppressively present?

Worse yet, the rebels who are making these defiant gestures toward existing institutional authority are, it might seem, rebels without a cause, some of the institution's own favorite sons. Harold Bloom is the former student of M. H. Abrams at Cornell; Geoffrey Hartman, of René Wellek at Yale. Even Paul de Man, as a teaching fellow at Harvard, served his time under Reuben Brower in one of the smaller but more fruitful vineyards of "close reading." Yes, there seems to be an element of Oedipal reenactment at work, with the overreaction on both sides, on the part of the fathers as well as the sons. When M. H. Abrams maintains the availability of literature's "obvious and univocal sense," or René Wellek reaffirms the achievements of Yale formalism against the "apocalyptic irrationalism" of its deconstructive successors, these academic patriarchs are insisting, like latter-day Lears, that in our dealings with language, something, even if it lacks the total conviction of ultimate certainty, is preferable to nothing: "Nothing will come of nothing. Speak again." Imagine their shock and dismay to hear their own beloved offspring reply that the something they cherish and affirm is based on and amounts to nothing more than philosophical nostalgia or wishful thinking. What else could the patriarchal reaction be when what is put in question is filiation itself, once conceived as a benign relationship upon which to base something precious—be it literary influence or real estate. All the more disturbing when those who raise the question are themselves—again like Cordelia—apples of the patriarchal eye.

From a sense of lèse majesté on behalf of the institutional superstructure, it is a short step to offense on behalf of the affronted subject. What is the subject, after all, except what it is defined by those who are officially—that is, institutionally—appointed to teach it? So that any critique of the institution, a fortiori a critique so radically skeptical, is necessarily construed as a critique, in this case virtually a dissolution or demolition, of the subject itself. In this respect, the reaction to deconstruction is analogous to an early and still persistent reaction to psychoanalysis: an irrational fear that, if this sort of analytical activity is pursued, the subject of it, be it literature, the personality, or even the very person, will in fact disappear, be analyzed, as it were, out of existence. The fear of self-annihilation in its extreme form, may also be akin to the superstition among some primitive tribes that photography steals the souls of its subjects. From the standpoint of deconstruction, what both fears—

that literature or human personality have their very existence imperilled by some ways of scrutinizing them—have in common is a superstitious or magical or sacramental view of language, within which the relation between signifier and signified is a sacred and inviolate given: words mean exactly what they say. Hence the primal terror aroused in some quarters by the very term "deconstruction"—after all, the word has (in part) the same root meaning as "analysis," an "unmaking"—quite aside from the actual disintegrative thrust of deconstructionist, indeed all structuralist and poststructuralist thinking, in which that fundamental relation of language is seen to be problematic.

Note, however, that this view of deconstruction as a nihilist plot is incompatible with the view of it as an elitist cult. Why would the high priests of a religion of literature want to abolish the source of their status and power? Such a state of affairs would be akin to the mafia lobbying for the extirpation of opium networks in Southeast Asia, or to the venerable comic routine of a man sawing off the bough on which he sits. Deconstruction cannot, within Aristotelian logic at least, be what each of its chief polemical opponents has claimed—a priestly cult and a nihilist plot—at one and the same time. Or can it? We could reply that within the current institutional politics, deconstruction may well seem elitist and conservative in relation to Marxism, though in relation to our established formalism it may seem utterly radical. But to leave it at that, would be to play into the hands of deconstruction by accepting its extension of the structural linguistic principle that what has its existence within a system of differences with no positive terms, is in the nature of the case contradictory, perverse, multivocal, mind-boggling, thus leaving the scandalous undecidability of its institutional position intact.

To leave it at that would also be to let deconstruction off the hook of its own real or potential anxiety, for what I am arguing in this essay is that deconstruction is, or ought to be, not only the cause of anxiety in the institution, but institutionally anxious in itself. This latter anxiety arises out of its own uncertain potential for institutionalization, the questionable capacity of a practice so profoundly oppositional, skeptical, and antisystematic to turn into a transmissible, teachable program in its own right. For there is great potential for anxiety in deconstruction's apparent desire to destabilize the interpretive structures and conventions through which institutional authority is manifested and perpetuated, while remaining unwilling quite to relinquish any claim to institutional authority for its own practices. In institutional terms, what the new Marxists and the old new critics have in common is the premise that authority in interpretation is necessary and resides in communal—that is, institutional—consensus; each is antiauthoritarian only with respect to the other's authority-conferring community. Both are threatened and scandalized by a deconstructive antiauthoritarianism so radically individualistic or solipsistic that it denies the interpretive authority and the communal basis for it, not only of other communities but of its own community—to the extent that it can be said to form one—as well, and then has the further audacity to insist on its own institutional pride of place.

These conflicting impulses within deconstruction express themselves in the apparent insouciance with which deconstruction transgresses the communal rules of the language game known as literary criticism while continuing to play it, in repeatedly exceeding the rules of the game by introducing an element of free play deriving from a heightened and ever-present awareness that the rules of the game were arbitrary in the first place. Such a gambit might be tolerable even to other players who are playing more "seriously"—that is, conventionally—who are so caught up in the game, and have so internalized its rules, that they have forgotten or repressed their own awareness (if they ever were aware), of the original arbitrariness or groundlessness of those rules. But it becomes intolerable once it is clear to these honest souls that the deconstructive transgressors, the disintegrated consciousnesses at the table, are not just kibitzing, but playing to win, and have one eye firmly fixed on the institutional stakes. That is having it both ways, or some would call it, cheating. In either case it is breaking the rules that the community has agreed to play by, the rules that, by virtue of this agreement, may be said to constitute the community.

Deconstruction's desire to have it both ways, to be in the community, even in its mainstream or bloodstream, but not *of* it, is more than a matter of wanting institutional prestige and influence, while violating some of the institution's most honored conventions and taboos, like making more puns that is thought seemly, or writing books without footnotes. It is a matter of putting into question the very constitutional and contractual basis, the social rationale of consent, on which the institutionalized interpretive community exists, what may be termed its major premise that there is something that requires and justifies, in social and historical terms, the service it renders, and for the sake of which it structures its activities.

That something, that sine qua non and raison d'être, is the presumed existence of literary or poetic, as distinct from ordinary, language. Here we encounter a further paradox that the one deconstructionist for whom, as far as I can tell, this distinctive category does not exist, is also the one who is least subject to, and least the object of, institutional anxiety. For Derrida, as for the late Barthes, the category of literary language has dissolved, through the powerful reagent of *différance*, into writing and textuality in general. The relative absence of anxiety over and in Derrida—this is admittedly hard to measure—may well have to do with the primarily philosophical context of his work. For the institution of philosophical, as distinct from literary, study has long since given away any social or missionary rationale and is to that extent less predisposed, if not quite immune, to institutional anxiety.

The idea has been around for some time now among philosophers, particularly Anglo-American philosophers, that theirs is a highly technical language-game of only marginal social and practical consequence, and whether or not they accept this view, the reemergence under the name of deconstruction of extreme language-skepticism in the mode of play is not likely to carry much shock value for those familiar with the work of Nietzsche, Heidegger, and Wittgenstein. We shall have to return to the marginal standing of philosophy as an institution; for literary deconstruction, as we shall see, continues to propose a dubious merger with it.

It is rather American—specifically Yale—deconstruction, proceeding, as it does very much upon the humanist premise of literariness, and aware of the increasingly imperilled centrality of its institutionalized study for culture at large, that occasions the anxieties I have been describing. Perhaps the richest irony of the situation is that the definitions of literary language it still feels compelled to produce, ought to be, as the only poststructuralist defense of poetry on offer, the shibboleth of institutional acceptance, indeed, respectability. But that defense is so uncanny and paradoxical that it does not feel to the institution like a defense at all. Rather, it seems more like a surrender of the power of literary language to engage with, let alone enhance, anything beyond itself that might, in turn, lend it privilege, validity, or in the language of the Supreme Court, "redeeming social value"—in particular, the moral, mimetic, or expressive value conferred on it by traditional poetics:

> For the statement about language, that sign and meaning can never coincide, is what is precisely taken for granted in the kind of language we call literary. Literature, unlike everyday language, begins on the far side of this knowledge.... The self-reflecting mirror-effect by means of which a work of fiction asserts, by its very existence, its separation from empirical reality, its divergence, as a sign, from a meaning that depends for its existence on the constitutive activity of this sign, characterizes the work of literature in its essence. It is always against the explicit assertion of the writer that readers degrade the fiction by confusing it with a reality from which it has forever taken leave.[1]

I have selected this definition of literary language from the work of Paul de Man, not because his definition is singularly fugitive or teasing. Definitions comparably threatening to the institution's sense of cultural mission could be culled from the work of Geoffrey Hartman, for whom art is characterized by the "generic impurity" of being "ambiguously involved with sacred and profane" and "always inauthentic vis-à-vis the purity of ritual and vis-à-vis a thoroughgoing realism," or even from the work of Harold Bloom, for whom a poem is not a relief or release from, or a resolution or expression of, an anxiety, but itself "an anxiety." I single out de Man's definition because it states in terms more unrecuperable and uncompromising, more austere and demanding, if you will, than the others, the deconstructive defense of poetry as a denial of precisely what the institution of literary study has traditionally thought of itself as being about. Literature, for de Man, remains an enlightened mode of language, "the only form of language," he calls it in the same passage, "free from the fallacy of unmediated expression." But its enlightenment consists precisely in its disclaimer of what is normally claimed for it—its special immediacy or at least its special power to mediate something outside itself and something important to us. The revelation that literature offers is that it can never be what the institution of its study blindly takes it to be.

Having brought out into the open, in luminous essay after essay, the anxiety of reference that blinds and vitiates the interpretive labors of the normal humanists who compose the institution, de Man might reasonably be expected to be urging that we write paid to those labors and dismantle the existing institutional support system that sustains them. Or at least that we radically change the departmental and curricular structures that promote in their *wissenschaftlich*, systematic way the ongoing misunderstanding of literature as something whose relation to and meaning for society can be ascertained by the historicist or formalist methods in place in the academy. It is just such a need for sweeping institutional change, after all, that the Marxists, given their own materialist demystification of bourgeois literary study, incessantly proclaim. They openly aspire to reconstitute the institution anew from the ground up, the ground being a not-so-new version of history and the study of literary forms giving way to the study of ideological formations. That may be, from the deconstructive viewpoint, only another and more intense manifestation of the old anxiety of reference, but at least it has the courage and candor of its conviction or fantasy. Indeed, some younger, self-styled deconstructionists of my acquaintance—none of them at Yale—would like to see the institutional structures that the old historicist and formalist anxiety of reference shores against its ruin give way to more expansive and flexible institutional structures that would bend with what they take to be the new bliss of difference that deconstruction—in its French forms at least—promises. They envision a carnivalization of the institution in which the old divisions between departments of national literature, between departments generally, disappears, and a new free play reigns, where students are given high marks for making puns and dispensing with footnotes.

The logical outcome, in institutional terms, of deconstruction would surely have to be some kind of anti-institution, where the full writerly fluidity of differential intertextuality could flourish without the guilt or anxiety induced and controlled by the oppressive superstructures and restrictive routines of departments, canons, methodologies, and footnotes.

Perhaps it was some such academy without walls that the late Roland Barthes had in mind when he answered an interviewer's question about the place of literary study in the university to the effect that "it should be the only subject." After all, if deconstruction stands, as Richard Rorty suggests, in the same relation to "normal" criticism and philosophy as "abnormal" sexuality or science do to their "normal" counterparts—"each lives the other's death and dies the other's life"—should not its chief practitioners outspokenly advocate the legal and constitutional reform of the institution, if not actively attempt to found a new anti-institution of an unabashedly utopian kind.

In fairness to the Yale deconstructionists, they have braved considerable communal opprobrium by proclaiming, up to a point, the unnegotiability of their differences with the institutional definition of the subject. "A critic must choose," wrote J. Hillis Miller, "either the tradition of presence or the tradition of difference, for their assumptions about language, about literature, about history, and about the mind cannot be made compatible." Yet the cry for large-scale institutional reform that such incompatibility ought logically to issue in has not been forthcoming. However different the deconstructive definition and defense of literature, it seeks neither blissfully to abolish a canon, nor radically alter it, nor even to rewrite afresh the institutional style-sheet of our dealings with it. Yale deconstruction may argue for, may even exemplify, the play of difference in its approach to literature, but there can be no mistaking that in so doing it is *hard* at play. No bliss, no *jouissance*, not even much *plaisir*, here in puritan New Haven, thank you; we prefer "rigor," "strenuousness," "ruthlessness," anxiety, and old-fashioned "hard work." For all its puns and abandonment of footnotes, this free play turns out to be very hard work after all.

The highest compliment Geoffrey Hartman can pay to the work of Paul de Man is to call it "a kind of generalized conscience of the act of reading," and conscience, as students of medieval allegory well know, is no figure of fun, at least not in his work. What prevents Yale deconstruction, unlike its Parisian cousin, from giving itself up to an abandonment of the institutional controls of method and system, and embracing a complete laissez-faire regarding the object of that method and system, is the distinctly puritan work-anxiety it continues to share with the older institution, whose forms it largely accepts despite its declared differences with the traditional rationale for those forms.

But what, then, is the point of all this sweat and strain? Having relinquished all claim that the strenuous study of literature will confer on its students any positive benefit of cultural or historical identity, moral goodness, psychological wholeness, or even philosophical wisdom—the traditional humanist justifications for the institutionalized study of the canon—Yale deconstruction seems content that the institution continue to exist for the sake of work alone, in so far as its *Aufhebung* of work is also an emptying out of work's former purposes and justifications:

> The whole of literature would respond in similar fashion [i.e., as Proust responds to de Man's deconstruction of his rhetoric], although the techniques and the patterns would have to vary considerably, of course, from author to author. But there is absolutely no reason why analyses of the kind here suggested for Proust would not be applicable, with proper modifications of technique, to Milton or to Dante or to Hölderlin. This will in fact be the task of literary criticism in the coming years.[2]

What is at issue here is not the logic or accuracy of de Man's prediction—as the present conference attests, his prophecy, uttered more than five years ago, is coming only too true—but its tone of equanimity. Deconstruction is indeed proving thoroughly amenable to routinization at the hands of the institution to whose authority it once seemed to pose such a challenge of incompatibility. More than that, it has all but become the institution, as its life and activity rapidly become indistinguishable from the life and activity of the institution at large, as one classic text after another is subjected to moves and reflexes increasingly predictable and programatic, and the aporias and undecidabilities, the *mises-en-abîme* and impasses, the deferrals and misprisions in the canonical literature are relentlessly unfolded. Deconstruction has made so much work for us all, it hardly seems to matter that, not only do the traditional justifications for that work no longer apply, but no justification other than the technical challenge of the work itself, seems to be offered.

It is at this point that the full anxiety of deconstruction begins to appear. The last thing deconstruction wants to be, or be seen to be, is an empty technology of the text, like its old rival, structuralist poetics. So it now emerges that the traditional humanist justifications of hermeneutics and history, according to de Man himself, may even *reappear*, if the institution only goes one step further in meeting the challenge:

> It would involve a change by which literature, instead of being taught as a historical and humanistic subject, should be taught as a rhetoric and a poetics prior to being taught as a hermeneutics and a history. The institutional resistances to such a move, however, are probably insurmountable. . . .

> Yet, with the critical cat now so far out of bag [sic] that one can no
> longer ignore its existence, those who refuse the crime of theoretical ruthless-
> ness can no longer hope to gain a good conscience. Neither, or [sic] course,
> can the terrorists—but then, they never laid claim to it in the first place.[3]

De Man's professed skepticism about the full institutionalization of
deconstruction is at this point surely rhetorical. The institutional "change"
he recommends is minimal and moderate—still no call for a full-blooded
utopia of differential bliss, but only for more "theoretical ruthlessness."
Such a change, in fact, has either already taken place, or soon will, as
courses, in conferences on, and centers for the study of methodology and
theory not only proliferate, but move from the periphery to the longed
for metaphorical "center" of the discipline.

But even if this change has already occurred, or is about to occur, why
would de Man be content to see it happen? Why would deconstruction
acquiesce in what, on its own terms, would be a form of self-destruction?
How can it accept its own institutional routinization with the same insouciance it once displayed in transgressing the institutional routines by which
literature was supposed, by being reduced to law and order, to yield up its
truth? If the diverse academic formalizations and normalizations, gram-
matizations and rhetorizations, have been revealed, by de Man's own
highly principled practice, *not* to be capable of negotiating the transition
from the semiotic to the hermeneutic and historical —that is, from sign to
meaning—how is studying them *first*, logically or chronologically, going
to help? That nostalgic or desired transition can *never*, by de Man's definition of literary language, be methodically made, no matter what new
priority is given to the study of rhetoric and poetics, or with whatever
"theoretical ruthlessness" that study of method is pursued.

The "critical cat" is indeed so far out of the bag that its existence
cannot be ignored, but why should de Man think, or wish to think, it will
find any ground, old or new, to stand on by seeking out departments of
philosophy or theory? The proposed merger of deconstructive criticism
with philosophy and theory no doubt identifies an area of hard work
shared by deconstruction and the traditional institution, but that area
would have to be, by de Man's own lights, one of continuing contention
rather than newfound accord. For the interests at stake are opposed and
incompatible. What has deconstruction taught us if not that there is no
theoretical "ground" so long dreamt of by philosophy outside writerly
practice, from which epistemology, ethics, and now writerly practice itself
can be positively described? What has Derrida taught us but that the
philosophical tradition, including deconstruction, *is* writerly practice.

De Man's proposed institutional merger with philosophy and theory
—if he means by it the Kantian kind, and what else has poetics proved

itself to be? — would be at once regressive and counterproductive. It would be like the managing director of a growing company recommending to its shareholders merger with an all but bankrupt competitor, whose imminent collapse will give the company a complete monopoly of the market. As Richard Rorty describes those "weak textualists" who think they are adding the prestige of philosophy to their criticism when they discuss a writer's epistemology: "Thus conquering warriors might mistakenly think to impress the populace by wrapping themselves in shabby togas stripped from the local senators." On the other hand, if de Man is recommending merger with what Rorty terms the "abnormal" philosophical tradition, culminating in Derrida and de Man himself, that variously denies the real or potential groundedness of discourse, he is recommending only what has already taken place. Whatever his Yale colleagues may mean by philosophy and theory when they recommend it, de Man is certainly no "weak textualist," and we must give him the benefit of the doubt by assuming it is the latter kind of merger he has in mind, which is to say, more of the same.

But in the very ambiguity of de Man's proposals, we sense the impasse confronting deconstruction as it ponders the possibilities of its institutional future and the full anxiety it quite properly feels in the situation. Too puritan and conscientious to abandon itself to the textual hedonism of its French counterpart, which in its utopianism could never be institutionalized anyway, Yale deconstruction has only two courses open to it, neither of which it can pursue without anxiety. Either it can continue to attempt its project of opposition, which would now mean to oppose the routinization of its own earlier practice by resisting the co-option of its techniques by the institution, now composed of its own graduate students and disciples, by withholding its blessing from the ongoing deconstruction of the canon by textual techniques now only too familiar and repetitive.

It is, of course, an open question whether and how long even such resourceful critical minds as we are dealing with could maintain such an adversary role, could continue to devise new ways of rescuing difference from the authoritative presence they have become in the work of their epigones. Even if they could so maintain the energy of deconstruction, the puritan dissidence of their dissent, they would have to abandon all hope of institutional détente. That eventuality must be a cause for anxiety. The alternative would be to acquiesce fully in their present institutionalization, to give their blessing to the wholesale routinization of deconstruction now under way. For deconstruction to do that would be for it to cease to be deconstruction, for it to pass into institutional history. That thought too must cause considerable anxiety.

Whether the conscience of deconstruction is good or bad, it certainly exists and is powerful enough to bring upon itself in its current dilemma an acute *malconfort*, an aporia with a vengeance. For Paul de Man was never more clairvoyant than when, more than a decade ago, he foresaw his own present situation:

> All true criticism occurs in the mode of crisis. . . . In periods that are not periods of crisis, or in individuals bent on avoiding crisis at all cost, there can be all kinds of approaches to literature: historical, philological, psychological, etc., but there can be no criticism. . . . Whether authentic criticism is a liability or an asset to literary studies as a whole remains an open question.[4]

This account of the nature of criticism as difference from institutional norm is of course perfectly consistent with de Man's account of the nature of literature, and indeed underwrites deconstruction's own aspiration to literary status. Were deconstruction now to avoid crisis by acquiescing in the assimilation of its critical difference, its questionable status as a liability or an asset, by settling down under institutional auspices to the no longer hard but now empty labor of processing the entire literary canon, it would no longer be "true criticism" but just another "approach to literature." For deconstruction will be "true criticism," by its own lights, only as long as whether it can be done at all, and what it means institutionally to do it, remain open questions. Just as a number of critics in the mid-sixties, among them the present charismocrats of deconstruction, were writing against formalist and historical interpretation and calling, from within the institutional routine that new and practical criticism had become, for different styles of reading, so essays are now beginning to emerge from within theory—the present chapter is just one of them—against the institutionalization of theory, including that of deconstructive theory.

Having all but prevailed within the academy and secured its institutional line of succession through the process described by Max Weber as the routinization of charisma, some exponents of deconstructive theory now envision its expansion beyond the walls of departments of English, French, philosophy, and comparative literature. Hillis Miller, for example, sees the time as right for colonizing the pedagogy of the schools. So it was always written. And despite his caveats concerning theory, Geoffrey Hartman aims at nothing less than the repossession in the name of literary theory of the wider cultural discourse by an adventurous band of well-trained, versatile hermeneuts for hire, offering their skills for the decipherment of textuality in law, medicine, and commerce. One cannot help wondering whether they are to be deconstructive textualists, and if so, imagining the sober justices of the Supreme Court listening to their briefs!

It was de Man himself who once cautioned that "a literal-minded disciple of . . . Frye is given license to order and classify the whole of literature into one single thing which, even though circular, would nevertheless be a gigantic cadaver." With its positive and positivist capability, its massive potential for reductive reification, Frye's protostructuralism once seemed the methodological antitype of deconstruction, with its insistence on negative capability, its inbuilt recalcitrance to being turned into "positive and exploitative truth." It was difficult indeed not to concur with Hartman that "to imagine children of the future performing little Anatomies as easily as they now do basic operations in mathematics may not be everyone's Utopia." Fortunately for all of us, Frye's utopia of "sweet science" did not quite come off. Perhaps that means there is still hope we may yet be spared all the potential utopias of deconstructive theory, where little aporias and *mises-en-abîme* are extrapolated from the world's textuality as easily, normally, and literal-mindedly as "close-readings" once were.

Part V

Deconstructing Translation

PRELIMINARY REMARKS

The essays in this part address the issue of deconstruction and translation. Translation is of sharpened interest for deconstruction, for here many
traditional assumptions about meaning, reference, and interpretation
become explicit. Treated deconstructively, translation is not completely
distinguishable from its original text and vice versa. Thus translation
includes a moment of undecidability of the same order as deconstructive
reading. Indeed, our contributors, all translators of Derrida, operate
according to the Derridean *"arche"* that any use of language is already
translative, and that the deconstruction of translation is therefore a deconstructive exercise par exellence. It not only renders explicit the traditional
(metaphysical) assumptions about meaning, it also thematizes its own
double nature as a reading that is a writing and a writing that is a reading.

The essays presented here were written for the IAPL symposium
entitled "Translating Derrida and Deconstruction." Each participant was
asked to produce "ten propositions on translation," but each noted that
this would imply, somewhat naively, that deconstruction as well as translation might be propositionally codified. Such, of course, is not the case.
Allison and Leavey incorporate the implications of this request into their
texts; Graham opts to ignore it. All the papers, however, explore the issue
of translation as a Derridean motif, each from a different perspective.

In "Around and About Babel" Joseph Graham takes up translation
theory as a contribution to the problem of meaning. This problem, he
notes, is structured around the question as to whether linguistic meaning
can be accounted for without appeal to intentionality or representation,
and has become central for both Anglo-American and Continental-
European philosophy. Graham opens his discussion with a review of
Walter Benjamin's notion of "complementarity" as developed in "The Task
of the Translator." Here, Benjamin suggests that a translation and its original text stand in complementary relation to one another. They are complementary because both ultimately refer to a "pure language," to which
access can be gained through the differences of translation. Meaning, for
Benjamin, is therefore an ideal limit that can only be approximated by
any given discourse or text, and becomes manifest in the difference
between a translation and its "original."

Graham proceeds to a reading of Derrida's "Des Tours de Babel" as a
deconstruction of, and complement to, Benjamin's text. He notes that
where Benjamin describes translation in terms of a final reconciliation of
languages (in "pure language"), Derrida begins with "Babel" as both the
origin and dispersion of languages. Moreover, Derrida stresses the reciproc-
ity inherent in the complementary relationship between a text and its translation. This renders the notion of "pure language" highly problematical,

even as an ideal limit. For the relation of complementarity would obtain as well between this language and any particular discourse for which it is a referent. Derrida's deconstruction of "Babel" illustrates this point.

As the name for an original confusion of language, "Babel" could have no significance in the language of Babel itself. However, the context for the utterance of the word, the language of Babel, does give it meaning beyond a mere designation—it comes to *describe* its referent. Nevertheless, as Graham puts it, the context for any use of language cannot be determined a priori. The context for an utterance is determined by whatever is relevant to that utterance, and relevance is not constrained within an identifiable form or structure. Thus the complementarity of languages, as evidenced in translation, cannot reveal a reference toward a unifying limit. Translation, as it were, always remains "around and about."

In "Coquilles St. Jacques" David Allison takes up the problematic of translation in terms of the sentence and the proposition. He examines three traditional theories: that a proposition is a type conveyed by sentence-tokens; that a proposition is the meaning content of a judgment; that a proposition is the common meaning of a sentence and its translation into another language. The first theory breaks down over the fact that two sentence-tokens of the same type may mean different things, depending upon the context, and that tokens of different types might mean the same thing. The second theory would render subjectivity constitutive of propositional meaning, and is therefore vulnerable to the myriad difficulties of subjectivistic metaphysics—for example, psychologism, transcendental illusion, false consciousness, and so forth. The third theory founders on the question of how a proposition might be known in the absence of translation, or how a translation could be verified as correct rather than incorrect. In summation, Allison claims that any theory of propositions must make reference *to* reference, which is impossible. Instead, we simply (or not so simply) use language, and all communication or translation is use. *Im Anfang war die Tat.*

This nonobjectifiable transitivity of language is taken up by Heidegger and then by Derrida. The early Heidegger, notes Allison, tries to account for the transitivity of signification within the grammar of objectifying discourse, and becomes caught within the "hermeneutical circle." But the later Heidegger realizes that the transitivity of language cannot signify itself, and Derrida takes his cue from here. In light of this irreducible transitivity, Allison suggests that rigor, not correctness, is the aim of the translator. The rigor of transitivity requires the inclusion of the "exotic" (nonobjectifiable, nonformalizable contextual moments) within "ordinary" discourse, for the transitivity of a text is translatable only in the doing, or writing, of a text. And so translation partakes of the oblique itinerary of deconstruction.

John Leavey focuses upon various aspects of transitivity in "Lations, Cor, Trans, Re, &tc*." Leavey offers this contribution not as an essay, but as "a series of propositions with interjections and notes." His remarks and digressions are loosely held together by etymological variations on the Latin roots of "lation" (*latus*, *lâtus*, *latere*, etc.) and by citations from Derrida.

Following Derrida, Leavey characterizes translation as *apotropoca- lyptic*—that is, as *apotropaic* and *apocalyptic* at once. Translation is apotropaic as a turning away from, or a warding off of, the "original" text. It thus preserves the original while supplanting it. On the other hand, translation is apocalyptic as *dis*closure of the text, but of course without disclosing the event of disclosure, or translation, itself. The original equally discloses and supplants the translation, and so the relation of trans-lation becomes undecidable. Moreover, in temporal terms, transla- tion is *telelation*. Leavey cites Derrida's "Living On: Border Lines" as an illustration of this point. Here Derrida traces the undecidable relation between the two (?) narratives in Blanchot's "Death Sentence." The ques- tion concerns the impossibility of textual closure, and specifically of tem- poral completion. This question impeaches the narrative voice that would provide a temporal unity and continuity between texts that are distin- guished from, yet are also interior to, one another—as in a text and its translation. Telelation, as Leavey indicates, is the ghostly voice through which one text haunts another, is already carried out for another, but is not presently sayable in the other.

Complementarity, transitivity, and telelation are features of the rela- tion between deconstructive practice and its text. As features of transla- tion, they are more explicit and more complex than when embedded in a critical reading or commentary, for here the dependence of one text upon another is obvious and indisputable. Furthermore, in taking their transla- tions of Derrida as points of departure, Graham, Allison, and Leavey multiply the complexity of these relations exponentially. Indeed, in Lea- vey's paper one encounters a self-implicating complexity raised to the nth degree, beyond all possible discursivity. From this example, we see that discursivity requires limitation of the very complexities celebrated in deconstructive practice. Would such limitation always be in bad faith— that is, arbitrary—as some deconstructionists suggest? Consideration of this issue is reserved for the next and final part.

G.E.A.

13

Around and About Babel

Joseph F. Graham

Recent debate about Derrida and deconstruction in America has been marked by acute if not complete disagreement on matters of principle, with more confrontation than real discussion, satisfaction, or resolution as a result. At times it has almost seemed as if there were no common language or no means of translation from one language to another, and thus no way of knowing whether the parties to the dispute really understood each other because no way of knowing whether they were in fact talking about the same things even when they used the same words. If that were indeed the case, polemics would remain futile until some topic could be found or some object identified that was not only the same for all but also accepted as such. There could be no basis for agreement otherwise. There would be little hope either in that confusion of tongues, unless we had at the very least a theory of language to explain the possibility and so to encourage the pursuit of serious discussion beyond such basic differences.

Reading about language in both French and English, some of us have been struck by a strong convergence of interests on the problem of meaning. Meaning has become problematic in both cases because of a no less striking divergence of opinions about the nature of meaning. On the French side, there was a reaction against phenomenology that went under the banner of structuralism. On the Anglo-American side, it has rather been a resurgence of mentalism against behaviorism. The differences between these two movements are considerable and hardly negligible, but their common effect has been to raise critical questions about the function of meaning in a theory of language and mind. Whether it be the primacy of intention against the principle of structure on the one hand or knowledge of grammar against indeterminacy of meaning on the other, the point of debate is the same in that it concerns the very possibility of ever explaining language without recourse to some concept of intentionality or mental representation. The same question could also be framed as a matter of whether something like meaning is a cause of language, both real and independent, or merely its effect and perhaps epiphenomenal.

There are various ways to present this convergence on the issue of meaning in French and English, along with various ways to promote discussion that might resolve some of the differences between the two traditions. What I have written here was prompted by my reading of Jacques Derrida on Walter Benjamin on the task of the translator. The result is comment by way of complement for reasons that pertain to translation in Benjamin and extend to interpretation in Derrida. They describe translation and interpretation as modes of complementation in language such that one text complements another. These same descriptions have their own complements in turn. They not only complement each other, but they also complement other texts on meaning and translation in a very different tradition. They do not refer to those texts but refer to matters of common concern. Whence my purpose has been to describe Derrida and Benjamin in terms of that other tradition by way of further complement.

Complements presume and even require common concerns by the very nature of their relation. Here it is not just a matter of meaning and its difference or identity in translation. There are also more specific concerns about the scope and limits of language itself. The discussion of meaning in both French and English turns on the question of whether or not to include proper names along with common nouns as integral parts of language. The issue also involves the basic function of language, whether it be simple designation or exact description, whether by reference alone or by meaning as well. These concerns for the nature of language have further consequences for theories about language, for their relations to their objects and to each other. Theories about designation and description clearly have consequences of their own including consequences for themselves.

What is finally most striking about both discussions of meaning is the way they turn back upon themselves to consider their own possibilities both past and future. In the analytic tradition that leads from Frege to Quine, language and theory are closely related if not actually equated. Problems of change in either language or theory are often discussed as a matter of how it would be possible to exchange one conceptual scheme for another and what it would be to translate from one to another especially if they were so radically different as to appear incommensurable. In the version that comes from Benjamin through Derrida, it is language itself that changes in translation as it develops purity with posterity. But this development of language also has consequence for history and theory, for the very history of theories about language and translation. So it is that what Benjamin and Derrida say about the real debt of complementarity between author and translator can apply to others, like Quine and Frege, in the process of elaborating through history a theory for language that would explain translation, with or without meaning.

In describing what he calls "the task of the translator"[1] (*die Aufgabe des Uebersetzers*), Walter Benjamin suggests how translation could, as indeed he urges it should, contribute significantly to something like a theory of meaning for language. Of course, he does not say just that, just that way. His account is very different, not only in tone, but also in tenor of argument, and in the use of common terms, like language and meaning, different enough to seem directly opposed rather than simply irrelevant, let alone equivalent, to anything in the analytic tradition of Frege or Quine. A positive correlation is less than obvious in that it requires a certain amount of translation, though translation not forced in principle, for both sides admit a distinction between description and designation that allows for the possibility of saying different things about the same thing and so allows for complementarity in different accounts of the same thing. Moreover, it is such a complementarity in language already that makes translation so difficult and yet so important for any theory of meaning.

Benjamin first considers bad translations and bad translators. Their success is a failure in itself, the failure of a mistake in purpose. They assume the wrong task and then do the wrong thing. The essential purpose of translation and the worthy task of translator does not consist in just getting the sense right by saying the same thing with the words of some other language. The real achievement is not the restitution of sense (*die Wiedergabe des Sinnes*) nor even the preservation of sense (*die Erhaltung des Sinnes*), rather it concerns the claim or the demand of literality and what Benjamin calls "the pure language" (*die reine Sprache*). Here the obvious crux is the pertinent notion of sense, for if what Benjamin means by *Sinn* is sense in the Fregean sense or meaning in the intensional sense, then his account becomes irrelevant because incoherent.

Benjamin explains what he means by sense with recourse to the scholastic idiom of *intentio* and that "fundamental law in the philosophy of language" that distinguishes the mode or manner of meaning (*die Art des Meinens*) from the thing meant (*vom Gemeinten*). But this is surely the difference between meaning, as the content of intention, and reference, as the object of intention. Bad translations get the reference right and the meaning wrong by neglecting the letter of the text and the form of the language. A true or real translation is transparent to the extent that it exhibits the literal difference of language in translation. Such differences are differences of meaning, different ways of meaning, from langugage to language. And so it is an error to oppose form and meaning, eventually sacrificing the one for the other, for the very object of translation is to resonate the meaning that adheres to the form in another language.

It is the idea of a pure language that gives real purpose to the task of the translator. Yet the exact nature of that language and its relation to translation remain enigmatic even for Benjamin. His use of metaphor and his own comments on the problem draw attention to the inherent diffi-culty of describing just what it is that he is talking about. Indeed, as he explains it, we have no direct access to that pure language, but only inti-mations or indications particularly, though not exclusively, through dif-ferences in translation. What is striking is not simply the fact that he should present a positive or constructive view of such differences. Still more striking is how well his description actually fits the medium of rep-resentation for mental states and processes, that veritable language of thought, as postulated in the theory and studied in the practice of recent cognitive psychology. The task of the translator, which Benjamin com-bines with that of the philosopher, then becomes part of a project in the science of mind.

There are many points of convergence to be mentioned. Translation in principle is directed to the expression of the innermost relation among languages, and the consequent relation of a translation to an original, like that of one language to another; it is complementary in nature. Text and translation complement each other much like the fragments of some larger whole, and just like different meanings with a common reference. The same complementarity (*Ergänzung*) applies to both.

The pure language is finally the object of reference for translation, and even the end of all linguistic reference, in that it is the ultimate object of reference for each and every language as such. In order to express that convergence of languages, translation cannot simply reproduce either the reference or the meaning of the original; it cannot be simply equivalent in content and arbitrarily different in form like any ordinary version. Trans-lation has somehow to signify or exemplify, and not just satisfy, that very relation of difference in meaning between languages if it is ever to con-tribute more than evidence for a theory of language.

The lexicon provides clear evidence for the claim that languages are related in what they want to say. Individual languages represent different functions or mappings between a specific domain of lexical items and a common range of concepts. Different languages have not only different means but also different powers of expression as a result. They do not all express the same concepts in the same ways. Such differences should appear in translation wherever the vocabulary of one language is richer than that of another, which could be either in number or in content. A difference in content could be a difference in structure and so a matter of the relations among concepts, but it could also be a difference in substance or wealth of description, so that differences in translation would bear on the issue of reference for general terms. If designation rather than description were the principal mode of reference, that difference should make translation easier in a given domain, and where translation is relatively easy, the language looks to be more like a conceptual notation, a strict correspondence of term and concept. The whole problem of syntax is more difficult, for the relations between grammatical form and logical form are more complex, as are those in this area between universal and particular aspects of grammar. But the idea for translation in the demand of literality is still to render all and only those morphological or formal differences that have semantic value and so realize a pure language of thought or a language of pure thought as represented in part by various languages of expression.

Languages are related in a rather special sense, for theirs is not simply a general relation (*Verhältniss*) but a real kinship (*Verwandtschaft*). They have a natural affinity, vitality, and finality. Like all members of a single species, they have the same biology in that they have the same history. And if the end of all life, in all forms of life, is the expression of some truth or specific essence, as Benjamin imagines, then the life of language merges with the representation of language, and through translation, in particular, that which ordinarily symbolizes finally becomes symbolized. This reflexive turn is clearly consistent in itself and quite consonant with the idea of a naturalized epistemology within cognitive psychology where our regular knowledge of language, or linguistic competence, and our science of language both figure as biological phenomena under the general capacity of our species to represent the world in thought.

There are, for Benjamin as for others, rather serious doubts as to whether that end of reflection with its promise of reconciliation could ever be reached. But any issue of intellectual or scientific competence as such comes down to the empirical question of whether our cognitive capacities with their intrinsic scope and limits can finally comprehend their own structure and function, which is also one version of the general question about the possibility of ever reducing designation to description, by exhausting designation in description, for a given domain. Whatever the answer may be in this case, the implication and indeed the inspiration of such an inquiry is to have translation, along with science and even literature, participate directly in the full adventure of humanity realizing itself in history. Such no less is the task of the translator.

When commenting on his own relation to Benjamin in "Des tours de Babel,"[2] Jacques Derrida emphasizes the fact of translation. He says that in some way, his own way, he is translating, and translating not only someone who was a translator, but also something on translation that served as a preface to a translation. He even says that he is translating a translation and so translating a text already in translation. Yet it is hardly obvious in just what way or in just what sense Derrida can be truly said to translate Benjamin. Certainly not in any simple or literal sense, and not in the sense that Maurice de Gandillac first translated Benjamin from German into French. Perhaps it is rather in the special sense that Benjamin gives to translation as its right or proper sense. In that sense, Derrida would be translating Benjamin by complementing his text with regard to some larger whole, some wider context, some purer language. And the sense of translation as complementation does indeed make sense of their relation to a fair extent.

Derrida complements Benjamin in many ways. There is even a complementarity in the very choice of text for discussion. Derrida chooses this text on the task of the translator rather than another, which actually mentions Babel with reference to proper names, and he thereby extends the context of discussion. Whereas Benjamin presents the task of the translator in relation to the common end and final reconciliation of languages, Derrida begins with Babel, the origin and dispersion of languages. Benjamin stresses not only teleological but also theological aspects of translation, whereas Derrida brings out the archeological, the political, and the legal. The same complementarity also shapes the actual commentary of Derrida on Benjamin. Not only is the missing supplied, but what was implicit in the one becomes explicit in the other, the minor becomes major and the peripheral becomes central, in an elaborate counterpoint of terms and themes. Such a complement may be rightly taken as a compliment, and Derrida clearly acknowledges a debt to Benjamin in the very act of elaborating the notion of debt that he finds in Benjamin.

The task of the translator involves a debt in that the translator is beholden to the author of the original. Yet a complement can also take the form of criticism, and Derrida insists upon the initial debt of any author to an eventual translator. If the relation of the translation to the original is that of complement, such that the translation complements the original, the relation is by nature symmetric, such that the original also complements the translation. But if the essential relation is symmetric, there is no provision to mark any essential difference between an original and a translation. They need each other in the same way and they complement each other in the same way; and to that extent they are equivalent.

Derrida insists that the debt of translation is not only mutual or reciprocal but also insolvent by nature. The author is no less beholden to the translator, and yet neither can possibly repay the other. They are complementary and so equivalent in structure, as in reference, but not in substance or in meaning. They lack a common coin, as it were. Here Derrida complements Benjamin first by emphasizing the paradox of that debt with its structure of complementarity short of identity, and further by exhibiting the very same structure in what he calls "the Babelian performance" or simply *Babel* and in what looks to be an essential, hence irreducible, complementarity of reference and meaning of language.

Derrida begins with the proper name and asks if we really know what it is that we are talking about. He asks if we know what we name when we say *Babel*. The biblical account and a philosophical, *cum* philological, commentary are then invoked to suggest that Babel represents not only the multiplicity of languages but also the impossibility of a certain construction or completion due to something like a formal limit, a limit to form or formalization. The story of Babel figures both the necessity and the ultimate or absolute difficulty of translation in a sequence of events. Moreover, the very word itself bears the same significance as an event, as a specific utterance in a specific language. The reference if not the meaning of the word, for Babel is precisely the confusion of meaning and reference at its original occurrence in the language of Babel.

The confusion of tongues at Babel represents a confusion of language as well as a confusion in language. The proper name for Babel was confused with the common noun for confusion in the language of Babel. That name given to Babel was given by God. It was both a name from God and the name for God, the name of God the father and thus a patronym, but it was not in the language as such and so it was received in confusion as a word in the language. *Babel* was confused, in a manner doubly confused, with the noun that actually meant confusion. In confusing one word with another, there was confusion over what belonged to the language as a matter of fact. And in confusing a name with a noun, there was confusion about the principal function of terms in language. The act of reference was confused with the concept of meaning, or the fact of reference as an act, with or without meaning, was confused with the fact of meaning as a concept. The difference in function between nouns and names, between description and designation, was confused. And the difference between what can and what cannot be translated was thereby confused in what was really a confusion of translation, the confusion of translating a proper name as a common noun. Furthermore, the very form of that confusion, the specific performance in the language of Babel, cannot be translated as such, in its peculiar economy, for it exemplifies the double bind of translation that it represents. You cannot rightly translate what belongs to the language itself any more than what does not belong at all.

The original naming of Babel was an act of language with reference to Babel yet with no significance for Babel in that the utterance of the word as a proper name could not convey any meaning at all. As such it could only designate rather than describe its referent. Still, what seemed to be one and the same act had meaning as issued in the language of Babel, a meaning determined for that word by the context of its utterance in that language. Once construed as a common noun, it served to describe rather than merely designate its referent. The real problem of duplicity in this case, with the vertiginous prospect of further multiplicity in some other, need not reduce to a puzzle about the identity of an act that appears to be two or more in one. It is enough to assume that a linguistic act is an action under a description and that a grammar is a system of such descriptions, for the same action or utterance could then satisfy different descriptions from different grammars and so constitute different acts of language. With syntactic and semantic properties duly relativized to a grammar, the same sound could be a noun in one and a name in another, whence it would regularly serve to describe here and designate there.

An action, like any object, can satisfy more than one description at a time, quite easily and quite normally, for the number of relevant descriptions usually has no limit. But there will always have to be some restrictions on the diversity if not the multiplicity of those descriptions, at least so that no one object or action could ever satisfy contradictory descriptions relative to any consistent system of valuation, if satisfaction is to be a form of truth and if truth is to have its standard values, surely exclusive and probably exhaustive.

The proliferation of actual descriptions is characteristic of language use where various systems ordinarily converge. The general significance of an utterance, like the sense of a sentence, depends upon context as a function of some independent variable assigning values in the form of descriptions that are broadly rhetorical or pragmatic rather than strictly linguistic or grammatical. And perhaps the grammar itself should only count as one of many contextual factors, something like a minimal context or partial specification of context with default values for utterances, even though grammars may differ considerably from pragmatic systems in specificity and autonomy.

What is peculiar about the confusion of *Babel* is the very way in which the grammatical and rhetorical values of that word get crossed by that context. The result is to render any full account almost incoherent, as if there were no real or right way to sort out the various differences in fact or even in principle. The case of that particular utterance clearly involves a difference in syntax between nouns and names, a difference in semantics between some meaning and none, as well as a difference in pragmatics between description and designation. Those differences constitute a crux with categories that are no less than contrary, which should make it impossible to qualify for more than one in any pair of opposites.

Yet somehow something of the sort does happen, and without any turn of speech or figure of language, which would simply add the other category to the original in a way consistent if not literal. There is a difference in that utterance between rhetorical force or significance and rhetorical effect or consequence, but that difference is not figural, for both are strictly grammatical. There is then a difference in grammar, yet one that cannot be resolved by appeal to the actual context, for it contains both: the grammar spoken and the grammar heard.

Again, it would not help to force the issue on the question of what *Babel* really meant in and of itself, as if the sound alone could have meaning independent of any semantic representation provided by some grammar or other system of interpretation. Whether they be phonetic, syntactic, semantic, or pragmatic, the phenomena of language as such are intensional. They are descriptions according to rule, so that the real or right form and meaning for a word depends upon the grammar. And just the way language is relative to grammar, so grammar is relative to context, in that the real or right grammar for an utterance depends upon the context. The problem of interpretation thus shifts to the context and its consistency, where the question is finally whether the context is relative to anything else or even whether it could possibly be anything but relative. This much already may seem like a major concession, if not simply a capitulation, with Derrida leading back to Babel and a skeptical conclusion about the specificity and autonomy of grammar.

It is true that the argument against meaning can also be mounted against syntax to the effect that there is no objective fact of the matter when it comes to assigning either semantic categories like synonym and antonym or syntactic categories like noun and name to utterances of any word. It would then make no sense to ask about the form or the meaning of a word like *Babel* prior to some choice of grammar and so prior to some decision about the right context. Granted as much, the critical claim is that no such choice, no such decision, can be anything but arbitrary. Neither the grammar nor the context is given or even justified by the available evidence. The example of confusion at the utterance of *Babel* does show an obvious limit of form as evidence for meaning. Yet that is merely the point about intensionality. The syntactic and semantic properties of language do not have acoustic counterparts, hence you cannot possibly know what they are if all you know is the sound. You have to know the grammar that assigns those descriptions. But you could only know the grammar if you could somehow learn it, and you could only learn the grammar if you could have sufficient evidence for it. This line of argument leads from language to the general problem of knowledge.

Evidence is also a matter of context, a matter of what counts as evident in context. Then there is further and deeper the matter of relevance, for not all evidence is relevant any more than all relevance is evident. What really counts as context for language use is finally whatever counts as relevant to the utterance in question, which may be the grammar alone, even less or a lot more, whether evident or not. But that will depend upon the specific interest or purpose of inquiry. Where the object is simply truth as an empirical fact, there is no abstract or absolute standard of evidence or any comparable standard of relevance. There can be no a priori definition or delimitation of context for language or its use as a result. Here is a further and perhaps final limit on form. It is impossible to calculate or even estimate the full extent of relevant context for any form of language, either grammatical or rhetorical. You could never know in advance what could only prove significant in the end. Still this conclusion does not warrant skepticism about language or its significance, unless you have to know everything to know anything—because the context of relevance for any empirical inquiry is neither given nor evident does not mean that it cannot be discovered or inferred and if not saturated at least approximated. The most relevant context is the one that offers the best explanation, whether it be the meaning of a sentence or the grammar of an utterance. Such a context is both right and real, for it is indeed the very causal mechanism that determines the phenomena in question. When it comes to the truth of a statement about meaning, grammar, or anything of the sort, that context is no less than whatever makes it true as well as whatever it makes true. If, then, you include complements along with antecedents and consequents, as suggested by Derrida and Benjamin, you have your hands full of relevance.

14

The *Différance* of Translation

David B. Allison

As the celebrated Walter Kaufmann long ago transformed Nietzsche into a cottage industry, so do we give the appearance, at least, of turning Derrida into a veritable monument—a Tour St. Jacques, perhaps even a Prussian Academy edition of one, a *Derridawerke A. G.* I'd like to spare you one more eidetic variation on the term 'deconstruction'—a word so often become flesh that, much as Macauley lamented the linguistic incapacities of County Derry's residents, we can no longer writhe our mouths to pronounce such cant. Well, that may well be there and not here, and if they're not there after what I'm here after, they'll be there after long after I'm gone—following the Jansenists down the Milky Way to Rue St. Jacques. Fortunately, there has been no shortage of mellifluous, indeed melodious, translations: a colportage of hymns, as well as litanies and odes, by the porte-paroles. Articles get translated, are retranslated, and retranslated in turn, with a seeming tropical efflorescence. Doubtless, the laundry slips attached to the Lanvin lapels and to the mauve shirts will form the next occasional volume—thence to be translated into Urdu or perhaps into one of the lesser Panoan dialects.

To come to the point. What can I say about translation, particularly about translating Derrida and the translations of Derrida? I was instructed to address these topics in the form of advancing a series of ten propositions about translation. I do this with certain obvious reservations, for, as Paul Ziff says, "What is said is not so easy to say." Likewise, the very nature of the medium of the proposition itself—exactly what it is—this hardly stands as a beacon to guide the way of the translator. Is, for example, the proposition a sentence? In this sentence, I raise the first proposition, but posed as a question. Is the proposition a sentence?

Derrida himself sometimes equates the declarative sentence with the proposition. But he also and in the same text—in "Signature, Event, Context"—just as readily equates propositions with hypotheses. Whether written, verbal, or mental, propositions are generally and traditionally held to be different from statements. Granted, one can state a proposition and propose a statement, but one cannot say the *same* things about both, at least, not in the same way—particularly in view of such nonhypothetical considerations as intention and extension. Surely, statements and hypotheses are both *communications* in some sense, and in "Signature, Event, Context" this is *the* problematic issue that commands the entire text, from the first to the last sentence. The issue is problematic at the start, for the discourse *of* or *about* communication is itself a communication. As Derrida there says, "To articulate and to propose this question, I already had to anticipate the meaning of the word *communication*: I have had to predetermine communication as the vehicle, the transport, or *site of passage of a meaning*."[1] At the end of this brief text, one finds a striking admission: "What goes *without saying will quickly have been understood*, especially in a   philosophical colloquium: As a disseminating operation, separated from presence . . . writing, if there is any, *perhaps communicates*, but does *not exist*, surely. Or *barely*, in the form of . . . (a) signature. . . . Where? There."[2]

"God's wounds!" the reader is tempted to say. Or, rather "Zounds!" Or even "Zut!" Different *sentence tokens*, but they *mean* the same. Or do they? The move—in more than one sense—is from profanation to consternation to irritation. From the violation of a commandment to respect the divine nature to its *bland equivalent*, "darn it!"—which even Mr. Rogers could plausibly say—even though the latter token has passed through a similar flattening. From the temptation of Job to that of Mr. Rogers. "G-d damn it!" "Damn it!" "Darn it!" From sacrilege and transgression to triviality—*yet*, in certain contexts, and for the large part, they are identical in meaning.

Bound to language—perhaps to a divine language, perhaps to French, bound to law and its injunctions (as St. Thomas explained, law or *lex* derives from *ligare*, to bind). Bound in any event by a *double bind*, one slides, or steps, practically unnoticed, in this translator's *démache*, to the *doubly bland*. Like the zut suit at Sims, the *bland*, the ten-buttoned Perry Como sweater of Mr. Rogers, testifies to the Gaelic mixture of milk whey and water (called *blanda*), and to the Latin *blandus*, for the soft, the mild, and genial, as well as to the more and less Gothic tongues, meaning to mix or to blend.

"Too intensive and recursive," you say. An etymology like *that* would well deserve to bomb in Gilead. Skip it. Leave it, rather, to the logic of the kettle—back in the Normale Sup kitchen. Let it lose or gain some semantic thrust by the logic of the sheath, a practice hardly spurned by those heretics on the corner of Rue de l'Epée, in the Eglise St. Jacques-du-haut-Pas. Add or delete a few more *tokens* and take a trip—a real trip, out into the suburbs of language with old Wittgenstein, or out into the Irish greenswards, where the *Glas* is always green. Been in Bonn too long? Break the codes, Green it up! Add or delete a few more *letters*, and we finally cook up a recipe for the faithful translator of Derrida: coquilles St. Jacques— which is probably not a proposition, although it may well be a concealed one, or the title for one. Fall from grace, as the Jansenists feared, and one has another recipe, this time for the post-Derridean translators: coquilles sans Jacques. But these coquilles—what by any other name for these letters are *typos*—the *a* and the *e*, or the you and I, sometimes never do get home. Sometimes they are meant to reach their destination, sometimes not. Sometimes one can rejoice in this *Finnegan's Wake* of the Quartier St. Jacques, sometimes not. Understandable and at home in the conventicles along the Rue des Ursulines, ruefully *unheimlich* for the rest.

Propositions, meaning, understanding, and communication. At once, this set limits and defines the possibility of translation. Severally, they are the borderlines *of* translation. We know from practically every text of Derrida that this *rubric* of the line/limit/border/step/partition/margin— or in other, older words, the work of the determinate *and* indeterminate dyad—that all this, which might also be called différance and dissemination, is Derrida's arena—it is the Jock's ballpark, and a wriggly field it is indeed. Or, just as well, it is the *blend* of 'blanda,' which fuses, distends, and distorts intension and extension, making up that cunning little pouch into which all those token postcards and letters are to be carried—from Dublin to Compostelle.[3] *As* such, it is the *portmanteau* of an earlier traveler. But the tour has just begun: carpetbag in hand, following the course of the sun, wandering in strange lands, "everywhere at issue, nowhere at rest," the strangest of all writes in four languages. And Ireland, the old sod, is always elsewhere, over *there*—to the mercenary, the nonconformist, the immigrant, the polyphone, and polylogue, even to the Greens. "The Frenchman who speaks many tongues," they might have said, years ago, at Oxford. The polyfrog, hopping over from the pas de Calais—the polywog. To cross over St. Jacques—to get to the wrong side of the Left Bank—the letter carrier might have silently walked past the Institute for the Deaf Mutes, along the way to hear Merleau-Ponty speak about the *chiasmus*, at the Tower of Babble, the Collage de France. But, that was the road not taken, the rue not crossed, by all accounts. One had to read the notes and scrawls—the *Geshrieben*—of others, all in a language not exactly "my" own.

Derrida says as much, in "Borderlines":

> One never writes either in one's own language or in a foreign language. Derive all the consequences of this: they involve each element, each term [or token] of the preceding sentence.[4]

Because this is an *imperative* addressed to the translator, one is literally sentenced: bound to respond. One *must*. Or is this only a token obligation? Curious context for this imperative. The two preceding sentences in the text are, properly speaking, not grammatical sentences at all. Rather, they are two phrases. I cite them:

> What will remain unreadable for me, in any case, of this text, not to mention Shelley, of course [of course], and everything that *haunts* his language and his writing. What will remain unreadable for me of this text, once it is translated, of course, still bearing my signature.

Curious. No verb in this veritable verbarium. That is, no connection between the subject and what is predicated about the subject, *no assertion*, in short. What is suppressed, crossed out, or suspended in this text about translation is *the* verb, 'to be.' *It* goes without saying. As does the last sentence of "Borderlines," which *says* the same. As does the sentence, by the same token, at the end of "Signature, Event, Context," what we raised earlier as the problem of translation: "What goes without saying will quickly have been understood, especially in a philosophical colloquium. Writing perhaps communicates, but barely . . . in the form of a signature." That is, in the form of a *sign*, signed or impressed, super-impressed—*Übersetzung*—by the unique author—the "J. D.," *which* letters he signs. An attenuated *mark* of Jacques Derrida, or, perhaps, over here, of James Dean, a notorious J.D., who lives on, even more so, *in* the attenuated form: J.D. Attenuated: the sign of an infirmity. Signed, as he *says*, in another language: authoritis in the St. James Infirmity, around the corner from Plato's drugstore and the law offices of Dr. J.

All this imputation, this limp aggregate of vague references, hints, suggestions, allusions, homonyms, syllepses, even laundry slips, all this is at least part of the *site of meaning*, the meaning communicated *by* an author *to* a translator.[5] Obviously, this is an extremely *generalized site*, one with no fixed borders, either national or international. It is the site of meaning's passage, which is structured, as he says, by "relationships of cryptic haunting—from *mark* to *mark*."[6] It is, in other words, the place of textuality—that site which is near and remote: as near as Heidegger's *Nachbarschaft* and as distanced as Mr. Rogers's neighborhood. It is the *transitive* site of passage—of crossing over, setting down, *and* of disclosure. Call it a floating opera. The transitivity of this site is itself generalized: its way is never fixed, it is always adrift, yet it is punctuated more than occasionally by marks, by *Wegmarken*: from "Anximander's Fragment," channeled through Humboldt's own currents, beckoning on along Heidegger's dark paths, *qui menent nul part*. The *author* who communicates is likewise at pains to generalize *himself* (almost obsessionally so), via Nietzsche's "All the names of history," or, more modestly, via Reb Derissa's ninety-nine names. "Don't tell me *what* you are, I can see that easily enough," says one of Pinter's characters: a real *operator*, a *macher*, they'd say at Ratners. For others, perhaps for Quine or Nolan, the *who* in question would become a generalized set of *discourse* operators: poetic flexions *here*—tense, a moody case operator *there*, always in deep cover, a cryptographer or cipher clerk. Doubtless poetic and a dubious philosopher. But then, *they* would have some*one* in mind. Someone who speaks his mind, and is bound by the rules: someone who gives the translator discrete propositions. The translator, in turn, could then set down or set forth his propositions—and maybe more than a perfect 10, if he, too, plays by the rules.

What could such propositions *be*, in any case? For a large part, philosophical tradition since Boethius has it that a proposition is a declarative sentence accompanied by its meaning. The problem with this view is that two sentence tokens of the *same* type can easily mean different things: "Dr. J. is hot." Thus, they would constitute *different* propositions. Likewise, two markedly different sentence tokens could mean the same thing: "James presented a marvelous communication." But if propositions are capable of assuming a truth value, then, especially in the absence of context, appropriateness, discrete intention, etc., one would be sorely pressed to ascertain the truth or falsity of many propositions, particularly when the truth seems to depend on the particular choice or form of words *in* the sentence.

Another tradition equates propositions with the meaning content of judgment—that is, with the mental acts of assent or denial. Rather than having truth-functional propositions depend on the particular words of a particular language, they must *also* depend on the individual's *mind*, the individual's mind who in fact speaks his mind and thereby judges. And while many easily grant that there *are* other minds, though perhaps not *many*, such a situation is far too *subjective* to be of practical use. To avoid this *impasse*, one of the most current accounts of the proposition defines it in the following way, and here I quote from Alonzo Church:

> For some purposes at least there is needed a more *abstract* notion, independent alike of any particular expression in words, and of any particular psychological act of judgment or conception—not the particular declarative sentence, but *the content of meaning which is common to the sentence and its translation into another language*—not the particular judgment, but the *objective content of the judgment*, which is capable of being the common property of many.[7]

The problem *this* view holds for translators in particular is interesting and classical. Classical in that the abstract proposition advances a notion of meaning that is shorn of space and time, the here and now. The ideal meaning content (what Husserl called the *Bedeutung* of the expression, what Frege called the *Sinn* of the proposition, the *Gedanke*, Bolzano's *Satz an sich*, or Meinong's "intentionally inexistent objectivity"), this ideal meaning content is sometimes conflated with its reference, sometimes not. When it is, for example, with the case of universals, the communication of a proposition's meaning may well be little more than a noetic dream.

The translation view of propositions is perplexing, of course, for in order to ascertain that there *is* such a thing as a proposition, I must *already have produced it.* Thus its possibility is limited exclusively to accomplished fact, to the factual accomplishment *of translation itself.* Even more problematic, however, is the question of how I *know* a proposition to *be* a proposition if it remains *in fact un*translated. More problematic still, how do I know that I or someone else has in fact *properly translated* the statement from one language to another, such that (a) it retains *its* meaning by *my* intervention, and (b) that it is thereby capable of being a true or false proposition? To do this, I would have to be less a cryptographer than the third man himself — of Viennese and Aristotelian provenance, circling around Plato's Ideas. Thus, I would have to interpose a *third* language to ascertain the truth of the proposition carried by the first and second; but that operation could only be guaranteed by interposing a fourth to the first three, and so on. Another Tower of Babble, a *collage de farce.*

In fact, the entire problematic of propositions can only be approached by reference to a consideration of reference itself, to truth and meaning.[8] There is *simply* no truth to truth, no language of languages, no Being of Being, no reason of reason — that is, not *simpliciter.* This is why, for example, Heidegger employs the *chiasmus*, the cross *over* Being, which is the cross *of* Being, in his *Principle of Ground*, of Reason: *Der Satz vom Grund.* The *Satz*, the proposition or principle, is also the jump, leap, or *step*, the *transitivity* that enables the crossing over and back of the *Grund*, the foundation, earth, ground, reason, terrain. The *Satz* is the step or *pas*, which is the *movement* of what Heidegger calls the "four-fold" or *Das Geviert*, but which has its many antecedents as well — for example, in Plato's *Gorgias* (507e-508a). The step that is *always* in the *there*, "the site of passage where meaning is communicated," but never stopped, never arrested, never simply hung up, or hung at all. Essentially nonobjective and transitive. Transitivity itself.[9]

We *use* language, we refer to things, we understand and communicate — and thus, *in fact, we translate* — in ways, always ways, that escape and outdistance taxonomic classification, much less univocality or simple correctness. And there is always the *exotic*, the eccentric, to contend with. Husserl foresaw this problem in his account of the *essentially occasional* expression, something that locates itself—essentially, but for him, unfortunately—*with* the movement of space, time, and individuation. The meaning of these *occasional* expressions, however, could never be fully recuperated in properly expressive propositions—that is, in *ideal* discourse, in the *Satz an sich*. In a somewhat different way, Heidegger thematizes transitivity itself in his discourse, which transitivity as we know, is not objectifiable. In fact, this is the entire problematic of *Being and Time*, what Heidegger termed the transcendental project: "We use the term 'transcendental' to designate everything that belongs by its essence to transcendence"—that is, of Dasein and its essential ecstasis, as well as the *world's* structure *as* transcendence.[10]

Of course process philosophy attempts much the same procedure—as does ordinary language. An example dear to Derrida, of these essentially occasional *usages* are *nonce-words*, which are defined as words used for the nonce. Is that a tautology? It depends. Closer still to the *translator* is one of the operations *by which* he com-poses, under-stands, and translates these nonce words—namely, the use of hendiadys, the rhetorical use of a figure in which a complex idea is expressed by two words connected by a copulative conjunction. *Hen Diadyoîn*, one *through*, one *via*, two. Once again, the way: the way from the *hen*, the one, to the *dyad*, the two—each operating on the other, sometimes supplementing, sometimes limiting, sometimes opposing and delimiting the other. But both coming through the copulative, which *is*, also, more and less than a simple copula. Of course, one can compound the procedure and suppress the *is*, the Being, of the copula, as has so often been done, to *form* the compound or complex—one can slam/dance the *neologism*, for example, for the nonce.

I'd like to push this rather figurative motion of the exotic a bit. Obviously, such a term is itself a bit of a portmanteau word for the well-known Derridean gang of operations: especially "supplement," "dissemination," "*différance*," and Lord knows what else next, perhaps *vaginitis senilias* or even "Schreberance."[11] It is a notion that bears finally on *understanding* and the status of *translation*, and Derrida recalls through this term and its allied figures an *itinerary* that is largely Heideggerian, one that takes him at least *one step* out of the tradition of representation—or, in a by now familiar shorthand, it would be another shake of the tree of presence. Of course this is no simple matter, and it duplicates much of the discussion we have already enjoyed here. It is an itinerary in any case, that passes through the issues of representation, intentionality, truth, and meaning, to arrive at a kind of understanding that is excessive and irrecuperable, one with, as Derrida says, a *general economy*. Economy, with the wealth of significations he finds in it—as did Heidegger, Nietzsche, and Aristotle before him: house, household, *Heimat, heimlich, Unheimlichkeit. Nomos, numis*, law, governance, agreement, money, value, name, exchange, etc.

Simply by way of literal reference: Koitchi Toyosaki mentions the term 'exotic' in his paper on "Translation and Citation," given at the Cerisy Conference, stating that for the translator, the exotic appears a bit like the local flash and glitter, the distinctively local color of a language, place, dress, or culture, which cannot easily be transported without loss, elsewhere.[12] Well, he should know, too, for he is the Japanese translator of Derrida. In the discussion following, Suzanne Gearhart mentions the issue again, and compares it to a problem Alan Bass mentioned in *his* translation of *Writing and Difference*: how do I make *this*, this text, comprehensible to *us*, to an English-speaking audience in the U. S., without torturing the text or without flagrantly anguishing English itself?

Underlying *this* conversation is the one Derrida has with his own text, "Living on/Borderlines," which is itself a sort of a dia-logue between two divided texts, one set above, the other below: *Übersetzung*, translation. A structure not unlike *Glas*, but more like "Signature, Event, Context," where he gives a communication about communication. In "Borderlines" he remarks:

> The ideal thing is translation into a foreign writing system (Japanese, for example, for a European). But that's valid in "my" language too. An impossible contract.[13]

Yet, indeed, there *was* a contract *and* a translation, *by* Toyosaki *into* Japanese. Almost a step-by-step reversal of Gore Vidal's remark about Herman Hesse: namely, that he brought the truths of the East to the suburbs of Cleveland. Why impossible then? Well, it's the exotic, the glitter and flash of local color—the tone, tonality, *Stimmung* of an unsaturable context. But *really impossible* if this is an *ideal* of transference, of setting forth *this thing*, over *there*, in discrete representational totality, without loss.

This is basically what Heidegger says *to* the Japanese interlocutor in one of *his* texts from *Unterwegs zur Sprache*, "A Dialogue on Language," a con-versation about language and translation. That is, in another, earlier communication on or about (and within) communication. The discussion with the Japanese concerns—among other topics—Heidegger's revision of Husserl's doctrine of signification, of propositional meaning. He tells the Japanese that the *Bedeutung* of Husserl's expression (*Ausdruck*) had to be replaced with the notion of *appearing (Schein, Erscheinen)*, in which "appearance does not name objects as objects"—*simpliciter*—"and least of all as objects of consciousness." He adds that this was the subject of his 1921 seminar, five years before the first draft of *Being and Time*. The Japanese explains the difficulty of his situation—that of translation:

> I *must* give a translation which makes our word for language look like a mere pictograph, to wit, something that belongs within the precincts of conceptual ideas; for European science and its philosophy try to grasp the nature of language only by way of concepts.[14]

Of course, Heidegger sees *this* way of thought, the representation of concepts, as the very determination of the West, as, for example, in "The Anaximander Fragment." Conceptual thought as representation is a categorial form of thought, which is a grasping together (*concipiere*) of discrete particulars, elevating them to genus and species in the universality of the concept.[15] Conceptual thought, however, presumes itself capable of expressing Being, which, for Heidegger, it is not—due precisely to the transitive, active, and incomplete nature of *Being*, and of its truth and meaning. Rather, conceptual thought is *framed* precisely to *represent* the particular being, the particular thing, in the form of an image or idea, which it then universalizes. The power of the concept and the interpretation of thinking as conceiving, these rest on the unthought: ultimately, on the Being process itself, which is always concealed by and made possible by an enigmatic relation to its other, to its nonground, its abyss, which is never simply presentable, nor thereby, *re*presentable, nor entirely conceptualizable, nor simply translatable.

What is required, then, for Heidegger, is a *transformed* way of *thinking*, of conceiving, of *understanding*, and not so much a doctrine of conventional *signification*, which would attempt to *express* and then *transfer* the conceptual meaning content of a proposition from one language user to another, from one subjectivity to another. Heidegger discusses this transformation briefly, in terms that could be Derrida's *own*. Moreover, this brief discussion is itself broken up by an exchange of discourses, in this "dia-logue on language":

> H. "The transformation occurs as a *passage* . . .
> J. . . . in which one *site* is left behind, in favor of *another* . . .
> H. . . . and that requires that the *sites* be placed in *discussion*.
> J. One site is metaphysics.
> H. And the other? We leave it without a name."[16]

Heidegger then refers the Japanese gentleman back to the text of *Being and Time*, section 34, entitled "Dasein, Discourse, and Language." There Heidegger had opened up language to the entire domain of *understanding*, perhaps the fundamental teaching of *Being and Time*. Language thus understood includes understanding of the totality of reference and involve-ment structures, which serve to make up worldhood, as the site of human existence—that is, the thereness, the openness, which is also the *Da* of *Dasein*. Interpretation articulates these reference and involvement structures, and speech, properly speaking, articulates them, voices them. What language includes in its domain, then, for Heidegger, is an enormity: the *prepredicative*, the *precognitive*, worldhood, understanding, interpre-tation, mood, silence, being-in, being-with, etc. Hence, when the reader insistently asks for *Heidegger's* doctrine of *signification*, he meets the positively opaque rejoinder, "To significations, words accrue." Come on, Martin, what kind of an answer is *that*? At the end of section 34, he adds, "A doctrine of signification will not emerge automatically even if we make a comprehensive comparison of as many languages as possible, and [even] those which are *most exotic*."[17] Rather, and as a precondition, any suffi-cient account of signification must reconsider *how* we *think* and *what it is* to represent anything to or by our understanding: thus, it entails the attempt to think through the ontological difference in *its* enormity of forms. In a rare moment of *irony*, Heidegger adds a footnote to close the section: "On the doctrine of signification, see Edmund Husserl, *Logical Investigations*."

Husserl's doctrine of signification. This was the point of incision Derrida made on Husserl's text: indication and expression are both forms of signification. How can one communicate a critical discourse on the sign when *it* makes up, quite literally, the body and soul of signification itself? I must *employ* the sign to signify anything about signification, or about anything else, for that matter.

This predetermined reserve of signification, which rarely exposes itself *as* an issue, is also Heidegger's issue in sections 32 and 34 of *Being and Time*, where he addresses the problem of hermeneutic circle. The problem arises in the section entitled "Understanding and Interpretation" (*Verstehen und Auslegung*), and concerns how our understanding is a pro-jective or ec-static interpretation of the world. To reduce this to an insultingly brief formula, Da-sein projects itself in the world and appro-priates what its possibilities yield up—namely, the involvement references or relations (e.g., the "in-order-to" or the *um-zu* relations, which define the "ready-to-hand," the things of our ordinary dealings: the *Umgang*). What then gets interpreted so as to be *explicitly* understood is the matrix or fabric of the *um-zu* relations, which have as their structure the notion of "something *as* something": *as* this, *as* which, *for* this, *from* or *by* this, *across* that, and so forth, which is to say, an entire nonlimited set of transitivities.

This essentially transitive *as* structure—which can productively be thought of in any many ways: as reference, performance, assertion, trope, metaphor, homonym, similie, textuality, trace, pointing, vector, and indeed, across lottsa neologisms—this *as* structure, at least for Heidegger, is a *"constituting* state for *understanding,* [it is] existential and a priori."[18] Moreover, it is precognitive and prepredicative. Because understanding *is* this projective ecstasis we have *in* the world, we who are *of* the world—Dasein—our understanding thereby takes its *mark from* the world, which world *is,* among other things, the *totality of involvement relations. We understand the thing* with regard to *its* involvement structures.

The understanding of a thing, a term, a token, a step, a letter, thus is a *disclosure* of that entity or event, *from* the implicit, nonevident ground of its involvements—this ground, which is not simply absence or nonpresence; it is not merely negation or opposition. The thematic interpretation need not explicitly grasp that involvement totality, although in some cases these relations may be articualted in depth. In any case, the thing is understood because we have some understanding of the totality of involvements—the world—beforehand. I thereby understand "X" *as* this, *as* that, because I *already understand,* even if implicitly, the constitutive functional, practical, material, economic, psychological, or intelligible involvements that subtend its emergence, its *appearance as* some*thing,* as how it is and as what it is. Understanding is thus and always a forehaving, a fore-conception, a fore-sight. Interpretation and experience itself "is never a presuppositionless apprehending of something presented to us."[19] For such a view, meaning (*Sinn*) functions as that process *by which* things get understood. For Heidegger, some *thing* or *being* is said to *have* meaning *when* it is disclosed from, or revealed upon, the ground of its involvements or reference structures:

> What is understood, taken strictly, is not the meaning but the entity, or alternatively, Being. Meaning is that wherein the intelligibility [or understandability: *Verständlichkeit*] maintains itself. . . . Meaning is the 'upon-which' of a projection in terms of which something becomes intelligible *as* something; it gets its structure from a fore-having, a fore-sight, and a fore-conception. Insofar as understanding and interpretation make up the existential state of Being of the 'there,' 'meaning' must be conceived as the formal-existential framework of the disclosedness which belongs to understanding.[20]

All of this *means* that, for Heidegger, meaning is not the ideal content of a proposition, nor is it something attaching to things, but rather it is one of Dasein's ways of Being—that is, the projective understanding that interprets the *as* structure of things with regard to the world of involvement relations.

One objection Heidegger raises to his own account is that meaning, or what is articulated through interpretation, seems to presuppose itself—that is, its own operative understanding. In other words, if interpretation draws upon understanding for its intelligibility, isn't this a vicious circle? Like Husserl's account of signification?—the essential elements of which, *expression and meaning*, Heidegger critiqued in a discussion with yet another Japanese, Count Kuki, in the 1921 seminar entitled "Expression and *Appearance*."

Heidegger replies that the situation is not a vicious circle. Understanding, the topic *here*, and ultimately of concern for communication and translation, understanding operates only within the structured field of the world—that is, in the *there*, with its involvement and reference relations. Yet, because this *there* is also constitutive of *who* I am, of my own Being, I shall never escape that aspect of the circle. Moreover, since all experience is interpretive, in that it grasps its objects by means of its *as* structure, my understanding can never occur without presuppositions of reference and involvement. No understanding can thereby be pure, no perception immaculate, no meaning without its necessary residue and ground. Understanding is thus not discrete: it entails an open fabric of reference and involvement. It indiscreetly refuses subsumption into a finite logic or grammar based on the axioms of a full presence.

By the time of Heidegger's conversation with the Japanese, he claimed that the very notion of the hermeneutic circle was superficial. The Japanese of the dialogue asks the question of Heidegger: "How would you present the hermeneutic circle today?" Heidegger replies, "I would avoid a *presentation* as resolutely as I would avoid speaking *about* language."[21] What Heidegger appreciates *about* language by the time of this later work is precisely what he had already shown in paragraphs 32 and 34 of *Being and Time*—namely, that language was not an *object* or *item* domain *at all*, but the very movement of interpretation—the generalized *as* structure by which our understanding articulates itself. This movement or transitivity is at work in the prepredicative and precognitive domain of behavior, of comportment and disposition—that is, in experience, and *also* in the predicative utterances of propositional assertions, themselves derivative from language in the broader sense. Thus, language in the narrower sense, discourse as assertion (*Rede* as *Aussage* or *Ausdruck*) derives its intelligibility from the wider sense; but in the move from the articulation of interpretation to that of predicative utterance, language imposes the demand that there be a discrete object, an entity or item, which serves as the subject for subsequent predications. Heidegger realizes his predicament in *Being and Time* by noting the peculiar incapacity of language to speak about itself. It seems circular. Indeed, he notes the reasons: the grammar of language has traditionally sought its grounds in the logic of the classical *logos*,—that is, of the traditional predicative assertion or the proposition of apophantic logic. But this logic was governed by the likewise classical ontology of the *item*, the entity, or the discrete bit or byte of information about the item—in other words, by what he termed the ontology of the present-at-hand.

The *problem* was, that Heidegger of *Being and Time* still felt obliged by this grammar, even though he had already successfully countered it, indeed even noting this with irony. The problem was much the same as Nietzsche encountered in the composition of *The Birth of Tragedy*. Doubly bound: to an ontology that subtends the discourse, his discourse—in German—which, to be intelligible, had to be expressed, significantly, in the logical grammar of that language.

But Heidegger had *already* shown the way out: "The task of liberating grammar from logic requires beforehand a positive understanding of the basic *a priori* [i.e., transcendental] structure of discourse in general as an *existentiale* [i.e., as a *way* of Dasein's *Being*]."[22] He had *made* this move, but did not fully appreciate it until later. The grammatical liberation that he had in fact made was also the basis for overturning the traditional notion of propositional expressiveness, so dear to Husserl; that is, Husserl's doctrine of a logically pure grammar, wherein signification would find scientific precision by the expression of an ideal and objective meaning content, without loss. Such expression is the classical ideal of communication *and* of translation: to *set forth* the discrete meaning content of a proposition to another mind, without loss or gain. The *grammatical illusion* behind this doctrine, which importantly governs the model of phenomenological intentionality and meaning, finds its origin, however, precisely *in the objective or accusative case of inflected languages themselves*.

Whether by form or position, the accusative case has the function of indicating the object of the verb, or of what follows a preposition implying direction of motion or destination of action. Grammatically, this is the relation that allows, or rather governs, the very foundation of Husserlian phenomenology: intentionality itself. For Husserl, inasmuch as intentionality *defines* consciousness as the relation *to* its objects, then every consciousness *must have an object*, intuitively ascertainable, verifiable, iterable; indeed, reiterable as a meaningful expression,—hence fully transferable, translatable, and exportable. The very name 'intentionality' derives from the Latin *intentio*, to point, to point *to*. Intentional consciousness is thus always consciousness *of*, it has an *object*: it is aware *that* "the things themselves" are the case. The act of seeing or touching has, for such an account, its *object* in the seen or touched. As well it might. But the case is complicated for the meaning-act, for the acts, for example, of expressive signification, of propositional assertion. *Where* are their objects? Literally, in the *topos noetos* of reduced consciousness, *or* floating, silently, omnitemporally, over Plato's Drugstore. The very *Idea*!—much less, that for Husserl, the *Bedeutung* of such propositions is the most objective of objectivities, so objective that it would ensure the *practice* of scientific exactness (univocity) and serve as the paradigm case of apodictic evidence and thereby serve as the guarantor of truth itself.

Heidegger's entire thematic of interpretation is constructed to avoid this problem, by employing a distinction well known to everyday understanding and to ordinary language—namely, that we *use* words, especially verbs and prepositions, differently. Propositional verbs such as "to say," or "to state," or "to commmunicate" *do not* or *need not* have *real objects* corresponding to their accusative case, whereas cognitive verbs, "I know that," or "I believe that," as well as the large part of transitive verbs, *are* generally held to have such objects.

But to generalize a *dyadic* model of meaning as *simple naming or reference* from the external accusative, thence to transfer it back to propositional usage, and hope to find *meaning*, so conceived, as the *object of* my discourse, my language, or even, intentional consciousness, all this is to transform syntax into the hot line to Solomon. Ultimately, this series of transfers valorizes the *correspondence* theory of truth, which in turn presides over classical metaphysics and epistemology. Truth and knowledge thereby have as their goal *correctness, exactness,* of the object referred *to* or represented *by* the *subject.* And spoken about. And translated.

Exactness in *this* sense, and except in certain specified conditions and for certain specified discourses, need *not* be the aim of the translator. Rather, it is rigor.[23] If something like the ontological difference *is* an issue, and surely the entire elaboration of Derrida's work testifies to this, then the very notions of representational thought, conceptuality, the status of the subject, the type and site of communication, the determinations of history and institutions, all these escape, to some degree or another, the determinations of a narrow and formally conceived language—and the propositions such a language would subtend; as well as the nature of *what* it is that would simply correspond to those propositions. Ordinarily, we include the infralinguistic, the supralinguistic, and the nonlinguistic, *within* our discourse, that is to *say,* within our writing—*such* that it is at once ordinary and exotic. The translator must operate with the sum of these other elements of discourse and understanding—writing—to achieve the *appropriate* goal of a rigorous and thoughtful work. Obviously, all this too is of the nonce, as is the site of passage. Indeed, even the once praiseworthy rigor of the translation *also* quakes and dies its little death— essentially transitive, that.

15

Lations, Cor, Trans, Re, &c.*

John P. Leavey, Jr.

. . . what follows *dis*joins. Originally presented as a series of propositions to be explained and discussed, what follows preserves the disjunctions of that first request. Interspersed among those original propositions that are printed in italics and with some modifications are, as an aid for reading, interjections and notes. This dispersal will result perhaps in a more disjointed graphics (to be sure, no essay will result), but that is the transliteration I am impelled to follow for this series.

LATIONS, COR, TRANS, RE, &c. *

*Is this to repeat the simple and by now tiresome play of language(s), either in translation or in deconstruction? Have I forgotten the hyphens? In other words, does the title already begin to fail to communicate (the enterprise of) translation? Does this note already indicate, even before the title, the inability to translate the work of translation beyond the preciousness of its own frontier back (is to translate back, to transrelate?) to the constituted, i.e., intended, simplicity of one's own tongue? The note crosses the frontier without crossing it, in my own tongue. I translate in my own tongue, but not in my own tongue: the double bind correlations of translation.

Whether carried with (*collation*), across (*translation*), or back (*relation*), or in any combination of these (*correlation, transrelation*), . . . lation involves the lateral (*latus*), the diffuse (*latus*), the carried past (*latus*), the hidden (*latere*). Whether of the family side (*latus*) or the carrying of the child (*ferre*), . . . lation carries within itself its other that is most close, most hidden, itself, a family scene.

191

(. . . lated . . . lating: the past, the ongoing, but the past, the ongoing of what is carried, here, back across, transrelat . . .*)

*Why do I refuse to translate? Can I translate? What reprieve does transla-
tion provide? These three dots, are they the result of indecision, a kind of
play I could avoid by writing "better"? If I mean transrelated, transrelating,
or transrelation, is the ellipsis only a matter of a shorthand, like the &c. of
the title? But shorthand itself translates. Who is to answer, to translate. . . .

I am in the process of translating several "propositional functions"*
on translating Derrida** and deconstruction.*** The double bind—what
is my intention? what is the metatongue**** by which I translate translation?—transrelates in translation.

*Is this an expression to be translated? A. R. Lacey, *A Dictionary of Philoso-
phy*, s.v. "Function," writes: "In fact predicates stand to functions rather as
sentences stand to propositions. A predicate is a linguistic or notational
representation of a function. *x is red* can be called a *propositional, state-
mental* (rare), or *sentential function*, according as *blood is red* is regarded as
a proposition, statement or sentence. Sentential functions are often called
open sentences. The term *closed sentential function* is occasionally used of
ordinary sentences." Propositions, sentences: the translation of intentionality
decides which is which, up to the point of ordinary sentences. This expression then is already a translation. Prolepsis: already a metaphrastics of
the sentence.

**How is a proper name to be translated? Can the proper name be trans-
lated? Is the proper name the ultimate shorthand or ellipsis, the signature
itself that must continually substitute itself for itself as what cannot take
place, even in the signing? Can the proper name be translated from one
occurrence to the next, in as much as the proper name is the idiomatic idiom,
the most idiomatic idiom? Is Derrida the only possible translation of Derrida?
In French and in English in the text, that is how one would have to differentiate these two that are never proper.
     Perhaps the name is to be semanticized. Or at least its siglum, the rush-
ing to sign that gets reversed in the rush, the J.D. to D.J., is to be read as the
déjà of *Glas*. Should that *déjà* be, can it be, translated as *already*? Even if it
could and should, is that to translate a proper name? Or a signature?

***Another term to be translated, the term has already been translated any
number of times. An example: "The word 'deconstruction' is in one way a
good one to name this movement. The word, like other words in 'de,' 'decrep-
itude,' for example, or 'denotation,' describes a paradoxical action which is
negative and positive at once. In this it is like all words with a double anti-
thetical prefix, words in 'ana,' like 'analysis,' or words in 'para,' like 'para-
site.' These words tend to come in pairs, which are not opposites, positive

against negative. They are related in a systematic differentiation which requires a different analysis or untying in each case, but which in each case leads, in a different way each time, to the tying up of a double bind. This tying up is at the same time a loosening. It is a paralysis of thought in the face of what cannot be thought rationally: analysis, paralysis; solution, dissolution; composition, decomposition; construction, deconstruction; mantling, dismantling; canny, uncanny; competence, incompetence; apocalyptic, anacalyptic; constituting, deconstituting. Deconstructive criticism moves back and forth between the poles of these pairs, proving in its own activity, for example, that there is no deconstruction which is not at the same time constructive, affirmative. The word says this in juxtaposing 'de' and 'con.' "[1]

Another example: In a parenthesis in his "Letter to a Japanese Friend," Derrida writes: "(and the question of deconstruction is also through and through *the* question of translation . . .)."[2] A note is added to this letter when reprinted in *Psyché*: "I add that the 'deconstruction' of the following article would not be without interest:

" 'DECONSTRUCTION.

" 'Action of deconstructing, of disassembling the parts of a whole. The deconstruction of an edifice. The deconstruction of a machine.

" 'Grammar: displacement that words are made to undergo when a written sentence is composed in a foreign language, by violating, it is true, the syntax of that language, but also by drawing close to the syntax of the maternal language, in order better to grasp the sense that the words present in the sentence. This term exactly designates what the majority of grammarians improperly call "Construction"; for in any author, all the sentences are *constructed* according to the genius of his national language; what does a foreigner do who tries to comprehend, to translate this author? He *deconstructs* the sentences, disassembles their words, according to the genius of the foreign language; or if one wants to avoid all confusion in terms, there is *Deconstruction* with respect to the language of the translated author, and *Construction* with respect to the language of the translator. (*Dictionnaire Bescherelle*, Paris, Garnier, 1873, 15th ed.)" (*Psyché*, pp. 388n-89n).

This entire letter is a letter of translation, on translation. Derrida ends with the statement that he does "not believe that translation is a secondary and derived event in relation to an original language or text." Translation involves "the risk and the chance of the poem. How to translate 'poem,' a 'poem'?" (*Psyché*, pp. 392-93; *Derrida and Différance*, p. 8).

****Is Latin a metatongue? Or Greek? *Meta-* sets going another series of substitutions in the attempt to translate translation: *metagraphein*, "to write differently: to alter, correct: *also*, to interpolate, falsify"; *metapherein*, "to carry from one place to another, transfer . . . to change, alter: to pervert" (*The Classic Greek Dictionary*); *metaphrazein*, to declare, to show, across or differently, i.e., to translate. *Phrasein*, an idiomatic root: "To show, say. Greek verb of unknown origin" (*The American Heritage Dictionary of the English Language*).

. . .

Translation is the science of old writings—paleographics.

The *translated** text is, to transform *Positions* on *paleonymics*, set aside, "held in reserve, limited in a given conceptual structure."[3] The *translating* text delimits, grafts, extends the translated text set aside. The translating text, in other words, *writes* the translated text in its (their) setting-aside, grafting, extension.

> *Is this the "original"? In a first case, I think so. The *translated* text is the text *to be translated*. But the *translated* text is also the text as *already translated*. The *translating* text is what translates the *translated* text; the *translating* text is the ongoing text of the text in translation.

Translation is the relation of two texts across their differences. In paleographics, the difference is that of the -*latus*, of the past (*paleo-*) carried on, laterally inscribed in the tongue translating. The difference, in other words, would be simple, a difference of signature and date, of the proper name. The translated text signed X is re-signed X in a lateral tongue later. The date is redated, carried back across. But the difference is inscribed within the difference itself, in the translation of the signature itself, in the dating itself never present even in its past. The signature is always lateral. Translation too.

Paleographics marks that language is several, that "the supreme one is lacking,"*[4] that "the relatedness (*Verwandtschaft*) of two languages" "rests in the intention underlying each language as a whole—an intention, however, which no single language can attain by itself but which is realized only by the totality of their intentions supplementing each other (*der Allheit ihrer einanderergänzenden Intentionen*): pure language (*die reine Sprache*)."[5] This conjunction of Mallarmé and Benjamin is Benjamin's. As Carol Jacobs remarks in her essay on Benjamin's preface, " 'pure language' [is] certainly not the materialization of truth in the form of a supreme language. Benjamin sets this temptation aside with a passage from the 'Crise de vers'. . . . He displaces his own text with the foreignness of Mallarmé's in which the latter insists on the insurmountable disparity between languages. The 'pure language' . . . does not signify the apotheosis of an ultimate language but signifies rather that which is purely language—nothing but language."[6]

Is there a contradiction here? The supreme language is lacking for Mallarmé; for Benjamin the relatedness of languages is the intentionality of pure language. Is Mallarmé's supreme language Benjamin's pure language? Is the pure language, like the supreme language, lacking? According to Mallarmé, the lack of the supreme language, of the desire for a term wedding timbre and sense, is necessary for verse to exist, a verse that philosophically remunerates the failing of languages. This lack is pure language, is as Derrida writes, "the being-language of the language, tongue or language *as such,* that unity without any self-identity, which makes for the fact that there are languages and that they are languages."**7 Paleographics remarks this lack as other as the trace, as the "language of the other," as the lateral of the tongue, possibly its collateral. Derrida writes: "The language of the other lets the spoken word have the word, and commits us to keep our word. In this sense, there is 'language of the other' whenever there is a speech-event. This is what I mean by 'trace.' "8

*"*Les langues imparfaites en cela que plusieurs, manque la suprême,*" writes Mallarmé in *Crise de vers.* This begins the passage cited but not translated by Benjamin in "Die Aufgabe des Übersetzers." As Derrida notes in "Des tours de Babel"—it is one of his persistent questions there: "Once again: how is a text written in several languages at one time to be translated?" (p. 176).

**A certain reading and translation of Benjamin (who leaves Mallarmé both translated and untranslated) are required here. As J. Hillis Miller points out in *The Ethics of Reading,* "Benjamin's formulations depend at crucial places on figures, the figure of the fragmented vessel, the figure of the circle and its tangent. . . . all readers tend to see the interpretation of these figures as crucial to any reading of Benjamin's essay."9 And, as Paul de Man and Carol Jacobs argue, the translation of these figures is crucial to any reading of Benjamin's essay. Recalling Jacobs's "exceedingly precise and correct" treatment and translation of the image of the vessel and fragments in her article "The Monstrosity of Translation," de Man argues that the fragments are " ' the *broken* parts of the vessel,' " they do not "constitute a totality," "the fragments are fragments," and "they remain essentially fragmentary. . . . What we have here is an initial fragmentation; any work is totally fragmented in relation to this *reine Sprache,* with which it has nothing in common, and every translation is totally fragmented in relation to the original. The translation is the fragment of a fragment, is breaking the fragment—so the vessel keeps breaking, constantly—and never reconstitutes it; there was no vessel in the first place, or we have no knowledge of this vessel, or no awareness, no access to it, so for all intents and purposes there has never been one."10
Derrida also reads and translates Benjamin's figures. On the way from the "larger language" to "pure language," the vessel (or in the translation of Maurice de Gandillac that Derrida works with, the *"amphore"),* "Like the urn which lends its poetic topos to so many meditations on word and thing, from Hölderlin to Rilke and Heidegger, . . . is one with itself through opening itself to the outside—and this openness opens the unity, renders it possible, and forbids it totality. Its openness allows receiving and giving" ("Des tours de Babel," pp. 190 and 234).

. . .

Translation is in other words, *autrement dit — transformation.*

How is this to be read? In other words, how am I to translate in other words this here called a sentence? In other words, how am I to metaphrase this here called a sentence? Translation is always *in other words,* mataphrase, always uses other('s) words, even in its "primordial" sentence. That is the collateral of translation, the lateral tongue collared by sense. That is, translation is transformation, self-transformation, metagraphic, if there were the identity by which the family relation could be identified, by which a self could be designated outside the translation of translation itself. A transformation without identity, and so always other in its repetition — in other words.

. . .

Translation forges its signature, paraphs it, signs the name of the other as the same, signs the other text as its own, and thereby maintains the translated text, seals it.

To paraphrase, this could mean that translation, like every signature event, is a forgery, for it must infinitely paraph its own signing, which here is the signature of the other as the same — that is, the signature of translation itself as the language of the other, as the trace. But also translation signs the text, the other text, the text of the other, its own text then, as its own. The other is the ownness of translation, whether in one language or more than one. Each text is signed as a translated text, at times countersigned and sealed in its doubled otherness from one language to another, at times within one language only.

. . .

By way of citation: "What this institution cannot bear, is for anyone to tamper with [toucher à; also 'touch,' 'change,' 'concern himself with'] language, meaning both the national language and, paradoxically, an ideal of translatability that neutralizes this national language. Nationalism and universalism. What this institution cannot bear is a transformation that leaves intact neither of these two complementary poles" (LO, 94).

Translation disrupts the university, the teaching institution of universal nationalism, of national universalism — that is, of racism — with the mark of the other. Racism's other: translation, the kinship without kinship, the lateral family, that is what the institution cannot bear — to translate.

. . .

Translation and Apotropocalyptics.

What language is spoken here? Apotropocalyptics and translation.[11] Why do I refuse to write in English? Can anyone write in English? Can anyone write without translating? To write in English is racist, even when I address myself to English-speaking readers. An impossible racism, but racism nonetheless.

. . .

(1) *As apotropaic, translation wards (off) the (translated) text, becomes its Medusa charm. ("The logical paradox of apotropaics: . . . renouncing life and mastery in order to secure them; putting into play by ruse, simulacrum, and violence just what one wants to preserve; losing in advance what one wants to erect; suspending what one raises: aufheben."[12])*

The Medusa charm: Medusa is charming, calls to her wide-open mouth all language. (a) Translation (as the translated) opens its mouth wide, calls all language to itself. It takes in and spews out, forever indigestible, languages; charmed, they speak as one, transliterated one in the other. (b) Translation (as translating), the defense mechanism, wards (off) (in other words, partakes in order not to be incorporated) the gaping mouth of the translated text, ready to receive all tongues in its (their) translatability. *Translating* defends against the *translated*. The translating takes part of the translated (the semantic, the formalistic, letters, puns, syntax, &c.) in order to ward off the translated. There is a kinship between the translating and the translated, a kinship of apotropaics, just enough of the other to make it possible but not itself be there.

The collateral of that wide-open mouth is Medusa's hair, the proliferation that for Freud only serves to erect the one. Apotropaics: from languages, language. Phallogoracism, Medusa's charm.

. . .

(2) *As apocalyptic, translation (dis)closes the (translated) text and partakes in the catastrophe or the apocalypse of the apocalypse: (dis)-closure without (dis)closure, "an apocalypse without vision, without truth, without revelation . . . an apocalypse beyond good and evil."[13]*

The apocalypse reveals, but it reveals according to the syntax of Blanchot's *X sans X*, without revealing. The *dis*sonnance of apocalypse closes without closing (the *claudication* of closure) the revealing language: the clause of closure in the *dis*lation of revelation and truth, of the destination of truth in a revelation—in other words, *dis*revelation, *dis*closure, clandestination. Translation *dis*closes the text; the catastrophic *dis* reveals the translation of the text, in and of itself.

. . .

(3) *As apotropocalyptic, translation wards (off)-(dis)closes without truth the (translated) text. Translation contaminates the text: there is no paradigmatic text, no original revelation or sin.*

Apotropocalyptic, to use Mallarmé's syntax, the uneasy hymen of the apotropaic and the apocalyptic. Defensive disclosure: reveal just a bit in order not to reveal, in other words reveal in order not to reveal: translation. The other marks the disclosure in its defense and its revelation, in its lateral dream, marks the translation as apotrope and apocalypse in exile, in errance, destinerrance, apotropocalypse, in metaphrase.

The text as apotropocalyptic, as translative, cannot be original, in all the senses of this word. The text can be no paradigm for the text, one for the other, one in the other, conceptually, textually. The text is other in relation even to itself, even in relation to other texts: the intertext of the intertext: *envois* without destination even in the text. The series is without paradigm, without series, erases itself as series in its series, *sériature.**

*Derrida: "A unique series of unique objects: each time the *hiatus* maintains and *scores out* [rature], in the serial interlacing, the reference to the other (elsewhere I've suggested calling this *seriature*) and to the other's other. How to describe this *fold* [pli] of internal or citational reference? Of this transformational grammar?"[14] The elsewhere refers to a reading of Levinas, "En ce moment même dans cet ouvrage me voici," in which Derrida proposes the word *seriature*: ". . . only after a series of words that are all faulty and that I have as it were erased (*raturés*) in passing, in tempo (*en mesure*), regularly, one after the other, while leaving them their tracing force, the trail (*sillage*) of their tracing, the force (without force) of a trace that the passage of the other will have left. I have written while marking them with, while letting them be marked by, the other. That is why it is inexact to say that I have erased these words. In any case I shouldn't have erased them, I should have let them be entrained in a *series* (a tied up suite of twisting *erasures*), an interrupted series, a *series* of interlaced interruptions, a *hiatus* series (wide-open mouth, a mouth open to the cut-in word or to the gift of the other and to-the-bread-in-his-mouth), what I shall call from now on to formalize economically and to dissociate no longer what is no longer dissociable in this fabrication [*fabrique*], *sériature*" (in *Psyché*, p. 189).

. . .

(Cor)relations of . . . lated and . . . lating.

Text can only be the correlation of texts, with the cor-, col-, the *cum*

that is without relation, thus a correlation of the other: such is the text in
its apotropocalyptic relations (kinship, references, &c.), in transrelation.

. . .

(1) Lated *and* lating *(cor)relate as the two récits of Blanchot's* Death
Sentence: *"These things happened to me in 1938."* — *"The truth will
be told, everything of importance that happened will be told. But
not everything has yet happened."*[15]

I do not know (Derrida doesn't either) whether *Death Sentence* is
made of two *récits*, or one, or a series in one. The blank across which
there must be communication to decide this question is the blank of translation, the blank that must be transliterated into all alphabets, against all
racisms, the blank of the telic (the near distance: telephone, telegram,
telepathy, telelation).

But the blank here is complicated in time. Telelation is chronic. The
distance is the distance between what has *happened* and what has *not yet
happened*, between the *lated* and the *lating* yet postponed in its present
truth, between the *tele* and the *paleo* (paleotelics, the pleonastic distance
inscribed in the Indo-European root *kwel*): "The truth will be told" (DS,
31; AM, 54), will always be told, not just told, but will be to come, in the
never present of the . . . lation.

. . .

(2) Lated *and* lating *(cor)relate as the "and immediately"* resurrection of the one by the call of the other: "She who had been absolutely
alive was already no more than a statue. . . . I leaned over her, I
called to her by her first name; and immediately* [et aussitot] — I can
say there wasn't a second's interval — a sort of breath came out of her
compressed mouth" (DS, 20; AM, 35-36).

*Derrida, in LO (pp. 126-27): "The 'and' ('and immediately,' 'and eternally')
weds in a timeless time the one called and the caller, the imperative 'come'
and the coming of the one who comes. In this sense, we can no longer
describe the call (demand, order, desire . . .) and the response in the usual
terms and according to the usual distinctions of an analysis of locutionary
acts. The 'come'-effect of the 'first name' transcends all these categories
(strictly speaking, it can thus be called 'transcendental': *qui transcendit omne
genus*), and this event, at once ordinary and extraordinary, is also what
L'arrêt de mort 'recounts.' "

Chronic telelation transcends chronicity in the exchange of "come" 's
and responses of the *lated* and *lating*. Each calls the other to come, and

immediately the other responds. The call is always already response. Of the first name, the proper name. What, however, is the proper name of the text? Of the translated text? of the translating text? And is the problem of translation how to translate the proper name? In other words and in response, for the text, how is the signature to be translated? How is the signature rendered even in its own tongue? *Lated*, and immediately *lating*, signature translates untranslatable, idiomatic, without paraphrase or metaphrase, belongs without belonging to no language (the double negation disrupts the semantics further), like "the very name of Babel: which at once translates and does not translate itself, belongs without belonging to a language and indebts itself to itself for an insolvent debt, to itself as if other" ("Des tours de Babel," pp. 174-75 and 218).

. . .

(3) Lated *and* lating *(cor)relate as the doubleness of the two women:* "But each woman is also the double, death mask, cast, ghost, body at once living and dead, of the other. Separated: joined" (LO, 164).

Translating and translated they are colossal, the double of each other in death. J. and N. translate—that is, double—each other. Two signatures double each other as the death mask ("a very beautiful cast of J.'s hands" [DS, p. 10; AM, p. 21]; "Nathalie said to me: 'I telephoned X., I asked him to make a cast of my head and my hands' " [DS, p. 75; AM, p. 119]) cast over each other. Separated:joined, separating:joining—to use Blanchot's syntax (*L'attente l'oubli*)—the translating and the translated texts haunt each other; never present (alive or death, always surviving) one to the other, yet always like the Turin Sudario, dual paleotelic.

. . .

(4) Lated *and* lating *(cor)relate as the mad hypothetical relation Derrida reads between the two women (of* Death Sentence*):* "And what if it were this—that the two women love each other and approach one another, before him and without him. . . . I am speaking here of the fascination of one woman by the other, across the uncrossable glass partition that separates the two stories. They do not know each other, have never met; they inhabit two utterly foreign worlds. They telephone each other ('Come') across the infinite distance of a no-connection [d'un sans rapport]. The narrator is between them, saying 'I,' with an 'I' identical and other, from one récit to the other. In him, before him, without him, they are the same, the same one, 'two images superimposed on one another,' a 'photographic' superimposing; they are utterly different, completely

other, and they unite and call to each other: 'Come' " (LO, 169-170).

Again, the two texts, like the two women, are in telelation.* The two texts, separated and joined across their languages, even in the same language, these two texts are in their idiom, as language, hymeneal. Their relation is the hymen (of the tongue), a hymen identical and other at once, language. As hymen, language joins:separates in its marriage partition the . . . lated and the . . . lating in a polyphony of "Come" 's.

*How is this to be translated? According to what languages? *Telelation: tel elation, tel e lation, tele lation:* such elation, such being carried out of the past, paleolation, metaphrastics.

. . .

(5) Lated *and* lating *(cor)relate as the marriage contract between Socrates and Plato on the apocalyptic* Postcard: *"That dossier between the two bodies, I know what I mean, is a marriage contract. I always think of those contracts that are only signed by one—they are far from being without value, on the contrary. And even when both sign, it's twice by a single one."*[16]

Why does this passage fascinate so frequently? It occurs as the legend for the color reproduction of the postcard front for *The Post Card.* The legend metaphrases from the back the pictorial; the postcard translates the "legend." Each wishes to sign the other as one, indifferent to chronic concerns. Who translates whom? Socrates? Plato? Who dictates? Who writes? This, like "Living On," is the place of the fantasy scene, the scene of all telelation, the fascinating fascinated scene. The translating text is fascinated by and immediately fascinates the translated text (*paraly"s"es* it, Derrida would say: *"Paralyse* is a new *name* useful to me to announce a certain movement of fascination (fascinating fascinated), a movement that analyzes what prevents and provokes at once desire's step [*pas*] into the labyrinth that it itself is—not [*pas*]"[17]); the translated text fascinates and immediately is fascinated by the translating text.

. . .

Does translation survive (the text's) clandestination?

Clan, kin of *celare* and *helan* (hell), kin of *kaluptein,* to hide, conceal. Does translation outlive the secret kinship of its own destination in apocalypse?

(a) Is the life death (in other words the living on) of translation played out in clandestination, in the clandestination that the text (translating or translated, translating and translated) remarks? The *envois,* the dispatches, that come from one knows not where (*atopia*) in the intussusception of the text, remark the double bind of translation, the translate and not translate of all translation, the sur-translation (translation beyond translation, translation without translation) of translation.

(b) Does translation survive the clandestination of its own trans-literation, its own translation as translation: metaphrase, metagraph, met-aphor, transfer(ence), transrelation, transreference, &c.? Its own translation as clandestination: paleotelics, telelation, apotropocalyptics, &c.? Are these all a metaphrastics (surtranslation) of a proper name, translation, here morseled into any number of bits and pieces, in the dispatches without destination of its near distance response?

To write is to write in other words, to . . . late then, to trans . . . then, &c., is to remark the impossible signature, the impossible proper name, the idiom of the idiom as the untranslatable in translation, here translating on, living on as translating, as an overtranslating defending against the possibility of rendering any transfer without survivors, as defending against the "Apocalypse of the Name," according to the seventh missive and missile of "No Apocalypse, Not Now (full speed ahead, seven missiles, seven missives)": *"The name of nuclear war is the name of the first war which can be fought in the name of the name alone, that is, of everything and of nothing."* In other words, without remainder, without survivors, without the survival even of the name: "that name in the name of which war would take place would be the name of nothing, it would be pure name, the 'naked name.' That war would be the first and the last war in the name of the name, with only the nonname of 'name.' It would be a war without a name, a nameless war, for it would no longer share even the name of war with the other events of the same type, of the same family." But that is the war of Babel, the war for the name, in the name of the name, except translation has long "deterred" that war, as if "God and the sons of Shem having understood that a name wasn't worth it . . . they preferred to spend a little more time together, the time of a long colloquy with warriors in love with life, busy writing in all languages in order to make the conversation last, even if they didn't understand each other too well."[18]

Part VI

Alternatives to Deconstruction

PRELIMINARY REMARKS

The preceding sections raised the question as to whether discursive limits upon deconstructive play are always to be dissolved, as some, following Derrida, have alleged. This question assumes that deconstruction does indeed seek to accomplish such a dissolution, and that any avowedly discursive language would be nondeconstructive, at least in spirit. Those who uphold discursivity against its dissolution could thus be said to present an "alternative" to deconstruction. The following chapters by Easthope, Wurzer, and Villani explore "alternatives" in this sense. However, where the first two present variant neo-Marxian critiques of deconstruction, Villani offers a "poststructuralist" alternative, which he suggests is more an alternative *for* deconstruction, because its possibility arises within the Derridean texts themselves.

In "Derrida's Epistemology," Antony Easthope carries out an Althusserian critique of Derrida's essay "Structure, Sign and Play." He notes that Derrida characterizes the traditional notion of structure as referring to a point of origin, or fixed presence, at the center of a system of variations. The function of this center is to ensure a limit to the play of the structure itself, to render meaning determinate. Derrida's deconstruction of this origin and its presence as a "transcendental signified," says Easthope, leads to an extreme dilemma: either there is a fixed origin, an absolute, discursive center, or there is simply a system of differences without any necessary order or coherence. In embracing the latter alternative, Derrida would seem to abolish the possibility of scientific discourse, a possibility that Easthope, following Althusser, would preserve.

Easthope faults Derrida for failing to distinguish between meaning and reference on the one hand, and for characterizing scientific discourse as "empirical" (in his reading of Lévi-Strauss) on the other. Althusser, by contrast, rejects empiricism and its assumed totalization, but also rejects the "either-or" between absolute totality and "the absolute obligation to play." Instead, as Easthope points out, Althusser maintains that truth is only available in a discursive process of signification limited by the finitude of a historically situated subject. Truth is thus relative to its subject, its situation, and its conditions of production, which include the materiality of language. What is produced, therefore, is better characterized, not as truth, but as knowledge. Citing revisions of Althusser by Hindess and Hirst, Easthope characterizes scientific discourse as pluralistic—each science has its own objects of discourse and its own methods for referring to what lies *outside* discourse. Reference to the extradiscursive guarantees the structural limits of science and preserves the coherence of discourse, without appeal to any internal origin or center of meaning. As Easthope remarks, discourse is shaped negatively by the extradiscursive, which is a resistance that varies among different discursive formulations. Thus, without benefit of an overriding principle or totalization, knowledge can be produced and increased incrementally, and discourse can find a limit whose alternative is not an unlimited play.

Wilhelm Wurzer explores a related view in "The Critical Difference: Adorno's Aesthetic Alternative." Like Easthope, Wurzer appeals to the possibility of a dialectical constraint upon discourse, and therefore to the possibility of preserving it from deconstructive dissolution. Wurzer's alternative is found in Adorno's aesthetic theory and its concomitant principle of dialectical idiosyncrasy. Adorno, like Althusser, rejects the Hegelian *Aufhebung* in favor of a dialectic of finitude, and so would not be implicated in Derrida's deconstruction of Hegelian totality. Nevertheless, Adorno maintains that dialectical negativity, as found in the work of art, still limits, shapes, and preserves discursive thought.

Extrapolating from Adorno's position, Wurzer characterizes Derrida's grammatological practice as lacking a "negative moment," or a reference to an exterior reality. Without such reference, he remarks, the multiple readings of *gram* lead to a "one-dimensional *travail de textes*," which is "lifeless" and "indifferent." So considered, Derrida's play of *différance* is dialectically abstract, homogenous, and empty. For Wurzer, Adorno's theory of the *Kunstwerk* avoids this abstraction as well as the dogmatism of a more traditional Marxian analysis. Adorno's art work is an *Augenblick*, a moment of negativity and heterogeneity that preserves both the autonomy of the work itself and the social constitution of its "intertextuality." Adorno characterizes this heterogeneity as *das Naturschöne*—the beauty of nature. Aesthetic idosyncracy is the finite understanding of natural beauty in light of its social context—a context the art work illuminates and surpasses. The art work, then, is a *trace* of nature. It offers the possibility of freedom in its phenomenal residue, a residue that is indissoluble "but not systematically permanent." As such, the trace gives direction and movement to dialectical thought without falling into a totalizing logocentrism. It thus escapes the internalization that would deliver it up to deconstructive erasure.

In "Poststructuralist Alternatives to Deconstruction" Arnaud Villani examines an alternative that emerges within deconstruction itself, particularly via analyses carried out by Laruelle, Roussel, and Deleuze. Villani focuses upon the development of poststructuralism in the period following Derrida's essay "The Ends of Man." He poses the question whether post structuralism is an "incident" in deconstruction or something irreducible to the latter. Beginning with Laruelle, Villani shows that poststructuralism attempts to answer Derrida's question in the last sentence of "The Ends of Man": "Who, we?" That is, who is the nonanthropological subject who deconstructs? The answer to this question will determine whether and what kind of discursivity is implied within the deconstructive strategy itself.

According to Villani, Laruelle's answer to the question of a deconstructive subject is the substitution of a "mechanical process" for the (still anthropolgical!) "practice" of deconstructive reading and writing. In this way, he believes to have found the "external lever" between Derrida's text and its "copies." Laruelle's mechanical process would erase the vestiges of structuralism and metaphysics within deconstruction, in the very terms "text" or "sign," and would absorb these into a repetition whose movement and direction are moments of a generalized libido. With this move, Laruelle claims to have found a hinge between Derrida and Deleuze.

Villani suggests that the relation between Derrida and Deleuze, a difference within deconstruction, perhaps mimics Heidegger's *Verwindung* of metaphysics. Heidegger accomplishes this *Verwindung* by taking a "step back" to the presocratics. This move differentiates philosophy into two "lines." The "classical line," from Plato through Hegel and Heidegger, is refracted via the "physical line" that runs from the presocratics through Schopenhauer, Nietzsche, and Heidegger, such that the presocratics are shifted into the classical line, creating a "symmetry" between Heidegger and the presocratics on both scales. In this way, says Villani, philosophy becomes undecidable—differs from itself, becomes "scattered," its meaning an *unregulated* polysemy. This difference, moreover, is nonpolemical and nonsymbolical.

Quoting Deleuze, Villani reviews the structuralist "voiding" of polemical or symbolical opposition. Structural difference is the "empty square" (*la case vide*) that allows for "moves" in the game of substitution, the empty square that can never be occupied because it shifts *itself* with every move that it enables. Roussel's contribution is to think this opposition as an "extradiscursive and yet nonmetaphysical immanence," as *force*, which functions as "desire" for Deleuze and "libido" for Laruelle. As Villani points out, this "disparitive function" takes the place of structuralism's "empty square"—an alternative already seen, but not developed, by Derrida. In Deleuzian terms, this function is the "rhizoma" that leaps from one series of significations to another, and also from one level *between* two series to another. Such a motive function already guides Derridean deconstruction, the poststructuralists would argue, though Derrida himself emphasizes the undoing of discursive series and levels. For Villani, this function marks a reemergence of "the real" as an "extradiscursive immanence" and motive force in the text. It is the answer to the question of the nonanthropological subject "who deconstructs"; it is the "real" who "we are."

G.E.A.

16

Derrida's Epistemology

Antony Easthope

The title is an abbreviation. I shall not consider the general range of epistemological positions taken in Derrida's writings but only that given in one essay. However, this essay, published in English in 1970, has been very influential, especially in America, acquiring there "the status of a sacred essay" in Lentricchia's phrase.[1] "Structure, Sign, and Play in the Discourse of the Human Sciences,"[2] the full title, invites us to read the essay in the context of both the human sciences and scientific discourse in general. In responding to this invitation I shall contrast the epistemological position of the essay with that put forward by Althusser and by some subsequent critics of Althusser.

"Structure, Sign, and Play" describes a conception of structure it claims is as old as the Western tradition itself, one in which the organization of structure is envisaged "by a process of giving it a center or of referring it to a point of presence, a fixed origin" (SSP, 278). The function of such centering is defined by saying its purpose is to ensure a limit to "what we might call the *play* of the structure." Established at the outset, this alternative—*either* "fixed origin" *or* "play"—is redefined progressively throughout the essay. A centered structure is one whose basis is imagined as "a fundamental immobility," an immobility that is itself "beyond the reach of play" (SSP, 279). The notion of a center as a "natural site" (SSP, 280) is criticized with implicit reference to the Saussurean principle that there can be no signified without a signifier: the center as "transcendental signified" is impossible because it can never be "absolutely present outside a system of differences (SSP, 280).

Either an absolute and transcendental signified *or* a system of differences: in proposing this alternative the essay omits to bring forward a distinction that forms a necessary condition for the possibility of scientific discourse. In denying that a discourse can provide a "natural site" and origin "outside a system of differences," it is not entirely clear whether what is being denied is a site and origin outside the system of differences, which constitute the order of the signifier or an origin outside discourse as well. The distinction needed is that between *meaning* and *reference*. At the level of the signified, meaning occurs within and only within discourse. Reference is a matter of the relationship between discourse and an independent reality outside discourse to which discourse—certain discourses—may refer.

As its chosen example of human science, Derrida's essay refers to the anthropology of Lévi-Strauss. In so doing it observes that "ethnology—like any science—comes about within the element of discourse" (SSP, 282) and notes the way "the language of the social sciences criticizes *itself*" (SSP, 284), a way exemplified when Lévi-Strauss thinks "he can separate *method* from *truth*" and so "the instruments of the method" from "the objective significations envisaged by it" (SSP, 284). Although Lévi-Strauss admits that his book on myths "is itself a kind of myth" (SSP, 287), his work is criticized by Derrida on the grounds that there is no book or study by Lévi-Strauss that "is not proposed as an empirical essay," and "empiricism is the matrix of all faults menacing a discourse which continues, as with Lévi-Strauss in particular, to consider itself scientific" (SSP, 288). The clear implication is that empiricism is the necessary condition for a scientific discourse. Yet it is now argued that empiricism entails a necessary failure in totalization.

Lévi-Strauss says his work on myth is not exhaustive and fresh data may come up. The essay describes the admission as exhibiting the "limit of totalization" and offers "two ways" of understanding it. Nontotalization can be judged *either* as the failure of an "empirical endeavor" to cover all the material that might be relevant *or* it can be conceived in terms of play and the fact that "the nature of the field—that is, language and a finite language—excludes totalization," excludes it because language is "a field of infinite substitutions" without a center (SSP, 289).

"Structure, Sign, and Play" proposes a number of oppositions with reference to the possibility of scientific discourse. Even with some slide between terms, these line up as follows: "fixed origin," "center," "point of presence," "transcendental signified," "truth," "objective significations," "empiricism," "scientific discourse" on one side; and on the other "the element of discourse," "play," "system of differences," "infinite substitutions." The essay concludes by reaffirming the central opposition or alternative on which it is itself elaborated.

> There are thus two interpretations of interpretation, of structure, of sign, of
> play. The one seeks to decipher, dreams of deciphering, a truth or an origin
> which escapes play and the order of the sign. . . . The other, which is no
> longer turned toward the origin, affirms play and tries to pass beyond man
> and humanism, the name of man being the name of that being who, through
> the history of metaphysics or of onto-theology—in other words, throughout
> his entire history—has dreamed of full presence, the reassuring foundation,
> the origin and end of play (SSP, 292).

The founding opposition here is unmistakable: *either* truth is absolute, centered in a transcendental signified outside all process of signification, *or* there is play and only play, only the system of differences that
constitute language, only the process of signification. Absolute truth on
one side of the *aut* is balanced precisely by absolute play excluding all
truth on the other—one side of the opposition generates the other.

The terms of this absolutist problematic have been brought about by
the identification of truth (and science) with *empiricism*. ("the matrix of
all faults"). There are varieties of empiricism but Derrida's essay assumes
a traditional and mainstream definition of empiricism as the view that a
knowledge of reality can be gained through observation such that there
can be access to truth unaffected by the process of signification, access
therefore that "escapes play and the order of the sign."

Derrida's identification of (scientific) truth with empiricism and the
either/or this leads to can be contrasted with the epistemological position
of Althusser and of work in the Althusserian tradition. This rejects empiricism without being driven to capitulate to the absolute obligation to play.
It acknowledges in effect the principle that it is "impossible to separate,
through interpretation or commentary, the signified from the signifier,"[3]
and accepts that truth is not available apart from its construction in a
process of signification, a discursive process that takes place always for a
historically situated subject. Inasmuch as that result accordingly is to
envisage truth as relative rather than absolute, constructed progressively
not given once and for all, it is best to distinguish what is so produced as
knowledge rather than truth (with its absolutist connotations).

The context for Althusser's critique of empiricism can be illustrated
with the assertion in Marx's *Introduction* that knowledge is the product
of a "working-up of observation and conception into concepts" and in
this respect "is a product of a thinking head," but that reality nevertheless
"retains its autonomous existence outside the head."[4] In Althusser's summary *"the empiricist conception of knowledge"* supposes a process that
takes place "between a given object and a given subject," one in which
subject and object are presumed as "given and hence predate the process

of knowledge."[5] Empiricism disavows the production of subject and object in relation to each other. And so:

> The whole empiricist process of knowledge lies in an operation of the subject called *abstraction*. To know is to abstract from the real object its essence, the possession of which by the subject is then called knowledge (RC, 35-36).

Thus it is possible for empiricism to dream of knowledge as an absolute, a truth, an origin which "escapes play and the order of the sign," for it assumes that knowledge is "already *really* present in the real object" (RC, 38) the subject has to know. Althusser attacks both "empiricist idealism," which reduces "thought about the real to the real itself," and "speculative idealism," such as that of Hegel, which reduces "the real to thought" (RC, 87). The epistemological position defended states that the process of knowledge takes place between subject and object, a process in which thought about the real and the real are related. This relation is "a relation of *knowledge*, a relation of adequacy or inadequacy of knowledge" (RC, 87).

Althusser's epistemological generalizations have in turn been criticized. Hindess and Hirst,[6] notably, have condemned Althusser's assertion that there can be a relation between thought and the real that is a relation of "adequacy or inadequacy of knowledge." They argue that this conception of a relation of knowledge assumes some form of *general* distinction and correlation between a realm of discourse (thought) on the one hand and an independently existing realm of objects (the real) on the other. The consequence is infinite regress. To privilege any general criterion of adequacy/inadequacy (whether defined in empiricist or rationalist terms) immediately exposes that criterion itself to epistemological interrogation, the result of that inquiry itself being subject to further investigation. And so on. From this argument Hindess and Hirst draw the conclusion that it is no longer possible "to refer to objects existing *outside* of discourse as the measure of the validity of discourse" (MPSF, 18) and that "the entities specified in discourse must be referred to solely in and through the forms of discourse, theoretical, political, etc., in which they are constituted" (MPSF, 1).

This critique of Althusser's epistemology is doing much more than repeat the tautology that objects of discourse are objects of discourse, that signifieds are signifieds. Although they accept that all discourses, including scientific ones, come about "within the element of discourse," they do not derive from this the view that there can be no discourse of knowledge. Their argument does not go that way because they do not start from the presumption that only empiricism can ground scientific truth. The attempt rather is to get rid of a residue of idealism from Althusser's theorization, a residue left over even despite Althusser's insistence that there is no question of "*guarantees* of the possibility of knowledge (RC, 56). Epistemology—in general—has to be rejected because there can be no absolute guarantee of the validity of scientific discourse, whether that guarantee is conceived to derive from reality (as in empiricist epistemologies), from reason (as in rationalist epistemologies) or from a supposed general relation of adequacy/inadequacy between thought and the real (as in Althusser). Instead, there are only a number of different discourses, some of them being discourses of knowledge. Each discourse of knowledge works with its own objects of discourse (signifieds) *and* its own methods of referring to the extradiscursive.

Paul Hirst has summarized the position as follows:

> There are no general criteria of adequacy or truth. . . . We would argue that discourses and practices *do* employ the criteria of appropriateness or adequacy (not of epistemological validity) but these are specific to the objectives of definite bodies of discourse and practice. None will pass muster as a general criterion of validity, but there is no knowledge process *in general* and, therefore, no necessity for such a criterion. Techniques of criticism of Biblical texts are of no use in garage mechanics. Questions of priority and relation in the Gospels, of the state of wear of a gearbox, elicit different types of tests and disputes about them. The referents and constructs, Gospels, motor cars, depend on conditions which differ, so do criteria and tests.[7]

There is "no knowledge process *in general*" yet there are discourses of knowledge operating specific criteria of adequacy. One qualification that needs to be added is made in an essay by Andrew Collier:

> It is perfectly true that the procedures of validation are quite different in different sciences; one does not prove propositions of chemistry, evolutionary biology and linguistics in the same way. But in each case what the science aims at is knowledge of its object; the differences stem from the differences in the objects.[8]

The differences between scientific discourses are determined by the process of signification and also by the extradiscursive reality each seeks to give knowledge of. The extradiscursive does not contribute positively to the shaping of the specific discourse (that would be to regenerate empiricism) but it may be said to contribute *negatively*, for it appears in a discourse as resistance to it, as what resists some formulations in a way that is different from that in which it resists others.

The consequences of Derrida's essay have been registered in literary studies more than anywhere else. It is appropriate to finish by rephrasing in relation to the literary text what I have argued here. The brutal empiricism of Leavisism asserts of a text that "this is so, isn't it?." The more developed empiricism of *The Verbal Icon* claims that "the poem belongs to the public," for it is "embodied in language,"[9] and thus that criticism may refer confidently to "the meaning expressed by the poem itself" (VI, 87). The procedure in each case assumes the text as a reality given unproblematically as "the words on the page" outside a process of signification. Yet such idealist empiricism of the text need not lead to a counteridealism, which affirms that the text can exist only in an infinite play of interpretation, a counteridealism evident for example in the statement "that there are *no* texts, but only interpretations."[10]

We can step aside from the absolutist either/or—either perfect knowledge or no knowledge at all—and still move forward on the basis of a relative knowledge as produced in the process of signification. Such knowledge is relative in four respects. It is relative to the theoretical problematic in which the text is produced, and to the subject for whom the text thus becomes an object. It cannot be "referred up" to some absolute epistemological principle. And it is relative also to the materiality of the text, a materiality that resists differentially any process of signification in which the text is read. Knowledge of literary texts is constructed within a specific form of discourse and that which is so constructed is knowledge. How could it be otherwise?

17

The Critical Difference:
Adorno's Aesthetic Alternative

Wilhelm S. Wurzer

The petals of time fall immensely
like vague umbrellas looking like the sky,
growing around, it is scarcely
a bell never seen,
a flooded rose, a jellyfish, a long
shattered throbbing:
but it's not that, it's something that
scarcely touches and spends,
a confused trace without sound or birds,
a dissipation of perfumes and races.
                                        —Pablo Neruda

Deconstruction's remarkably significant bearing for contemporary criticism and philosophy may be attributed to Derrida's grammatological claim that the text does not reveal a pure dynastic presence of itself. "The present in general is not primal, but rather, reconstituted ... it is not absolute."[1] The dismantling of the presence/absence distinction and of other binary philosophical forms of the logocentric fallacy is not limited to the deconstructive method. Indeed, Adorno's aesthetics of negativity reveals the paradox of presence in the proposition: "The whole is that which is false."[2] Disintegration of meaning and subversion of metaphysics within an "originary" text are emphasized throughout Adorno's aesthetic enterprise. *Minima Moralia*, *Negative Dialectics*, *Prisms*, and *Aesthetic Theory* disclose a philosophical writing that is strikingly similar to Derrida's post-Saussurean reading of logocentrism. It is not my purpose here to enumerate the similarities but, rather, to point to the "essential" difference between Derrida's *différance* and Adorno's dialectic *idiosyncracy*. I intend to describe this difference primarily in relation to the conflict that arises between dialectic and grammatology. From this perspective I hope to show how Adorno's critical-aesthetic alternative to deconstruction may provide the reader with a creative understanding of the social and cultural traces of writing. Concomitantly, I will argue that the dialectical alternative does not negate the deconstructive strategy in its dynamic and fruitful criticism of subjectivity; instead, it restrains the reader's willingness to subvert the significance of such possible exterior textual references as the *aesthetic* and *social* dimension.

Let me begin with the core of the problem concerning deconstruction and dialectic—that is, with the way deconstruction thinks the "concept" of trace (*Spur, ichnos*). Derrida affirms the affinity of trace and *différance*, but denies the necessary relation of dialectic *and différance*—"because the trace itself could never itself appear as such."[3] Since *différance* too does not present itself, it is thought, by Derrida, to irrevocably surpass the dialectic relations of signifier/signified. Hence the very trace of *différance* seems to vanish from the negative "eye" of dialectic. "Tout est abîme!"[4] In the absence of dialectic aqua vitae, what will prevent Derrida's "flowers" of deconstruction from wilting? Is it necessary for deconstruction to disrupt the dialectic when the latter may have no desire to refurbish the representational ground of metaphysics?

Adorno's negative dialectic renounces the determination of being as presence without recanting the "presence" of dialectical thinking. The dialectical enterprise is involved in the process of decentering the rationality of Western ideology, and, therefore, need not be designated as logocentric. Neither the disintegration of the subject nor *Rezeptionsästhetik* is able to efface the dialectic trace.[5] Thinking, according to Adorno, cannot abdicate the conceptual activity of mediations, even, if in its modern stream, it has, from time to time, advanced upon the political bank of melancholy. On the other side of the stream, there may yet lie hope for *das Naturschöne. Ratio* may still be linked to the perspective of "the beauty of nature" without being muffled by the absolute consciousness of Hegel's *Geist*. Disinterest in dialectic may detach readers from a concrete analysis of the text and isolate them in "interpretive" *free play*. The dialectic does not erase "the silent spelling mistake" of *différance*. Instead, it "presents" *différance* as a historic play of differences without submitting to a system of *Identitätsdenken*. "Dialectical mediation is not a recourse to the more abstract, but a process of resolution of the concrete in itself."[6]

Let me, more tangibly, show why Derrida need not step outside negative dialectic to determine the movement of *supplementarity* in order to reveal the textual violence of *différance. Supplementarity* involves a dimension of free play that attacks totalization and judges nontotalization from an immense interpretive view. No longer is the text assumed to have a unity of meaning, for such a unity would merely formalize a limited interpretation. The horizon of dialectic is "thought" to be breached in favor of a process of seminal *différance* called *dissémination*. "Dissemination . . . although producing a non-finite number of semantic effects, can be led back neither to a present of simple origin . . . nor to an eschatological presence. It marks an irreducible and *generative* multiplicity."[7] Infinite substitutions of "meaning" are brought into play in Derrida's *travail de textes*, a process that permits the absence of a field of reference. The horizon of center or origin vanishes like the notion of time in Márquez's "Monologue of Isabel Watching It Rain in Macondo": "What should have been Thursday was a physical, jellylike thing that could have been parted with the hands in order to look into Friday."[8]

The deconstructive fate of the dialectic may indeed be that of "the last voyage of the ghost ship" called metaphysics. When the foundation of thinking is shattered, the Nietzschean deconstructor may be surprised to hear only "the neat destruction of ninety thousand five hundred champagne glasses breaking, one after the other."[9] The literary work of art may then appear as "a swarm of objects that call without being answered, and a ceaseless movement"[10] and the artist may fade as *un hombre confuso*. What is to prevent Heidegger's "house of being" from becoming *una casa sola*, "where the guests come in at night wildly drunk, and there is a smell of clothes thrown on the floor, and an absence of flowers?"[11]

Challenged by the urgent task of thinking, Adorno, the apparently abandoned one, were he alive today, might gently say to the deconstructionist: "You are, you are perhaps, the man or woman or the tenderness that deciphered nothing . . . on treading you did not know that from the blind earth comes forth the *ardent day of steps* that seek you."[12] Aesthetic dialectic is a new sonata which reveals "the ardent day of steps," or the future traces of disseminating unities gathering around us. There is mist in every open space, but the dialectic "clock" has not yet fallen into the sea. Abandoning eternal identity, *chronos* unites with works of art by transmitting diverse, dynamic images from the controlled field of representations to nonconceptual constellations of hope. Nietzschean readers may want to actively forget the *via negativa* and meditate upon Derrida's *via rupta* where "the clock that in the field stretched out upon the moss and struck a hip with its electric form runs rickety and wounded beneath the fearful water that ripples palpitating with central currents."[13] Adorno's dialectic, however, seeks no oblivion of "foundations".

To think that aesthetic dialectic is still in complicity with a teleological metaphysics of presence is structurally alluring. Dialectic may remain historical without being "conceived as the movement of a resumption of history."[14] Kant had already begun to disengage the dialectic from its logocentric moorings. Adorno completes the disruption of eschatological presence by letting dialectic "immigrate" into the "region" of the art work. This aesthetic orientation overturns the traditional meaning of dialectic (Plato, Hegel, Marx) without devitalizing the "dialectic energy" that confronts the dissolution of the subject. Dialectic theory remains outside the realm of totality and penetrates into the immanent nonidentity of the text. The latter is not conceived as a signified structure that a knowing signifier may readily represent. Adorno recognizes that "fidelity to one's own state of consciousness and experience is forever in temptation of lapsing into infidelity, by denying the insight that transcends the individual and calls his substance by its name."[15] Thus deconstruction's aim of a reductio ad absurdum of any dogmatic claim to finality is not dismissed by negative dialectic.

Adorno's method, schooled in Hegel's *Phänomenologie des Geistes*, insists that negativity be affirmed as the "essential" movement of the disseminating text. His aesthetics does not concede the *free play* of turning away from the negative. In accordance with Hegel's thought:

> The life of the mind only attains its truth when discovering itself in absolute desolation. The mind is not this power as a positive which *turns away from the negative*, as when we say of something that it is null, or false, so much for that and now for something else; it is this power only when looking the negative in the face, dwelling upon it.[16]

The work of art is such a negative and its dialectic does not evaporate disagreeables.

To avoid *die leere Tiefe* (empty profundity), thinking must delimit the grammatological project so that its heterogeneity does not develop into a(n) (in)different "ground." The missing center of deconstruction assents to indefinitizing modes of reading *gram*. What is written, or on a wider textual scene, what is painted, composed, and performed is still a structure consisting of elements that are interrelated. The polysemy of a text is only possible on the "basis" of the "interactive" relation of words. Words may not be returned to the author as subject and may not be absolved from the free play of substitutions. Words are not free from the disseminative process of *spacing* "defined" as "the impossibility for an identity to be closed on itself."[17] Nor does *spacing* surmount the disintegrating movement of negative dialectic, which shares deconstruction's disenchantment with logocentrism.

Adorno's "adherence" to the heterogeneous retains its fidelity to the dialectic *and* to philosophy's radical alterity. The nonconceptual may be experienced beyond the logocentric sphere, as, for instance, in *The Trial*, where Kafka shows Joseph K's unbroken urge to determine his situation. As he "spaces" from one building to the next, through halls and lobbies, up and down staircases and passageways, his confrontations with the law expose displaced images of life's darkling moments. The completely unnatural world of *The Trial* may not be understood by K., but he is still not less reflective because of it. Indeed, he repeatedly observes the desolation of human feelings and thoughts. Adorno realizes that Kafka does not pump metaphysical substance into the text. In fact, for Adorno, "the artist is not obliged to understand his own art, and there is particular reason to doubt whether Kafka was capable of such understanding."[18] Dialectic undertakes to reveal precisely this nonteleological understanding. Were this not so, "the work of art would be stillborn; it would exhaust itself in what it says and would not unfold itself in time."[19] Hence, negative dialectic is kept from the hermeneutic short-circuit "which jumps directly to the significance intended by the work."[20]

A deconstructive reader cannot throw to the winds the fact that the closure of identity rests upon relating one element of thought to another. Interminable textual analysis inscribes a multiplicity of generative positions. "Inscription is not a simple position: it is rather that by means of which every position is *of itself confounded (différance)*: inscription, mark, text, and not only *thesis* or *theme*—inscription of the *thesis*."[21] Determining different positions involves thinking dialectically, for a determinate negation does not entail a single position. "*Omnis determinatio negatio est*."[22] Spinoza's terse description of the dialectic should urge deconstruction to reflect more seriously upon negative dialectic, lest deconstruction fall victim to a linguistic abstraction of presence.

In *Die Phänomenologie des Geistes*, Hegel illuminates the dubiety of a mode of thinking that claims that difference is not derived from any dialectic. Such difference may eject the world from the text, leaving behind a writing that emerges as a "lifeless indifference" similar to the Stoic self-reflection: "The aim of self-consciousness is to be free and to maintain that lifeless indifference which steadfastly withdraws from the bustle of existence, alike from being active or passive, into the simple essentiality of thought."[23] Hegel is fully aware of the deceptions philosophy may yield to when it disconnects its thinking from the text of social reality. This kind of "free" thinking may be a delightful solace as Boethius occasionally thought during his stay in prison. It may even provide "metaphysical comfort" as Nietzsche discerned in his nihilistic reflections on Western culture.

Hegel, however, never relates philosophy to the comfort of renouncing the dialectic *via negativa*. Such free play is "*indifferent* to natural existence and has therefore *let this equally go free*."[24] Dialectical phenomenology refuses to assent to a notion of freedom that is rooted in the *interval* of an exclusive difference. In such a deconstructive state both freedom and reflection remain unmediated. And then: "Freedom in thought has only *pure* thought as its truth, and truth lacking the fullness of life."[25] Hegel discounts the "non-dialectical" mode of consciousness because it *plays* abstractly with its capacity to think by approaching the "infinity" of the text carelessly. "During thought, consciousness effaces its content, indeed, as an estranged being"[26] Dialectic is then "eradicated" as a "foreign *being*" and the "self-identity of thought is only the pure form in which nothing is determined."[27] It is not difficult to see that thinking is not what is called thinking when determinate nothingness is "playfully" absent.

Dissemination, therefore, cannot relinquish "the ardent day of steps" recognized by an aesthetic dialectic whose "difference is here understood as a relational concept, rather than as the mere inert inventory of unrelated diversity."[28] If grammatological displacements no longer refer to "negative moments" of exterior reality, a disseminative procedure of multiple readings may inevitably lead to the "semination" of a one-dimensional *travail de textes*. The presence of writing would then "establish" a grammatological self-identity not unlike the "lifeless indifference" of pure self-reflection. Without the dialectic trace of textual negativity, Derrida's *différance* may cut itself off from "the possibility of differencing itself as all difference degenerates to a nuance in the monotony of the supply"[29] of *gram*.

This kind of academic *jeu* would serve to energize a circle of interpretations beyond social and historical forces of production by projecting a thinking that thinks writing within the deferring process of thinking alone. Even Derrida admits this possible "error," unconsciously, when he writes: "We shift and recommence the very project of philosophy under the privileged heading of Hegelianism."[30] Thus, thinking, if it will be called thinking, will be, invariably, dialectical with or without a center, which means, of course, that it must relate its *Sein* to *différance*—beyond the scene of writing.

The dialectic suggests that readers may deconstruct a text expressing the reality of material production, but not deconstruct "the growing barbarism of economic hegemony."[31] The reader's "inability" to deconstruct the negative exterior text of society "influences" their "ability" to displace the "content" of the literary work. This "positional influence," if you will, imprints its form in a *deconstructive judgment* that may reveal the social tendencies of powerful interests without legitimizing a systematic interpretation of these interests. Consequently, a disseminative convergence of deconstruction *and* aesthetic dialectic would not only mean a "vigilant practice of textual division"[32] but also "intransigence towards all reification."[33] Adorno's later philosophy of *Ästhetische Theorie* attempts to confront the supplementary way of reading inherent in the dialectical enterprise with a "prismatic reference" to society. Thus his "theory" of the *Kunstwerk* avoids both the abstract contamination of meaning discovered in a non-dialectical process of interpretation and the concrete contamination of meaning discerned in a dogmatic social analysis.

I will show how Adorno counteracts the "hermeneutic short-circuit" and how his "idiosyncratic" dialectic generates a productive critical-aesthetic alternative to deconstruction.

Interpretation and *Kunstwerk* are no longer merely conceived in a subject-object relation. The decline of a reconstructive hermeneutics is apparent in Adorno's critique of *prima philosophia* in general and in his critique of the idea of aesthetic origin in particular. "Art has its concept in a historically changing constellation of moments. Its essence *cannot be ascertained by its origin*."[34] The reader's quest for a discursive social framework transcends the habitual crutches of a hermeneutics that purports to know what the art object is about. Readers may delight not only in contemplative textual pleasures but are also expected to participate in the inner movement of the art work's technique. This involves "the most acute attention to simultaneous multiplicity, the intensive perception of the unique and specific,"[35] without desiring to look for "the best theory." The notion of complementarity is primary in Adorno's aesthetic "theorizing." This means that an artwork may require diverse points of view, which are guided by historical constellations interminably challenging a singular description. For instance, the work of art is "read" not as an invariant phenomenon but as an *Augenblick* (lit., a look of the eye). Each work of art "expresses" the intensity and "truth" of the moment (*Augenblick*).

The paradox of Adorno's notion of aesthetic reality lies in the twofold character of the text: autonomy and social *mimesis*. "Art as social antithesis of society is not to be directly ascertained by it."[36] This suggests that the literary text is always a *work in progress* and as such *opposes* and "*presents*" the negative movement of society. Its form, however, is never determined entirely by society. As the radical other, the art work is not "repressed" by the Marxist intention, though it may be linked to it momentarily. The autonomy of art negates the social "spirit of gravity" without destroying those social moments that "determine" aesthetic intertextuality. Presenting social truth, the work of art is not a *mimesis* in the logocentric sense, but is a *promesse du bonheur*.[37] The heterogeneity of Adorno's aesthetics lies in *das Naturschöne*, a concept that—as I shall briefly explain —may disappoint both the "left" and the "right" deconstructors.

Dialectical thought "immigrates" into the work of art in order to free itself from the presence of the subject and the dominance of *die Sachen selbst*. It thereby withdraws from the logocentric devastations of Hegel's aesthetic idealism and Marx's social realism. But in the process of dialectic's ontological exodus and its aesthetic emergence, the work of art does not forsake the concept. "Art is reason, which it criticizes without leaving it behind."[38] Thus art needs the concept, for it cannot express itself conceptually.

The text never appears as a *system* of meanings that may simply be elucidated by interpreters. If the text appears at all, it shows itself as a crisis, indeed as *the* crisis of art itself. Therefore, a theory of art becomes necessary again. But this necessity is not to be affirmed from a solely Marxist or purely deconstructive perspective, or merely from a constellation of these positions. The reason for this is deceptively simple: Adorno's *Kunsttheorie* deconstructs Marx's master theory of society and other originary ideologies. Aesthetic *idiosyncracy*, however, does not depart from the social text; instead, it directs our interests in "understanding" the work of art to the phenomenal aspects of that text, namely to *das Naturschöne*.

"*—Hypocrite Lecteur,—mon semblable,—mon frére!*"[39] The dialectic is now idiosyncratic: empirical or intellectual intuition is no longer its reference. It is free *from* the presence of identity and free *for* the "presence" of the beauty of nature. The dialectic is still knowledge oriented, but knowledge is not directed toward objects but *Kunstwerke*. Together with art, dialectic has become dissonant in its diverse "expressions of meanings." Therein lies the idiosyncracy of an aesthetic theory that veiws the work of art as a "windowless monad," both *social* and *natural* in its negative activity. The dialectic elicits the text as a modern monad that reveals the interpretive constellations of society (*Gesellschaft*) and the beauty of nature (*Naturschöne*). The beauty of nature is conceived as the free model of the nonidentical, which is no longer superseded by the metaphysical coercion of identity. It appears that *das Naturschöne* becomes what nature could be, if it were freed from domination. The work of art is now "dis-played" as a trace of that possible freedom. Adorno's *goût du néant* is not enhanced by nature but by *the trace of nature*, which is beautiful yet not systematically permanent. Akin to music, the *Naturschöne* is indefinite. It shines beautifully through the darkness of the text and—like Derrida's *différance*—it cannot be appropriated. It is not a thing; it is *nothing*, as is the dialectic. "The beautiful in nature is the trace ["*Spur*"] of the non-identical in things within the spell of universal identity."[40]

Aesthetic dialectic does not defer appropriation of meaning; it negates any attempt to appropriate a *system* of thought. Instead of describing the presence of beings, the dissonant theory "inscribes" the *apparition* of textuality. *Apparition*, a term Adorno employs to "subvert" the idea of essence in a text, enables the beautiful image to *appear* and *disappear* in the work of art so that it may never emerge as a fixed idea. Art may then become what nature desires to—but cannot—write; this idiosyncracy occurs when the dialectic is engaged in intertextuality. The aesthetic "harmony" that is attained is merely the dialectic adventure of the trace of nature, an adventure that is not foreign to *écriture*. "That is why art needs philosophy to interpret it and to say what art cannot say, although art alone can say it: by not saying it."[41]

18

Poststructuralist Alternatives to Deconstruction

Arnaud Villani

In "The Ends of Man" (delivered at a 1968 colloquium in New York), Jacques Derrida reviews French philosophy in the preceding three decades. In an uncommonly clear fashion, he provides a critical panorama emphasizing two distinct discontinuities: the one, a break with humanism and metaphysics through deconstructive strategy (and conjointly with structuralism, the opening of the epistemic terrain of contemporary French thought); and the other, induced symmetrically by the former, but stated without the same precision: "In order to mark in boldface the traits that opposed this period to the following one, the one we are in, and which is probably also undergoing mutation. . . . "[1] Correspondingly, I shall try to be explicit about the changes that must have taken place between 1968 and 1973, and which, for short, I shall call "poststructuralism." And keeping in mind Derrida's own aversion to any kind of *Aufhebung*, I shall attempt to define the discontinuity by asking whether it is simply an event of deconstruction, an augmentation of deconstruction, or something radically irreducible to deconstruction altogether.

Like Plato's *Parmenides*, which offers a critique of the theory of Ideas, Derrida comments upon alternatives to deconstruction and the strategies that are compatible with the maintenance of a self-criticism. Thus "the reduction of meaning"[2] that appears as a feature of structuralism also belongs to the *Aufhebung* of hermeneutics, even if (and because) it constitutes a "critique of phenomenology" (and hence of the Husserlian "reduction of meaning"). If there is to be a real alternative, it will have to be "the strategic bet." As Derrida puts it, one can:

(1) Attempt an exit and a deconstruction without changing terrain . . . by using against the edifice the instruments or stones available in the house. . . . One risks ceaselessly confirming, consolidating, *relifting* (*relever*), at an always more certain depth, that which one allegedly deconstructs.
(2) Decide to change terrain, in a discontinuous and irruptive fashion, by brutally placing oneself outside, and by affirming an absolute break and difference. Without mentioning all the other forms of *trompe-l'oeil* perspective in which such a displacement can be caught (thereby inhabiting more naively and more strictly than ever the inside one declares one has deserted) the simple practice of language ceaselessly reinstates new terrain on the oldest ground.[3]

Derrida considers a third possibility located in the Nietzschean difference between the "superior man" and the "overman." The former will be abandoned to its last movement of pity. The second "awakens and leaves, without returning to what he leaves behind him. He burns his text and erases the traces of his steps. His laughter will then burst out. . . . He will dance, outside the house, . . . the active forgetting and the cruel feast of which the *Geneology of Morals* speaks."[4]

By contrast to this very programatic text, François Laruelle returns to Derrida's project. In *Les machines textuelles*, he attempts to "carry out an analysis of deconstructive techniques and to displace their problematic onto neighboring positions."[5] Laruelle is particularly conscious of the "blind" traps that Derrida invokes when speaking of "*trompe-l'oeil* perspective." He even writes: "So as to reduce the violence of deconstructions, at the risk of an ideological regression. . . ." But like Diogenes, he takes the next step. This step is resolutely opposed to representation, opposed to structuralism, but also opposed to the infinite text (commentary upon commentary), the sort of lay Talmudic text with its play of mirrors (*mimesis* without priority given to the imitated). Laruelle takes from deconstruction what Hyppolite had already discovered in Mallarmé — namely, a "materialism of the idea" (or what might be called "strategic dissymmetry"[6] — but not at the level of an (empirical) fact nor at the level of a (transcendent) Idea but rather as a transcendental-immanent function. This major preoccupation with the transcendental parodies itself in order to avoid appearing as the starting point of a system (as, for instance, in the systematic and ironic replacement of every "e" by an "a" in important philosophical terms). Laruelle's thesis goes as follows:

In deconstruction, the way to bring an end to whatever there "can" still be of representation, of secretly linguistic and structuralist presuppositions, and in particular the presupposition that there might be nothing other than the text and that all referents might be ideologically reduced to textuality, is to transform it into a mechanical process, to transfer it to the libido *qua* libido of writing.[7]

In this way Laruelle tries to substitute the "orphan" theme of "the desiring function" for the anthropological theme of practice, "machine processes" for deconstructive techniques, machines for those who operate them. He clearly shows that this is an alternative to deconstruction (taken to its highest degree of intensity—even to the nth power), and thereby surpasses it in a non-Hegelian way. Considering all the possible objections against the *other* deconstruction, Laruelle comments:

> We cannot see any other way to specify deconstruction, to distinguish it, except radically, from the signifying practices of linguistic, structuralist, or textual representations of textuality, where it begins to place under erasure, but where, in our view, it perhaps does not place under erasure vigorously enough.[8]

Laruelle has read his Derrida quite well. He remembers the final sentence of "The Ends of Man" where Derrida writes: "Perhaps we are between two eyes, which are also two ends of man. But who, we?"[9] "Who deconstructs?," asks Laruelle. And, furthermore, what can be said of the non-anthropological, deconstructing *subject*?

The process of differentiating deconstruction from its doubles, which are still metaphysical, is certainly inscribed in deconstruction itself. But the virtue of Laruelle's contribution (already following Derrida) is that he finds an external lever in Nietzsche that allows the "blank," the "fold," the "hymen" to appear between Derrida's text and its copies. This "veil which is hardly perceptible between Platonism and itself, Hegelianism and itself,"[10] must also pass between Derrida and himself. This lever bears the names of "Eternal Return" and "Will to Power." Transposed into a "generalized economy," it acquires the new names of "generalized repetition" and "intensive libido."[11] "Generalized libido is a supple and plastic function and the only energy in change sufficient to bring about the unconscious differential syntheses of any text."[12] This generalized repetition (as in a theatrical performance or *répétition*, as in Kierkegaardian "repetition," or, as in what can be called "differential repetition") applies primarily and strategically to deconstruction itself. The deconstructive return of the same is an affirmative disengagement from what is most specific in deconstruction—namely, its desire for its own end: "The deconstruction of the sign: 'text,' or 'sign,' is the greatest task of deconstruction, which must also wish its own decline, its consummation in the very libido which it seeks to liberate."[13] Once these metaphysical, idealist, hermeneutic, and structuralist signs have disappeared, what remains is "a machine-like process, a power to metamorphose, which can be characterized as textual, a process of production, reproduction, and consumption of signs."[14] Laruelle speaks of "disengaging" (by means of a kind of analytic

cure) that which is a "mechanical and energetic possibility" in deconstruction, and of "tapping" its "own power of repetition."[15] Two most
interesting themes arise from this procedure: (1) post-structuralism and
(2) the bridging of Derrida and Deleuze.

The machinelike process as reproduction and consummation of signs
has "placed structuralism and linguistics six thousand feet under."[16] This
involves an "auto-dislocation of structuralism,"[17] a "*séisme* which upsets
the structural order in structuralism itself."[18] At the same time, this
machinelike process, borrowed from *Anti-Oedipus*, makes the linking of
Derrida and Deleuze possible. And Laruelle writes:

> Is it a matter of *difference* in the systems . . . of Derrida and Deleuze? Between
> the two series, one Derridean, the other Deleuzian, I have employed a tool
> that is more or less capable of capturing and redistributing the resonance
> effects between repetition and textuality.[19]

In order to assess whether Laruelle's strategic approach is viable, and
in order to see whether it constitutes a real alternative to deconstruction,
let us place both Derrida and Deleuze in direct juxtaposition. In this way,
we will be able to determine whether the relation between them is one of
alternative, one of development, one of *Aufhebung*, one of a break, or
whether it remains simply "indecidable."

If one wants to fully grasp the concept of deconstruction, one cannot
avoid detecting a trace of positivity in the negative movement appropriate to the *Aufhebung*. Although this is precisely what Derrida refuses,
and for absolutely valid reasons, there is nevertheless an "*other*" to the
Aufhebung—namely, the Heideggerian *Verwindung* (a concept that can
also be translated as "surpassing" as well as "overcoming"). This concept
will take us to the very heart of what is at stake here. As Derrida remarks,
in "The Ends of Man," since "every humanism remains metaphysical"[20]
the primary task is to get rid of humanism by "surpassing" metaphysics.[21]
Let us remember that Heidegger comments on *Verwinden* by appealing
to the expression: "overcoming one's tears." This implies self-control and
presumption, pretense, persistence of the negative, and refusal to surrender to it.

From the very outset, overcoming is already a matter of minute discrepancies. According to Heidegger, "going beyond metaphysics" means
"stepping back," which is neither a long detour, nor one more search
after an original cause. Rather it is a quest for difference, for deviation.
This genetic difference can only be reached through repetition (by asking
the question of Being). And that difference—as minimal as a Lucretian
"swerve" (i.e., nothing more than what Michel Serres would describe as
the representation of a *tangent point* or an *eddy* in fluid physics)—

produces an even wider *gap* between the classical presocratic line (to which Heidegger returns) and the natural philosophy line (which takes over in Plato). The latter forces a *refraction* of the presocratic point of view into its virtual image (which has no factual existence except in the *classical perspective*). It is no surprise that the presocratics were distorted even long before Hegel, Nietzsche, and Heidegger (see figure below).

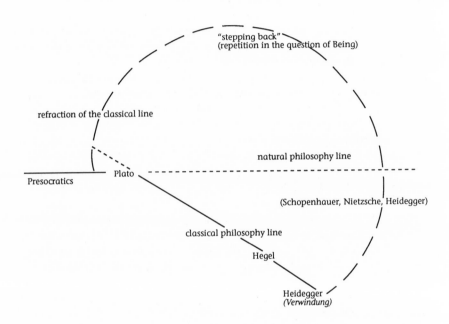

We need to be clear about the meaning of this division of philosophy into two lines, for perhaps deconstruction is only trying to mimic this division. It is not a matter of two types of philosophy established in order to discover a relation between domination and dominated, of putting a "computer" tradition in place, of the *Gestell* as "mastery" of the *ratio*— with its meditation on the simple, the clearing (*Lichtung*), or the enigma of *physis*—in short, of replacing a "philosophy of value" with a "philosophy of Being." Philosophy, now double, becomes *indecidable* as well (namely, both poison and remedy, rationalist and meditative, maximalist and infinitist, continuous and discontinuous, perennial and subterranean). Fundamentally doubled, obverse and converse (Sophists/Plato; Spinoza/Descartes; Herder/Kant; Schopenhauer/Hegel; Heidegger/Husserl), philosophy has not in any case ceased to function. After Socrates and before

Nietzsche, like an *unhappy consciousness* that elicits its own exteriorized image—that is, "the figure of the ideal"—philosophy at the same time devalues its own "changing consciousness."

However, in order to retrieve philosophy's duality, have we been sufficiently warned against the "return of the tragic," a repeat of dual unity (*unitas multiplex*) or simple "rivalry" (*polemos*)? A certain reading of Heidegger could make such thinking possible. However, inasmuch as deconstruction involves "dissemination" (and not "gathering"), it is formally forbidden. In fact, deconstructing speech does not imply writing as *arché* or *telos*. And dissemination is not only the "in-between" (*l'entre-deux*) or "quasi-sense" as the "impossible return to a rejoined unity, reinfused with meaning." Nevertheless dissemination does "reaffirm the still divided generation of meaning" without the negative prohibition of unitary meaning as virgin substance. Dissemination is what Mallarmé calls "*l'épars*" (the scattered). Dissemination is diffraction of meaning and not regulated polysemy. The question, which brings together all alternatives to deconstruction (should they exist!), is thus: What is the status of a nonsymbolic (nonpolemical) duality?

Structuralism *per se* is asymbolic. Certain texts by Roland Barthes[22] indicate that the symbolic (in the sense of a "plural language," "a constructive ambiguity," and a "dramatic discourse") is, in reality, parody. As Ferdinand de Saussure's archetypal scheme shows, the relation between the signifier and the signified is, in the structural sense, the *empty form* of a *symbolon*. What is missing is "the unity," "the break," "the *polemos*," and "the infinity." This "emptying" (*évidement*) facilitates the recreation of meaning as *immanence* by means of "relations," "serial combinations," and "games involving couples" (paradigm/syntagm, diachrony/synchrony, denotation/connotation, metaphor/metonymy, etc.).

In a 1967 article, Gilles Deleuze provides a very clear account of the identifying marks of structuralism.[23] Seriality, differentiality, "symbolic" elements, metaphor, metonymy, and the "empty square" are its distinctive features. In particular, a rather constant element in structuralist and "Tel Quel" literature is the role of the "empty square" or "empty space."[24] This idea reintroduces the lack appropriate to desire (of the Hegelian variety) by way of the "black box." The trap in the "return of the tragic" brings about a negativity that recovers everything. The *paradoxal object*, the "$= x$," the nectarine, the neuter, the eighth part, the empty chair, the what-is-not-in-its-place—each according to its particular form of denomination—makes it possible to link up Hjelmslev and Bataille, Lévi-Strauss and Blanchot, de Saussure and Levinas. The lack, in its very ambiguity, surreptitiously authorizes the reintroduction of *force* in a system of pure relations. The lack is in effect a symbolic split, an unfulfilled metaphor, a "hole in Being," a culpability, a sense of ungrounding [*effondement*], and the Other—all this is indissociably theological and atheological, metaphysical and deconstructive, pacifying ("oh, what a shame!") and violent, mediator and cause of disruption.

This "empty space" or "empty square" in structuralism makes the thought of the 1960s and 1970s particularly anti-Hegelian, while also maintaining in its recovery of a negative desire, barred, and lacking its object in a nonaccidental way. To be anti-Hegelian in this way brings comfort to Hegel, while also enlarging his field of action. The essentials remain present and allow for the view that an *Aufhebung* cannot be surpassed. Derrida has understood the trap quite well. His reaction is different from that of Deleuze and Lyotard (who are violently anti-Hegelian on the question of desire). For them, desire is not at all negative. Derrida considers Hegel unsurpassable,[25] but not insurmountable. He respects the master and enters into a double game with him, resulting not in anti-Hegelianism but para-Hegelianism. It is a "minute discrepancy" but one that pretends to say the same thing while also being very different.

The "blank," "the hymen," the "fold," the "veil"—these *"differences without decidable poles"*—eliminate the signified and are therefore no longer subject to the imperative of the "empty space" or "empty square," nor to the hidden sense of "Totality" that it presupposes. Here then, discursivity and textuality together change the sense. A new status for duality surpasses the empty space and the obsession for metaphor and metonymy —like syntagmatic and paradigmatic interserial relations— which "leap out of the discursive system and are kept from functioning as discourse." This is perhaps the genius of Raymond Roussel, who links discursivity (which remains enclosed in its narratives) with the machine-like (where the imagination continually races toward the genetic).[26] Thus the bill/pill [*"billiard/pilliard"*] which inspired Foucault[27] and Deleuze[28] is not just a minute discrepancy but a link between unmatchable series of words and things, of "eating" and "speaking" (as in Artaud and Lewis Carroll with their different word combinations [*mots valises*].

Discourse is therefore neither immanence nor a transcendental condition. Yet there exists an "immanence outside discourse, which is nevertheless not metaphysical," which involves force as function, fit, "desire to love," "desiring machine. . . ." And Derrida's "in-between,"[29] as well as his "dissymetry"[30] or "parting" (*l'épars*),[31] are also found in Deleuze at approximately the same time, along with "asymmetrical zig-zag," "intermezzo," and "dispersal" (*dispars*). What these terms announce, accompany, or follow indecidably is the central theory of disparative encounter. With Deleuze, this kind of "acephalous, anarchic, and orphan" short-circuit, which pairs up the major points of the two series, activates the "tangent point of the differential" and carries it to the nth power. And furthermore, Deleuze's account also makes the dissymetrical link between the wasp and the orchid, between words and things, between humans and animals, all according to stages of becoming.[32]

Inasmuch as Laruelle tries to designate the textual as machine-like and transcendental, what he envisions becomes clear. Laruelle wants to open up the textual aspect of Tel Quel structuralism into what Derrida had already foreseen but insufficiently developed by breaking up the transfer of genetic and violent themes in the textual circle. There is insufficient space here to develop and ascertain the limits of the rich promise that this theory carries with it. However, it is important to note that the "dispersal" (*dispars*) surpasses the blank space by taking its place and by fitting exactly into it. However, the "dispersal" (*dispars*) does not carry the mark of the "horrible *Ananké*" which turns against its own desire (in accordance with Freud's theory of Thanatos). With a real, radically new alternative we finally reach full, positive, affirmative desire. This tour de force is rendered possible by the total dispersal of the one, totalized, unary (*unaire*) subject's point of view. This "dispersal" (*dispars*) is affirmative, because it is indecidable. The immediate possibility of metamorphosis, as a "surmounted" metaphor, as a positive "escape"—leaping constantly not only from one series to another, but from a plateau formed by two series to the plateau of two others—sketching out Deleuze's picture of the *rhizome*, of "crabgrass," of what is "minor" and "stuttering."

The alternative to deconstruction thus appears in the "immanent use of the fourth synthesis of escape," which is both a key to Deleuzianism and a bridge from Derrida to Deleuze (and also to Foucault, Roussel . . .). This is accomplished not only by elaborating the necessary disappearance of the subject—and the "end of man"—but also by its profound finality. If one looks in the insurpassable direction inscribed since *Speech and Phenomena*, there is no alternative to deconstruction as a critique of *telos*, *arché*, "voice," "presence," "property/propinquity". . . . But, beyond the text, deconstruction itself becomes alternative (as in "alternating current"), establishing a "two-way switch," a "flash of lightning" between the series that constitutes the real (up to its minutest detail), and that which makes up our very *tissue*.

We, that is, the set of our own dispersals, are disseminated throughout the whole text of the real.[33]

Notes

Chapter 1
Christopher Fynsk: The Choice of Deconstruction

1. Translated by Marjorie Grene and collected in *Martin Heidegger and the Question of Literature; Toward a Postmodern Literary Hermeneutics*, ed. William V. Spanos (Bloomington: Indiana University Press, 1976), pp. 1-15.

2. I refer to Jacques Derrida's presentation of May 19, 1983, at Cornell University, "The Principle of Reason and the Idea of the University." A related argument concerning the demand that speaks in the principle of reason is developed in "Living On: Borderlines," in Bloom et al., *Deconstruction and Criticism* (New York: Seabury, 1979), pp. 75-175.

3. See in particular their contributions to the meetings of the Centre de recherches philosophiques sur le politique, collected in two volumes which they edited together: *Rejouer le politique* (Paris: Editions Galilée, 1981) and *Le retrait du politique* (Paris: Editions Galilée, 1983). See also the proceedings of the seminar on politics in *Les fins de l'homme; A partir du travail de Jacques Derrida*, eds. Philippe Lacoue-Labarthe and Jean-Luc Nancy (Paris: Editions Galilée, 1981).

4. I refer to an unpublished essay delivered at the IAPL conference in Orono, Maine, in May 1980: "Remarks on Thought and Science in *De la grammatologie*."

5. Martin Heidegger, "What is Metaphysics?," in *Basic Writings*, ed. David Krell (New York: Harper and Row, 1977), p. 96.

6. In Martin Heidegger, *Kant and the Problem of Metaphysics*, trans. James S. Churchill (Bloomington: Indiana University Press, 1962), p. 245 (translation slightly modified).

7. Jacques Derrida, *The Post Card*, trans. Alan Bass (Chicago: University of Chicago Press, 1987).

8. For the kind of philosophical treatment of the question of *mimesis* to which I am referring, see Derrida's essay "The Double Session" in *La dissémination* (Paris: Seuil, 1972), pp. 172-285, as well as Lacoue-Labarthe's "Typographie" in *Mimesis: des articulations* (Paris: Flammarion, 1975), pp. 165-270.

Chapter 2
Kathryn Kinczewski: Is Deconstruction an Alternative?

1. Wlad Godzich, "Introduction: Caution! Reader at Work!," in Paul de Man, *Blindness and Insight* (University of Minnesota Press, 1983), pp. xv-xxx.

2. Paul de Man, "Hypogram and Inscription: Michael Riffaterre's Poetics of Reading," in *The Resistance to Theory* (Minneapolis: University of Minnesota Press, 1986), pp. 27-53. (Hereafter, HI).

3. Godzich, "Introduction"; emphasis mine.

4. Martin Heidegger, *What Is A Thing?* (Chicago: Henry Regnery, 1967), pp. 1-2.

5. Martin Heidegger, *Qu'est-ce qu'une chose?* (Paris: Gallimard, 1971), p. 13.

6. Reinhard Kuhn, "Michael Riffaterre, *Semiotics of Poetry*," *Modern Language Notes* 94 (1979): 1199-1202.

7. Paul de Man, "Sign and Symbol in Hegel's *Aesthetics*," *Critical Inquiry* 8 (Summer 1982): 761-75.

8. The Riffaterre articles referred to and which often serve as cross-references to one another, are as follows: "Sémiotique intertextuelle: L'Interprétant," *Revue d'esthétique: Rhétoriques, sémiotiques* 1-2 (1979): 128-50; "Syllepsis," *Critical Inquiry* vol. 6, no. 4 (Summer 1980): 625-38; "L'Intertexte inconnu," *Littérature* 41 (February 1981) 4-7; "Interpretation and Undecidability," *New Literary History* vol. 12, no. 2 (Winter 1981): 227-42; and "La Trace de l'intertexte," *La pensée* 215 (October 1980): 4-18.

9. See Barbara Johnson's "Editor's Preface" and her article, "Teaching Ignorance: *L'Ecole des Femmes*" in *Yale French Studies*, no. 63 (1982): iii-vii and 165-82, respectively. In the preface Johnson writes,

> The gloss represents the desire to transform linguistic knowledge into existential knowledge and to fill gaps and discontinuities with causal explanations, moral judgments, or, at the very least, evaluative descriptions. The gloss, in other words, stands for a pedagogy that would repress the very stuff that literature is made of. But on the other hand, a reading . . . would suggest that teaching is a compulsion: a compulsion to repeat *what one has not*

understood. The locus of that non-understanding, the point at which rational continuity is eclipsed ... that blank is precisely what must—and cannot—be taught. And literature is the means by which such a blank—the very agony of teaching—can somehow, nevertheless, be captured [pp. vi-vii; emphasis mine].

10. See Michael Riffaterre, *Semiotics of Poetry*, p. 168, note 13, on abduction in Peirce's sense.

11. "Syllepsis," p. 638. See *La Production du texte*, (Paris: Seuil, 1979), p. 117, note 2, or "Syllepsis," pp. 625-26, concerning Riffaterre's distinctive use of the meaning/significance distinction (in particular, in contrast to E.D. Hirsch's).

12. Paul de Man, "The Purloined Ribbon," *Glyph* 1 (Johns Hopkins University Press, 1977), p. 46.

13. See not 5 above.

Chapter 3
Michael Fischer: Does Deconstruction Make Any Difference?

1. All page references are to Christopher Norris, *Deconstruction Theory and Practice* (London and New York: Methuen, 1982).

2. Subsequent page references are to J. Hillis Miller, "The Function of Rhetorical Study at the Present Time," in *The State of the Discipline 1970s-1980s*, ed. Jasper P. Neel (New York: Association of Departments of English, 1979).

Chapter 4
Eugenio Donato: Ending/Closure; On Derrida's Margining of Heidegger

1. Among the exemplary forms of argument used by the opponents of deconstruction, let me just quote the following two. The first is from Denis Donoghue's "Deconstructing Deconstruction," published in the June 12, 1980, issue of *The New York Review of Books*; the second is from Donald Reiman's letter to the editor of the February 18, 1983, issue of *The Times Literary Supplement*:

> I have only two or three thoughts on the subject. I think Deconstruction appeals to the clerisy of graduate students, who like to feel themselves superior to the laity of common readers, liberated from their shared meanings; liberated, too, from the tedious requirement of meaning as such, the official obligation to suppose that words mean something finite rather than everything or nothing. Deconstruction allows them to think of themselves as forming a cell, the nearest thing the universities can offer in the form of an avant-garde. The wretched side of this is that Deconstruction encourages them to feel superior not only to undergraduates but to the authors they are reading [p. 41].

Paul de Man, in particular, but the entire Yale school in effect, are mystifying literary studies in an effort to cut off students from the reformist and egalitarian values inherent in literary studies in America. By developing an arcane technical terminology and by demanding an exhausting apprenticeship in the reading of their own criticism (as well as in the works of selected European critics and philosophers), they close off from careers in teaching literature students of working-class background and those who began their studies at public (i.e., nontuition) schools in the American heartland (where the foreign language most widely taught is Spanish), or those who took undergraduate degrees at small colleges, where strong programmes in classical rhetoric, German philosophy, or contemporary French thought are rare and where interest in the relationships of literature to life is paramount [p. 159].

2. Rodolphe Gasché, "Deconstruction as Criticism" in *Glyph 6: Textual Studies* (Baltimore: Johns Hopkins University Press, 1979), pp. 177-215.

3. A recent text by Derrida himself—"The time of a thesis: punctuations," in *Philosophy in France Today*, ed. Alan Montefiore (Cambridge: Cambridge University Press, 1983), pp. 34-50—goes a long way toward clarifying part of the intellectual history that subtends his work. Derrida underscores how his interest in Husserl began as a reaction to the use of Husserlian phenomenology by Sartre and Merleau-Ponty. Derrida's statements in fact complicate considerably Gasché's history of deconstruction.

4. Jonathan Culler, *On Deconstruction: Theory and Criticism after Structuralism* (Ithaca: Cornell University Press, 1982), p. 85.

5. Jacques Derrida, *De la grammatologie* (Paris: Editions de Minuit, 1967), p. 90. All translations throughout this essay are my own. Subsequent quotations from Derrida's writings will be noted in the text as follows:

G: *De la grammatologie.*
VP: *La voix et le phénomène: introduction au problème du signe dans la phénoménologie de Husserl* (Paris: Presses Universitaires de France, 1972).
M: *Marges de la philosophie* (Paris: Editions de Minuit, 1972).
E: *Eperons: Les styles de Nietzsche* (Venice: Corbe e Fiore, 1976).
F: "D'un ton apocalyptique adopté naguère en philosophie," in *Les fins de l'homme: à partir du travail de Jacques Derrida* (Paris: Editions Galilée, 1981).

6. Defined elsewhere in the text as "appropriation, expropriation, prise, prise of possession, gift and exchange, mastery, servitude, etc." (E, 84).

7. See his "Typographie" in *Mimésis des articulations* (Paris: Aubier-Flammarion, 1975), pp. 165-270, and his *Le sujet de la philosophie* (Paris: Aubier-Flammarion, 1979).

8. Heidegger, *What is Called Thinking?*, trans. J. Glenn Gray (New York: Harper and Row, 1968), pp. 134-35.

9. Philippe Lacoue-Labarthe, *Le sujet de la philosophie*, (Paris: Aubier-Flammarion), p. 14.

Chapter 5
David Wood: The Possibility of Literary Deconstruction

1. Jacques Derrida, *Of Grammatology*, trans. Gayatri Chakravorty Spivak (Baltimore: Johns Hopkins University Press, 1967), (hereafter G).

2. Jacques Derrida, *Positions*, trans. Alan Bass (Chicago: University of Chicago Press, 1972), p. 10, (hereafter P).

3. Martin Heidegger, "Overcoming Metaphysics" in *The End of Philosophy*, trans. Joan Stambaugh (New York: Harper & Row, 1971), p. 85.

Chapter 6
Tina Chanter: Derrida and Heidegger: The Interlacing of Texts

1. Jacques Derrida, *De la grammatologie* (Paris: Editions de Minuit, 1967); *Of Grammatology*, trans. G.C. Spivak (Baltimore and London: Johns Hopkins University Press, 1976), p. 24/12). References will be given in the text, hereafter as G.

2. In 1956, twenty years after the lecture was first delivered, Martin Heidegger wrote an addendum to *Der Ursprung des Kunstwerkes* ("The Origin of the Work of Art"). Four years after it was written, the addendum was published in the Reclam edition (Stuttgart, 1960), trans. A. Hofstadter, *Poetry, Language, Thought* (New York: Harper & Row, 1971), pp. 17-87, hereafter UK. These notes draw the reader's attention to some key points in the essay, one of which is concerned with the unsatisfactory treatment of the relation between Being and human being. Heidegger's admission of the problematic status of this relation in "The Origin of the Work of Art" signals that the principal concern of that essay lies elsewhere. It lies in presenting a notion of truth that is not dependent upon resolving the problematic relation between Being and human being. Instead, it lies in presenting the disruptive experience of the strife of earth and world. Heidegger describes this experience in terms of rift (*Riss*) and framing (*Gestell*), where *Gestalt*—that which is fixed in place—"is always to be thought in terms of the particular placing (*Stellen*) and framing or framework (*Ge-stell*)" (UK, 71-2/64). Any allusion that Heidegger makes in such a context to what is proper to the self, any allusion to belonging, is far from naive. Moreover Derrida acknowledges Heidegger's caution in questioning what it means to belong, not only in his description of *Gestell* as an "out-of-work-supplement" that "cuts out but also sews up again" (R, 346/35, see Note 4 below), but also by reference to the trace. Which is not to say that the notion of the trace is foreign to Heidegger's thought. Nor is it to suggest that the same features, merely rearranged, exist in Heidegger's own text as in Derrida's commentary on it. It is perhaps to say that what constitutes Heidegger's 'own' text—or Derrida's for that matter—is up for question. Perhaps it is also to say that the trace is effective in the relation between Heidegger and Derrida—the trace effects their relation.

3. Meyer Schapiro, "The Still Life as a Personal Object—A Note on Heidegger and Van Gogh," in *The Reach of Mind: Essays in Memory of Kurt Goldstein* (New York: Springer, 1968), pp. 203-9.

4. Jacques Derrida, "Restitutions de la vérité en pointure," in *La vérité en peinture* (Paris: Flammarion, 1978), pp. 291-436. The first part of the French text of this essay was translated by J.P. Leavey and appears in *Research in Phenomenology*, vol. 8, 1978, pp. 1-43. Translations from the latter part of "Restitutions" are my own. References will henceforth be given in the text as R, followed by the English translation page numbers where possible. (An English translation of *La vérité en peinture*, by Geoff Bennington and Ian McLeod, has now been published by Chicago University Press as *The Truth in Painting*).

5. Jacques Derrida, "*Geschlecht: différence sexuelle, différence ontologique,*" in *L'Herne Martin Heidegger* (Paris: Editions de l'Herne, 1983), pp. 419-30. Trans. by John Leavey in *Research in Phenomenology*, vol. 13, 1983, pp. 65-83. References will henceforth be given in the text as GS.

6. In order to focus on the question of property, this account has left out much that is pertinent to Derrida's reading of Heidegger in "Restitutions," not least the details of Heidegger's undermining of the classical distinction between form and matter, Derrida's discussion of fetishism, and the significance of the shoes as a pair, and as therefore tied to a subject. For treatment of these issues, see the essays by N.J. Holland, "Heidegger and Derrida Redux: A Close Reading," and Dorothea Olkowski, "If the Shoe Fits—Derrida and the Orientation of Thought," both in *Hermeneutics and Deconstruction*, ed. H.J. Silverman and Don Ihde (Albany: SUNY Press, 1985).

7. Jacques Derrida, *Eperons: Les styles de Nietzsche/Spurs: Nietzsche's Styles*, a bilingual edition (Chicago: University of Chicago Press, 1979), (hereafter, S).

Chapter 7
Irene Harvey: The Différance Between Derrida and de Man

1. Paul de Man, *Allegories of Reading* (New Haven and London: Yale University Press, 1979), p. 17 (hereafter, AR).

2. Jacques Derrida, *Of Grammatology*, trans. Gayatri Spivak (Baltimore: Johns Hopkins University Press, 1976), p. 23 (hereafter, G).

3. AR, 187.

4. Jacques Derrida, *Positions*, trans. Alan Bass (Chicago: University of Chicago Press, 1981), pp. 40-41: "If there were a definition of *différance*, it would be precisely the limit, the interruption, the destruction of the Hegelian *relève wherever* it operates. What is at stake here is enormous. I emphasize the Hegelian *Aufhebung . . .*" (hereafter, P).

5. G, 24.

6. AR, 144.

7. Ibid., 125.

8. Ibid., 249.

9. P, 8.

10. G, 24.

11. Ibid., 99.

12. AR, 130.

13. Ibid., 125.

14. Ibid.

15. Ibid., 217.

16. Ibid., 199-200.

17. Ibid., 245.

18. Ibid., 298.

19. Ibid., 269.

20. Ibid., 299.

21. Jacques Derrida, *Margins of Philosophy*, trans. Alan Bass (Chicago: University of Chicago Press, 1982), p. 26n (hereafter MP).

22. MP, 19.

23. For more on this notion, see Derrida's essay entitled "From Restricted to General Economy" in *Writing and Difference*, trans. Alan Bass (Chicago: University of Chicago Press, 1978).

24. For Derrida's earliest work on this topic, especially concerning Rousseau, see G, pp. 95-317. For a later development, see *Glas*, trans. John R. Leavey, Jr. and Richard Rand (Lincoln: University of Nebraska Press, 1986).

25. Jacques Derrida, "White Mythology" in MP, 271: "The heliotrope can always be *relevé*. And it can always become a dried flower in a book. There is always, absent from every garden, a dried flower in a book; and by virtue of the repetition in which it endlessly puts itself into *abyme*, no language can reduce into itself the structure of an anthology."

Chapter 8
Paul de Man: Phenomenality and Materialism in Kant

1. Michel Foucault, *Les mots et les choses* (Paris: Editions Gallimard, 1966), p. 255: *"Le retrait du savoir et de la pensée hors de l'espace de la representation."* [Note that de Man emphasizes *retrait* as "retreat" as opposed to the standard English translation given in *The Order of Things* (New York: Random House,

1973), p. 242: the *withdrawal* of knowledge and thought outside the space of representation—ED.]

2. Immanuel Kant, *Kritik der Urteilskraft*, vol. 10 of *Werkausgabe* (Frankfurt am Main: Suhrkamp, 1978), ed. Wilhelm Weischedel, p. 90. English edition, *Critique of Judgement* (New York: Hafner, 1951), pp. 17-18. Subsequent references to this work cite two page numbers, the first for the German edition and the second for the English translation.

3. Blaise Pascal, *Pensées*, ed. Louis Lafuma (Paris: Editions du Luxembourg, 1951), 1: 199-390, 138.

4. Kant, *Logik* in *Werkausgabe*, 6:457.

5. Kant, *Betrachtung über das Gefühl des Schönen und Erhabenen* in *Werkausgabe*, 2:875.

6. Denis Diderot, *Lettre sur les sourds et les muets* in *Oeuvres complètes*, ed. Roger Lewinter (Paris: Club français du livre, 1969-73), 2:573-74.

7. Kant, *Kritik der Reinen Vernunft*, in *Werkausgabe*, 4:696.

Chapter 9
Rodolphe Gasché: On Mere Sight: Response to Paul de Man

1. For a discussion of the reasons why the *Third Critique* has given rise to relatively few critical works, see Donald W. Crawford, *Kant's Aesthetic Theory* (Madison: University of Wisconsin Press, 1974), pp. 3-7.

2. Ernst Cassirer, *Kant's Life and Thought*, trans. J. Haden (New Haven: Yale University Press, 1981), pp. 326-27.

3. Immanuel Kant, *Critique of Judgement*, trans. J. H. Bernard (New York: Macmillan, 1951), p. 107.

4. Ibid., p. 108.

5. Ibid., p. 115.

6. Alexander Gottlieb Baumgarten, *Aesthetica* (Hildesheim: Olms, 1961), p. 13.

7. Kant, *Critique of Judgement*, pp. 109-110.

8. A more elaborate discussion of the problem of *Augenschein* with respect to de Man's thought in general is to be found in my essay "In-Difference to Philosophy: de Man on Kant, Hegel, and Nietzsche," in *Reading de Man Reading*, ed. W. Godzich and L. Waters (Minneapolis: University of Minnesota Press, 1989.)

Chapter 10
Gregory Jay: Paul de Man and the Seduction of Literary History

1. See Jonathan Culler, "Literary History, Allegory, and Semiology," *New Literary History* 7:2 (Winter 1976): 259-69.

2. Cleanth Brooks, "The Language of Paradox," in *The Well-Wrought Urn* (New York: Harcourt, Brace, Jovanovich, 1947; 1975), pp. 3-21.

3. Paul de Man, "Form and Intent in the American New Criticism," in *Blindness and Insight: Essays in the Rhetoric of Contemporary Criticism*, 2nd edition, rev. (Minneapolis: University of Minnesota Press, 1983), p. 237 (hereafter, BI).

4. Paul de Man, "The Resistance to Theory," *Yale French Studies* 63 (1982); Reprinted in *The Resistance to Theory* (Minneapolis: University of Minnesota Press, 1986), pp. 3-20.

5. Paul de Man, *Allegories of Reading* (New Haven: Yale University Press, 1979), p. 4 (hereafter, AR).

6. I do not mean, however, to assimilate de Man's deconstruction of the production of meaning effects to any naive semiotics of signification. As de Man states, "instead of containing or reflecting experience, language constitutes it. And a theory of constituting form is altogether different from a theory of signifying form" (BI, 233). Much work remains to be done in disclosing the complexity of de Man's troping of semiotics.

7. Paul de Man, "Hypogram and Inscription: Michael Riffaterre's Poetics of Reading," *Diacritics* 11:4 (Winter 1981): 33, (hereafter, HI).

8. Paul de Man, "Autobiography as De-Facement," *The Rhetoric of Romanticism* (New York: Columbia University Press, 1984), pp. 75-76 (hereafter, RR). For further discussion see my "Freud: The Death of Autobiography," *Genre* 19:2 (Summer 1986): 103-28.

9. For more on prosopopeia, see Ned Lukacher, *Primal Scenes: Literature, Philosophy, Psychoanalysis* (Ithaca: Cornell University Press, 1986), pp. 68-96; Cynthia Chase, *Decomposing Figures: Rhetorical Readings in the Romantic Tradition* (Baltimore: Johns Hopkins University Press, 1986); and Michael Riffaterre, "Prosopopeia," in *Yale French Studies* [special issue on Paul de Man] 69 (1985): 107-23.

10. Barbara Johnson, "Rigorous Unreliability," *Critical Inquiry* 11:2 (December 1984): 284.

11. Like Rodolphe Gasché, de Man frequently cautions against mistaking deconstruction for the fallacy of imitative form—self-reflexive or not. For example, commenting on the fragmentary style of Auerbach and others, de Man counters that "I feel myself compelled to repeated frustration in a persistent attempt to write as if a dialectical summation were possible beyond the breaks and interruptions that the readings disclose. The apparent resignation to aphorism and parataxis is often an attempt to recuperate on the level of style what is lost on the level of history. By stating the inevitability of fragmentation in a mode that is itself fragmented, one restores the aesthetic unity of manner and substance that may well be what is in question in the historical study of romanticism" (RR, ix).

12. The paradox between generational imperatives and the lessons of close reading, as well as most of the generalizations on the problems of writing a his-

tory of romanticism, appear summarized in de Man's "Introduction" to a special issue of *Studies in Romanticism* 18 (1979): 495-99.

13. The language of appearance and sheltering here is (ironically) Heideggerian, recalling the latter's many meditations on *aletheia* and on language as the House of Being. Allen Stoekl documents how "de Man reads Heidegger against himself, valorizing division—what he calls dialectic (and later aporia)—against the common ground as unity, which comes to be identified in Heidegger with dwelling. . . . Poetically man dwells, yet the poetic, unlike complacent dwelling, is defiance and combat. . . . Poetic activity is not a bridge but is opposition or difference *in* language and time. . . . We should note here that 'history' for de Man, and 'the dialectic,' refer to the incessant process of the upheaval and destruction of permanence" ("De Man and the Dialectic of Being," *Diacritics* 15:3 [Fall 1985]: 40-41).

14. Paul de Man, "The Epistemology of Metaphor," *On Metaphor*, ed. Sheldon Sacks (Chicago: University of Chicago Press, 1979), p. 28. This essay also treats the figure of prosopopeia quite suggestively.

Chapter 11
Brian Caraher: Recovering the Figure of J.L. Austin in Paul de Man's
Allegories of Reading

1. This essay is a revised and expanded version of section 3 of my review-article "*Allegories of Reading*: Positing a Rhetoric of Romanticism; or Paul de Man's Critique of Pure Figural Anteriority," *PreText*, 4, 1 (Spring 1983) and is used here with the permission of the journal's editor, Victor J. Vitanza.

2. George McFadden, "Review" of *Allegories of Reading*, *JAAC*, 39, 3 (Spring 1981): 339. All quotations from Paul de Man's *Allegories of Reading: Figural Language in Rousseau, Nietzsche, Rilke, and Proust* (New Haven: Yale University Press, 1979) will be noted by the abbreviation AR and the relevant page numbers in parentheses.

3. Rodolphe Gasché, " '*Setzung*' and '*Übersetzung*': Notes on Paul de Man," *Diacritics*, 11, 4 (Winter 1981): esp. 36-40. Gasché offers a fair summary of Austin's position in *How to Do Things with Words*, yet I think he tries to lead Austin and speech act theory where they probably do not want to go: into "the problematics of reflexivity" (39) and "the metaphysics of transcendental subjectivity" (54). This move is accomplished essentially by isolating and recharacterizing Austin's notion of the "illocutionary act" and by linking "the status of the performative act, constitutive of the speech act," to Fichte's notion of "positing," that "pure activity" of the self (though not as a subject or agent), which posits and constitutes the self (see esp. 37-40, 52-54). Gasché contends that de Man critiques Austin's 'doctrine' by refusing "to endow the concept of the act with the totalizing explicative power it has in Speech Act Theory" (50) and by representing "an attempt at developing a more fundamental notion of the performative than the notion of self-positing on which Austin's Speech Act Theory rests, and which

keeps it locked within the boundaries of philosophical idealism and the metaphysics of subjectivity" (56).

There may be, however, a too abrupt collapsing of terminologies and philosophical lines of development here. Austin's sense of the subject or agent or speaker of speech acts must be valued and appraised a bit differently than Fichte's self-positing self, and indeed so must be Austin's notion of performatives or speech acts and Fichte's notion of 'act' or activity (*Thathandlung*). Austin's use of the word 'total' in the phrases "the total speech act" or "the total speech situation" really does not operate in the same ways or toward the same ends as the words 'totalizing' or 'totalization' in Fichte's, de Man's, or Gasché's discourses. Essentially, Austin's terminology and project are not situated within a traditional European metaphysical framework; they are neither idealist nor foundational, but are pragmatic and phenomenalist. Quite contrary to his claim that "Austin's philosophy is tributary to the metaphysics of subjectivity" is what Gasché dismisses in a parenthetical phrase: "which, by the way, cannot be escaped in any way by opting for a philosophy of the social, the communal, the collective, etc." (53). Such a philosophy indeed lies implicit in Austin's conception of action. "Austin's speech acts are undoubtedly acts of subjects"; but, quite unlike Fichte, they are not "in fact, of subjects before all social mediation" (53).

For investigations that build upon a pragmatic and phenomenalist sense of 'action' and 'a philosophy of the social, the communal, the collective,' see John Dewey, *Human Nature and Conduct: An Introduction to Social Psychology* (New York: Modern Library, 1930; orig. pub., 1922), Stephen Pepper, *Concept and Quality: A World Hypothesis* (LaSalle, Ill.: Open Court Press, 1966), Mary Louise Pratt's *Toward a Speech Act Theory of Literary Discourse* (Bloomington: Indiana University Press, 1977), and Charles Altieri's *Act and Quality: A Theory of Literary Meaning and Humanistic Understanding* (Amherst: University of Massachusetts Press, 1981).

4. I quote from AR, pp. 120-21. De Man quotes from the Nietzsche fragment at length, using and slightly altering the W. Kaufmann and R. J. Hollingdale translation of it as it appears as section 516 of *The Will to Power* (New York: Random House, 1967), pp. 279-80.

5. See esp. pp. 1-3 of Austin, *How to Do Things with Words*, ed. J. O. Urmson (New York: Oxford University Press, 1965). Additional references to and quotations from this text will be designated by the abbreviation HDTW and the relevant page numbers in parentheses.

6. This also is the clear recommendation of Austin's brief but well-known paper "Performatif-Constatif" written and presented in French in 1958 and published in *Cahiers de Royaumont, Philosophie*, no. 4, *La Philosophie Analytique* (Paris: Editions de Minuit, 1962), pp. 271-304. An English translation of the essay appears as "Performative-Constative" in the collection *Philosophy and Ordinary Language*, ed. Charles E. Caton (Urbana: University of Illinois Press, 1963), pp. 22-54. The essay seems to have influenced some of the work of Oswald Ducrot and Tzvetan Todorov, and to have left traces upon Michel Foucault's *The Archaeology of Knowledge*.

7. Here I am in agreement with an observation made by Jonathan Culler in his essay "Convention and Meaning: Derrida and Austin," *New Literary History*, 13, 1 (Autumn 1981): 17. With regard to Austin's strategy in *How to Do Things with Words*, Culler observes:

> Starting from the philosophical hierarchy that makes true or false statements the norm of language and treats other utterances as flawed statements or as extra—supplementary—forms, Austin's investigation of the qualities of the marginal case leads to a deconstruction and inversion of the hierarchy: the performative is not a flawed constative; rather, the constative is a special case of the performative.

I think that Culler blunts the force of this crucial observation by deflecting his discourse into "a deconstruction and inversion" of another purported 'hierarchy' to be found in Austin's text—namely, the privileged status of 'serious' speech acts vis-à-vis 'nonserious' or 'parasitic' ones (see Culler, pp. 19-28).

Austin's singular remark on drawing lines of difference between 'normal' or 'serious' performative utterances as opposed to 'parasitic' ones is indeed a residual problem and difficulty of Austin's text, but I basically concur with Stanley Cavell's quite astute comments concerning this issue in the essay "Politics as Opposed to What?," *Critical Inquiry*, 9, 1 (Sept. 1982): 165-67. Cavell here takes Stanley Fish to task for reading a distinction and hierarchy into the terms 'serious' and 'parasitic' (and 'ordinary' and 'literary') from which Austin might otherwise have wished to dissociate himself. I do not think Austin's *How to Do Things with Words* turns dependently upon the 'hierarchy' of 'serious' and 'nonserious' performatives. If anything, Austin seeks to foreground "standard," "typical" or "proto-typical" samples of performative utterances for discussion and analysis. This move seems to be a matter of convenience for him and not a rhetorically and philo-sophically suspicious and "seductive" one. Indeed a later comment by Culler, which indicates the arbitrariness of positing a hierarchy of 'serious' and 'parasitic' performatives, yields an observation with which I think Austin—John Searle per-haps notwithstanding—might have found himself in agreement:

> For the 'standard case' of promising to occur, it must be recognizable as the repetition of a conventional procedure, and the actor's performance on the stage is an excellent model of such repetition. The possibility of 'serious' performatives depends upon the possibility of performances, because per-formatives depend upon the iterability that is most explicitly manifested in performances [pp. 21-22].

The "possibility of performances" and their "repetition" or "iterability" or con-ventionality are the crucial notions. The status of samples or appropriate examples of performances and performatives is another issue, and one that I think Culler's essay draws attention to, though obliquely. The work of literary theorists such as Charles Altieri and Mary Louise Pratt (cited in note 3 above) as well as the work of such cognitive linguists as Charles Fillmore, George Lakoff, Mark Johnson, and others confront most directly speech acts, the nature of cognitive perform-ance, and the confluent status of 'serious' and 'parasitic' samples or examples.

8. 'Rhetoric' here, of course, is not restricted to tropes or figural language but broadened to include the various strategies and techniques of persuasion. Austin, though, does employ some resonant figural language. Note, for instance, his troping of the use of concepts as those instruments that can "crack the crib of Reality, or as it may be, of Confusion" (HDTW, 25). Besides the pun on Reality's rib, concepts are imaged as capable of breaking into and decoding that concealed *book* of glosses and clues that figure forth 'Reality' (or 'Confusion') to us.

In the third and final section of "With Compliments of the Author: Reflections on Austin and Derrida," *Critical Inquiry* 8, 4 (Summer 1982): 712-21, Stanley Fish explores, through the assistance of an insightful and persuasive reading of Jacques Derrida's "Signature Event Context" in *Glyph 1* (1977), the "radical provisionality" of the concepts and rhetoric of Austin's *How to Do Things with Words*. I find myself in agreement with many of the particulars of Fish's attentive reading of Austin's rhetoric, a reading that seems fully perceptive of the subtle and rhetorically self-aware performance involved in Austin's text. Fish also notes that Austin's preliminary distinction between 'constative' and 'performative' is one that "the book is devoted to blurring" in the end (p. 713). That is, "the true structure" of Austin's book "is its gradual dissolution as the distinctions with which it begins are blurred and finally collapsed" (p. 720).

9. Like the positivists, de Man would seem to foreground the systemic and instrumental features of language and concepts, regardless of how problematized they become in the end. Notice that, for both modes of thought, epistemology and the sense of the self as an active agent are elided in favor of a self-regulating grammatical system—though, for the former group, the system is regarded positivistically and, for de Man, the system yields only aporias.

10. See also my remarks on Derrida, de Man, irony, illusion, and positivism in Brian Caraher, "Metaphor as Contradiction: A Grammar and Epistemology of Poetic Metaphor," *Philosophy and Rhetoric* 14, 2 (Spring 1981): 282-84. Stanley Cavell notes Austin's intentions in philosophically undermining positivism as well as Paul de Man's misappropriation of Austin's terminology; see Cavell, "Politics as Opposed to What?," esp. pp. 163, 167-72. Cavell also examines de Man's use of the Archie Bunker gag in a manner that I believe well complements my discussion of it in the following paragraph.

Chapter 12
Howard Felperin: The Anxiety of American Deconstruction

1. Paul de Man, *Blindness and Insight: Essays in the Rhetoric of Contemporary Criticism* (Minneapolis: University of Minnesota Press, 1983), p. 8.

2. Paul de Man, *Allegories of Reading: Figural Language in Rousseau, Nietzsche, Rilke, and Proust* (New Haven: Yale University Press, 1979), pp. 16-17.

3. Paul de Man, "The Return to Philology," *Times Literary Supplement*, vol. 4158, no. 10 (December 1982): 1355-56.

4. De Man, *Blindness and Insight*, p. 8.

Chapter 13
Joseph F. Graham: Around and About Babel

1. See Walter Benjamin, "The Task of the Translator" in *Illuminations*, trans., Harry Zohn (New York: Schocken, 1987), pp. 69-109.

2. See Jacques Derrida, "Des Tours de Babel" in *Difference in Translation*, ed. Joseph F. Graham, (Ithaca: Cornell University Press, 1985), pp. 165-207.

Chapter 14
David B. Allison: The Différance of Translation

1. Jacques Derrida, *Margins of Philosophy*. Trans. Alan Bass (Chicago: University of Chicago Press, 1982), p. 309. My emphasis.

2. Ibid., p. 330. My emphasis.

3. For a recent discussion of ellipses, pouches, and envelopes, see "Comment," by P. A. Chambige, in *International Studies in Philosophy*, vol. 17, no. 2 (1985): 97-98.

4. Jacques Derrida, "Living on. Borderlines," trans., J. Hulbert, in H. Bloom, et al., *Deconstruction and Criticism* (New York: Seabury Press, 1979), p. 101.

5. "I have amassed references (to 'things' and 'texts,' they would say) but in truth what I have just written is without reference. Above all, to myself or to texts that I have signed in another language. Precisely *because of* this jubilant multiplicity of self-references. 'In order to come into being as text, the referential function had to be radically suspended' " (Paul de Man, "The Purloined Ribbon," in *Glyph 1*. Quote in full.). "Transference." *Ibid.*, pp. 173-75.

6. Ibid., p. 137. My emphasis.

7. Cited by Richard Gale in his "Propositions, Judgments, Sentences, and Statements" in *Encyclopedia of Philosophy*, ed. P. Edwards (New York: Macmillan, 1967), vol. 6, p. 500.

8. The question had been succinctly stated by Derrida in "Borderlines" as perhaps the central issue for understanding, and hence, for translation: "*What is a reference*, a reference to a thing, to a text, to one text, to the other? What is this word 'reference'?" (p. 154).

9. For an extended and extremely insightful analysis of these issues, see especially Dominique Janicaud and J.-F. Mattei, *La Métaphysique à la limite* (Paris: P.U.F., 1983).

10. Martin Heidegger, *The Essence of Reasons*, trans. T. Malick (Evanston: Northwestern University Press, 1969), p. 41.

11. For Schreber himself perhaps the most exotic notion was his beguilingly elusive "not thinking of anything thought" (*der Nichtsdenkungsgedanke*). Senseless? Absurd? Intentionally intentionally inexistent? *Fiat!*

12. Koitchi Toyosaki, "Traduction et/ou citation" in *Les Fins de l'homme*, eds. P. Lacoue-Labarthe and J.-L. Nancy (Paris: Editions Galilée, 1981), pp. 245-53.

13. Derrida, "Borderlines," p. 145.

14. Martin Heidegger, "A Dialogue on Language" (*Aus einem Gespräch von der Sprache*) trans. P. Hertz (New York: Harper & Row, 1971), p. 45.

15. Martin Heidegger, "The Anaximander Fragment," in *Early Greek Thinking*, trans. D. Krell and F. Capuzzi (New York: Harper & Row, 1975).

16. Heidegger, "A Dialogue on Language," p. 42.

17. Martin Heidegger, *Being and Time*, trans. J. Macquarrie and E. Robinson (New York: Harper & Row, 1962), p. 209.

18. Ibid., p. 190.

19. Ibid., pp. 191-92.

20. Ibid., p. 193.

21. Heidegger, "A Dialogue on Language," p. 51.

22. Heidegger, *Being and Time*, p. 209.

23. The play of the 'as' as over the 'that' resonates throughout the "Borderlines" text, especially. Tied to the trace of the ontological difference, it figures prominently in "Ousia and Grammé." as the movement of the trace, Derrida practically devotes the entirety of "*Différance*" to this issue; also, *in extenso*, in his *Of Grammatology*. The peculiar and elusive vocabulary of the *as* fairly well suffuses his work. (The vocabulary tied to the *economy* of the 'as' in "Borderlines" alone: syllepsis, superimprinting, psychoanalytic transference, insaturable context, exhibitionism, apocalypse, revelation, immodesty, metaphor, transferential magnetization, monstrous association, homonymic transference, transreference, transgression, etc. Add the terms that concern this economy of understanding—as— from "White Mythology," "The Retrait of Metaphor," "The Pit and the Pyramid," and "From a Restricted Economy," and the International Monetary Fund itself would seem little more than a credit to the national debt.) As mark, and especially as a mark of understanding, the 'as' structure that opens up transitivity in all its richness, receives a unique treatment in "Borderlines," one that remains thoughtfully attentive to the germane issues raised by Heidegger, not the least of which concerns the fluidity and consequentiality of those reciprocal relations between our understanding and our grammar. That these relations render our own language problematic is a truism. But that we can resolve such problems through the play of the 'as,' within ordinary language, is also a truism: "The *arrêt de mort* as *verdict*: it is obvious, and the translators must take this into account, that in 'everyday' language, in 'normal' conversation, the expression *arrêt de mort* is unambiguous" (pp. 115-16).

Moreover, that the resources of *ordinary usage* enable us to deal with what would ordinarily be called an extraordinary use of language, is likewise fairly well taken for granted. Moving from "everyday" language to the assertions of "literary" convention—or "parasitism"—which suspends "normal contexts," even there:

> The . . . usage of the language, in short, *everything that makes it possible to move* from 'death sentence' to 'suspension of death' in the French expression *arrêt de mort*, can always come about in 'everyday' usage of the language, in language and discourse [ibid., pp. 118-19].

Practically the same itinerary as Heidegger's: understanding, interpretation, assertion, and finally translation. The last step, however, now brings the *translator* back to the first, to understanding: and to understand understanding—via the detour of the *as* and the *that* (and *whose!*)—in terms of its generalized transitivity, its economy. For *such* an economy, there must be loss and gain, for the accounts (at least two of them for the translator) are never fully receivable, and one always keeps double books, anyway.

Recalling a remark by Koitchi Toyosaki, about the problems of translating— especially, concerning items of the accusative or objective case, as well as those of the genitive case—Derrida speculates on this last step, and on the necessary trace of *différance* it entails. And this trace is not so much a question of words:

> If there is something that arrests translation, this limit is not due to some essential indissociability of meaning and language, of signified and signifier, as they say. It is a matter of *economy* (economy, of course, remains to be *thought*) and retains an essential relationship with time, space, counting, words, signs, *marks*. The unity of the word is not to be fetishized or substantialized. For example, with more words or parts of words, the translator will triumph more easily over *arrêt* in the expression *arrêt de mort*. Not without something left over, of course, but more or less easily, strictly, closely, rightly [ibid., pp. 169-70].

To *be* fair, even rigorous, that sum in question, the *différance* of translation, the translation effect (which even escapes the minimal qualifications for *entry*, because it is not quantifiable, objectifiable), may hardly be extravagant, exotic. Nor is the site of passage exotic. But, then, it is not exactly home, either. Perhaps the passage from the West (the *Abend-land*) to the East may well be one of intensity, as Deleuze tells us. Or with the exotic always there, it may just as well be one of intensivity. Not a great difference.

Chapter 15
John Leavey: Lations, Cor, Trans, Re, &c.*

1. J. Hillis Miller, "The Critic as Host," in *Deconstruction and Criticism* (New York: Continuum, 1979), pp. 250-51.

2. Jacques Derrida, "Lettre à un ami japonais," in his *Psyché: Inventions de l'autre* (Paris: Galilée, 1987), p. 387; "Letter to a Japanese Friend," in *Derrida and Difference*, eds. David Wood and Robert Bernasconi (Coventry, England: Parousia Press, 1985), p. 1.

3. Jacques Derrida, *Positions*, trans. Alan Bass (Chicago: University of Chicago Press, 1981), p. 71.

4. Stéphane Mallarmé, *Crise de vers*, in *OEuvres complètes*, eds. Henri Mondor and G. Jean-Aury (Paris: Gallimard, Bibliothèque de la Pléiade, 1945), p. 363.

5. Walter Benjamin, "The Task of the Translator," in *Illuminations*, ed. Hannah Arendt, trans. Harry Zohn (New York: Schocken, 1968), p. 74; *Illuminationen* (Frankfurt a. M.: Suhrkamp, 1955), p. 54.

6. Carol Jacobs, "The Monstrosity of Translation," *Modern Language Notes* 90 (1975): 760-61.

7. Jacques Derrida, "Des tours de Babel," in *Difference in Translation*, ed. Joseph F. Graham (Ithaca: Cornell University Press, 1985), pp. 201 and 245.

8. Jacques Derrida, "Living On: Border-Lines," trans. James Hulbert, in *Deconstruction and Criticism* (New York: Continuum, 1979), p. 149 (hereafter, LO).

9. J. Hillis Miller, *The Ethics of Reading* (New York: Columbia University Press, 1987), pp. 123-24.

10. Paul de Man, *The Resistance to Theory* (Minneapolis: University of Minnesota Press, 1986), p. 91.

11. See also my "Destinerrance: The Apotropocalyptics of Translation," in John Sallis, ed., *Deconstruction and Philosophy: The Texts of Jacques Derrida* (Chicago: University of Chicago Press, 1987), pp. 33-43.

12. Jacques Derrida, *Glas* (Paris: Galilée, 1974), p. 56a. *Glas*, trans. John P. Leavey, Jr., and Richard Rand (Lincoln: University of Nebraska Press, 1986), p. 46a.

13. Jacques Derrida, "Of an Apocalypatic Tone Recently Adopted in Philosophy," trans. John P. Leavey, Jr., *Oxford Literary Review* 6:2 (1984): 34-35.

14. Jacques Derrida, "Cartouches," in *The Truth in Painting*, trans. Geoff Bennington and Ian McLeod (Chicago: University of Chicago Press, 1987), p. 240; in *La vérité en peinture* (Paris: Flammarion, 1978), p. 276.

15. Maurice Blanchot, *Death Sentence*, trans. Lydia Davis (Barrytown, N.Y.: Station Hill, 1978), pp. 1 and 31 (hereafter, DS). *L'arrêt de mort* (Paris: Gallimard [L'imaginaire], 1948), pp. 7 and 54 (hereafter, AM).

16. Jacques Derrida, *La Carte postale: de Socrate à Freud et au-delà* (Paris: Flammarion, 1980), p. 268; *The Post Card: From Socrates to Freud and Beyond*, trans. Alan Bass (Chicago: University of Chicago Press, 1987), pp. 250-51.

17. Derrida, "Ja, ou le faux-bond," *Digraphe* 11 (1977): 89.

18. Derrida, "No Apocalypse, Not Now (full speed ahead, seven missiles, seven missives)," trans. Catherine Porter and Philip Lewis, *Diacritics* 14:2 (1984): 30-31.

Chapter 16
Antony Easthope: Derrida's Epistemology

1. Frank Lentricchia, *After the New Criticism* (London: Athlone Press, 1980), p. 168.

2. Jacques Derrida, *Writing and Difference*, trans. Alan Bass (London: RKP, 1978), pp. 278-93 (hereafter, SSP).

3. Jacques Derrida, *Of Grammatology*, trans. Gayatri Spivak (Baltimore and London: Johns Hopkins University Press, 1976), p. 159.

4. Karl Marx, *Grundrisse*, trans. Martin Nicolaus (Harmondsworth: Penguin Books, 1973), p. 101.

5. Louis Althusser and Etienne Balibar, *Reading Capital*, trans. Ben Brewster (London: New Left Books, 1975), p. 35 (hereafter, RC). It might well be objected that the historical movement usually called empiricism does not really answer to the Althusserian description. The description, however, does apply precisely to the notion of empiricism assumed by Derrida. In a much longer essay it would have been possible to discuss the critique of empiricism conducted over the past twenty years by Anglo-American analytic philosophy. A starting point here might be W. V. Quine's essay "Two Dogmas of Empiricism" (1951) [see *Challenges to Empiricism*, ed. Harold Morick (London: Methuen, 1980)].

6. Barry Hindess and Paul Q. Hirst, *Mode of Production and Social Formation* (London: Macmillan, 1977) (hereafter, MPSF).

7. Paul Q. Hirst, *On Law and Ideology* (London: Macmillan, 1979), p. 21.

8. Andrew Collier, "In Defense of Epistemology," *Radical Philosophy* 20 (Summer 1978): 9.

9. W. K. Wimsatt, *The Verbal Icon* (London: Methuen, 1970), p. 5 (hereafter, VI).

10. Harold Bloom, "The Breaking of Form," in Harold Bloom, Paul de Man, Jacques Derrida, Geoffrey Hartman, and J. Hillis Miller, *Deconstruction and Criticism* (London: RKP, 1979), p. 7.

Chapter 17
Wilhelm Wurzer: The Critical Difference: Adorno's Aesthetic Alternative

1. Jacques Derrida, "Freud and the Scene of Writing," in *Writing and Difference*, trans. Alan Bass (Chicago: University of Chicago Press, 1978), p. 242.

2. Theodor W. Adorno, *Negative Dialektik* (Frankfurt: Suhrkamp Verlag, 1966).

3. Jacques Derrida, *Speech and Phenomena*, trans. David B. Allison (Evanston: Northwestern University Press, 1973), p. 158.

4. Charles Baudelaire, *The Flowers of Evil* (New York: New Directions Books, 1955), p. 146.

5. Adorno employs the term trace (*die Spur*) in relation to the dialectic notion of *das Naturschöne*.

6. Theodor W. Adorno, *Minima Moralia* (London: NLB, 1974), p. 74.

7. Jacques Derrida, *Positions* (Chicago: University of Chicago Press, 1981), p. 45.

8. Gabriel Garcia Márquez, "The Last Voyage of the Ghost Ship," in *Leaf Storm* (New York: Harper and Row, 1972), p. 135.

9. Ibid., p. 128.

10. Pablo Neruda, "Ars Poetica," in *Residence on Earth* (New York: New Directions Books, 1973), p. 47.

11. Ibid.

12. Ibid., "El Abandonado," p. 225.

13. Ibid., "El Reloj Caido en el Mar," p. 197.

14. Jacques Derrida, "Structure, Sign and Play in the Discourse of the Human Sciences," in *Writing and Difference* (Chicago: University of Chicago Press, 1978), p. 262.

15. Adorno, *Minima Moralia*, p. 16.

16. G. W. F. Hegel, *Phenomenology of Spirit*, trans. A. V. Miller (Oxford: Clarendon Press, 1977), p. 36.

17. Derrida, *Positions*, p. 94.

18. Theodor W. Adorno, "Notes on Kafka," in *Prisms*, trans. S. and S. Weber (Cambridge: MIT Press, 1981), p. 247.

19. Ibid.

20. Ibid.

21. Derrida, *Positions*, p. 96.

22. Benedict de Spinoza, *The Ethics*, trans. R.H.M. Elwes (New York: Dover Publications, 1955).

23. Hegel, *Phenomenology of Spirit*, p. 121.

24. Ibid., p. 122.

25. Ibid.

26. Hegel, *Phanomenologie des Geistes, Samtliche Werke*. Jubiläumsausgabe, vol. 2, ed. Hermann Glickner (Stuttgart: Frommann, 1927-30), p. 158: "*Das*

Bewusstsein vertilgt den Inhalt wohl als ein fremdes Sein, indem es ihm denkt." This and all subsequent translations are my own.

27. Hegel, *Phenomenology of Spirit*, p. 122.

28. Fredric Jameson, *The Political Unconscious* (Ithaca: Cornell University Press, 1981), p. 41. See also Catherine Belsey, *Critical Practice* (London & New York: Methuen, 1980).

29. Adorno, *Prisms*, p. 21.

30. Derrida, *Speech and Phenomena*, p. 151.

31. Adorno, *Prisms*, p. 24.

32. Derrida, "Semiology and Grammatology," in *Positions*, p. 36.

33. Adorno, *Prisms*, p. 31.

34. Theodor W. Adorno, *Ästhetische Theorie* (Frankfurt: Suhrkamp Verlag, 1980, p. 11: *"Kunst hat ihren Begriff in der geschichtlich sich verandernden Konstellation von Momenten. Ihr Wesen ist nicht aus dem Ursprung deduzibel."*

35. Adorno, "Arnold Schönberg", in *Prisms*, p. 49.

36. Adorno, *Ästhetische Theorie*, p. 19: *"Kunst ist die gesellschaftliche Antithesis zur Gesellschaft, nicht unmittlebar aus dieser zu deduzieren."*

37. Contrary to traditional interpretations of Adorno's philosophy, I would like to emphasize the affirmative side of aesthetic dialectic in view of Adorno's frequent allusions to *promesse de bonheur.*

38. Adorno, *Ästhetische Theorie*, p. 87: *"Kunst ist Rationalität, welche diese kritisiert, ohne ihr sich zu entziehen."*

39. Baudelaire, *Flowers of Evil*, "Au Lecteur."

40. Adorno, *Ästhetische Theorie*, p. 114: *"Das Naturschöne ist die Spur* [trace] *des Nichtidentischen an den Dingen im Bann universaler Identität."*

41. Ibid., p. 113: *"Deshalb bedarf Kunst der Philosophie, die sie interpretiert, um zu sagen, was sie nicht sagen kann, indem sie es nicht sagt."*

Chapter 18
Arnaud Villani: Poststructuralist Alternatives to Deconstruction

1. Jacques Derrida, "The Ends of Man," in *Margins of Philosophy*, trans. Alan Bass (Chicago: University of Chicago Press, 1982), p. 117.

2. Ibid., p. 134.

3. Ibid., p. 135.

4. Ibid., p. 136.

5. François Laruelle, *Les machines textuelles* (Paris: Seuil, 1976).

6. See Derrida, *Dissemination*, trans. Barbara Johnson (Chicago: University of Chicago Press, 1981), p. 207n.

7. Laruelle, p. 12.

8. Ibid., p. 13.

9. Derrida, *Margins*, p. 136.

10. Derrida, *Dissemination*, p. 207.

11. In order to understand precisely how Laruelle uses these terms, see, in particular, Gilles Deleuze, *Différence et répétition* (Paris: Presses Universitaires de France, 1969).

12. Laruelle, p. 13.

13. Ibid., p. 15.

14. Ibid., p. 14.

15. Ibid., p. 23.

16. Ibid., p. 14.

17. Ibid., p. 35.

18. Ibid., p. 36.

19. Ibid., p. 18. See, in particular, the reciprocal deformations of the two proper names.

20. Martin Heidegger, "Letter on Humanism" in *Basis Writings*, ed. D. Krell (NY: Harper & Row, 1977), pp. 193-242.

21. See, for instance, Heidegger, "Overcoming Metaphysics (1936-46) in *The End of Philosophy*, trans. Joan Stambaugh (New York: Harper & Row, 1973), pp. 84-110.

22. See Roland Barthes, *Criticism and Truth*, trans. Katrine Pilcher Keuneman (Minneapolis: University of Minnesota Press, 1987), where he addresses the question of asymbolism in the older criticism [*ancienne critique*].

23. Gilles Deleuze, "*A quoi reconnaît-on le structuralisme?,*" in *La Philosophie au XXe siècle*, vol. 4, ed. François Châtelet (Paris: Marabout, 1973), pp. 293-329.

24. The *case vide* ("empty space" or "empty square") is the place in a game that remains free and available such that the pieces which are in another location can move there. In such games (checkers, chess, etc.), the empty space itself moves around as well. Without the empty space, the game could not go on. [Ed.]

25. See, for instance, Derrida's prudent responses concerning Hegel in *Positions*, trans. Alan Bass (Chicago: University of Chicago Press, 1981).

26. Raymond Roussel, *Locus Solus* (1914) (Paris: Gallimard, 1963) and *Impressions d'Afrique* (1910) (Paris: Pauvert, 1963).

27. Michel Foucault, *Death and the Labyrinth: The World of Raymond Roussel*, trans. Charles Ruas (New York: Doubleday, 1986).

28. Deleuze distinguishes "differential" (or the virtual) from "differencial" (or the actual). See *Différence et répétition*, passim.

29. See Derrida, *Dissemination*, p. 212.

30. Ibid., p. 207n.

31. Ibid., pp. 253 and 267.

32. See the whole corpus of Deleuze's work since *Différence et répétition*, and most notably (and often coauthored with Félix Guattari): *Anti-Oedipus, Kafka, Rhizome, A Thousand Plateaus*, and the more recent *Logique de la sensation*.

33. This essay and the passages not currently available in translation were rendered into English by Hugh J. Silverman.

Selected Bibliography

Adorno, Theodor W. *Aesthetic Theory*. Trans. C. Lenhardt. Eds. Gretel Adorno and Rolf Tiedmann. London: Routledge and Kegan Paul, 1984.

— — —. *Negative Dialectics*. New York: Continuum, 1973.

Allison, David B. "Destruction/Deconstruction in the Text of Nietzsche." *Boundary 2*, vol. 8, no. 1 (Fall 1979): 197-222.

— — —, ed. *The New Nietzsche*. Cambridge: MIT Press, 1977, 1985.

Althusser, Louis, and Balibar, Etienne. *Reading Capital*. Trans. Ben Brewster, London: New Left Books, 1975.

Altieri, Charles. *Act and Quality: A Theory of Literary Meaning and Humanistic Understanding*. Amherst: University of Massachusetts Press, 1981.

Altizer, Thomas J.J., et al. *Deconstruction and Theology*. New York: Seabury Crossroads, 1982.

Arac, Jonathan, ed. *The Yale Critics: Deconstruction in America*. Minneapolis: University of Minnesota Press, 1983.

Artaud, Antonin. "Van Gogh, the Man Suicided by Society" In *Antonin Artaud: Selected Writings*. Trans. H. Weaver. Ed. Susan Sontag. New York: Farrar, Strauss, and Giroux, 1976, pp. 483-512.

Atkins, G. Douglas, "J. Hillis Miller, Deconstruction, and the Recovery of Transcendence." *Notre Dame English Journal: A Journal of Religion in Literature*, vol. 13, no. 1 (Fall 1980): 51-63.

— — —. "The Sign as a Structure of Difference: Derridean Deconstruction and Some of Its Implications." In De George, Richard T., ed., *Semiotic Themes* Lawrence: University of Kansas, 1981, pp. 133-147.

— — —. *Reading Deconstruction/Deconstructive Reading*. Lexington: University Press of Kentucky, 1983.

— — —. "Count It All Joy: The Affirmative Nature of Deconstruction." *University of Hartford Studies in Literature: A Journal of Interdisciplinary Criticism*, vol. 15-16, nos. 3-1 (1983-84): 120-28.

Austin, J.L. *How to Do Things with Words*. J.O. Urmson, ed. New York: Oxford University Press, 1965.

— — —. "A Plea for Excuses." In *Philosophical Papers*. J.O. Urmson and G.J. Warnock, eds. Oxford: Clarendon Press, 1961.

— — —. "Performative-Constative." In *Philosophy and Ordinary Language*. Charles E. Caton, ed. Urbana: University of Illinois Press, 1963. (Also "Performatif-Constatif." In *Cahiers de Royaumont, Philosophie*, no. 4: *La Philosophie analytique*. Paris: Editions de Minuit, 1962.)

Barthes, Roland. *Criticism and Truth*. Trans. Katrine Pilcher Keuneman. Minneapolis: University of Minnesota Press, 1987.

Baumgarten, Alexander Gottlieb. *Aesthetica*. Hildesheim: Olms, 1961.

Baynes, Kenneth, et al. *After Philosophy: End or Transformation?* Cambridge: MIT Press, 1987.

Belsey, Catherine. "Constructing the Subject: Deconstructing the Text." In *Feminist Criticism and Social Change*. London: Methuen, pp 45-64.

Benjamin, Walter. "The Task of the Translator." In *Illuminations*. Ed. Hannah Arendt. Trans. Harry Zohn. New York: Schocken, 1968.

Blanchard, Marc E. "The Sound of Songs: the Voice in the Text." In Hugh J. Silverman and Don Ihde, eds. *Hermeneutics and Deconstruction*. Albany: SUNY Press, 1985, pp. 122-35.

Blanchot, Maurice. *Death Sentence* (1948). Trans. Lydia Davis. Barrytown, N.Y.: Station Hill, 1978.

Bloom, Harold, et al. *Deconstruction and Criticism*. New York: Seabury/Continuum, 1979.

Blum, Roland P. "Deconstruction and Creation." *Philosophy and Phenomenological Research*, no. 46 (Dec. 1980): 293-306.

Brodsky, Gary M. "Comments on Reading, Writing, Text: Nietzsche's Deconstruction of Authority." *International Studies in Philosophy*, no. 17 (1985): 65-67.

Butler, Christopher. *Interpretation, Deconstruction and Ideology: An Introduction to Some Current Issues in Literary Theory*. New York: Oxford University Press, 1984.

Caputo, John D. *Radical Hermeneutics: Repetition, Deconstruction, and the Hermeneutic Project*. Bloomington: Indiana University Press, 1988.

— — —. "From the Primordiality of Absence to the Absence of Primordiality." In Hugh J. Silverman and Don Ihde, eds. *Hermeneutics and Deconstruction*, pp. 191-200.

— — —. "From the Deconstruction of Hermeneutics to the Hermeneutics of Deconstruction." In Hugh J. Silverman, et al., eds. *The Horizons of Continental Philosophy*. Dordrecht: Nijhoff-Kluwer, 1988, pp. 190-202.

Caraher, Brian. "Metaphor as Contradiction: A Grammar and Epistemology of Poetic Metaphor." *Philosophy and Rhetoric*, vol. 14, no. 2 (Spring 1981): 69-88.

— — —. "*Allegories of Reading*: Positing a Rhetoric of Romanticism, or Paul de Man's Critique of Pure Figural Anteriority." *PreText*, vol. 4, no. 1 (Spring 1983): 9-51.

Cascardi, A.J. "Skepticism and Deconstruction." *Philosophy and Literature*, vol. 8, no. 1 (April 1984): 1-14.

Casey, Edward S. "Origin(s) In (Of) Heidegger/Derrida." *Journal of Philosophy*, vol. 81 (Oct. 1984): 601-10.

Cassirer, Ernst. *Kant's Life and Thought*. Trans. J. Haden. New Haven: Yale University Press, 1981.

Cavell, Stanley. "Politics as Opposed to What?" *Critical Inquiry*, vol. 9, no. 1 (September 1982): 157-78.

Collier, Andrew. "In Defense of Epistemology." *Radical Philosophy*, No. 20 (Summer 1978).

Cousins, Mark. "The Logic of Deconstruction." *The Oxford Literary Review*, vol. 3, no. 2 (1978): 70-77.

Crawford, Donald W. *Kant's Aesthetic Theory*. Madison: University of Wisconsin Press, 1974.

Culler, Jonathan. "Jacques Derrida." In John Sturrock, ed. *Structuralism and Since: From Lévi-Strauss to Derrida*. London: Oxford University Press, 1979, pp. 154-80.

— — —. "Convention and Meaning: Derrida and Austin." *New Literary History*, vol. 13, no. 1 (Autumn 1981): 15-30.

— — —. *The Pursuit of Signs: Semiotics, Literature, Deconstruction*. Ithaca: Cornell University Press, 1981.

— — —. *On Deconstruction: Theory and Criticism After Structuralism*. Ithaca: Cornell University Press, 1982.

Cumming, Robert Denoon. "The Odd Couple: Heidegger and Derrida." *Review of Metaphysics*, vol. 34 (1981): 487-521.

Davis, Robert Con, and Schleifer, Ronald, eds. *Rhetoric and Form: Deconstruction at Yale*. Stillwater: University of Oklahoma Press, 1987.

Deleuze, Gilles, and Guattari, Felix. *Anti-Oedipus*. Trans. Robert Hurley, Mark Seem, and Helen R. Lane. Minneapolis: University of Minnesota Press, 1977.

— — —. *A Thousand Plateaus*. Trans. Brian Massumi. Minneapolis: University of Minnesota Press, 1987.

— — —. *On the Line*. Trans. John Johnston. New York: Semiotext(e), 1983.

De Man, Paul. *Blindness and Insight: Essays in the Rhetoric of Contemporary Criticism*, second edition. Minneapolis: University of Minnesota Press; London: Methuen, 1983.

— — —. "The Purloined Ribbon," *Glyph I*. Baltimore: Johns Hopkins University Press, 1977.

— — —. *Allegories of Reading: Figural Language in Rousseau, Nietzsche, Rilke, and Proust*. New Haven: Yale University Press, 1979.

— — —. "Hypogram and Inscription: Michael Riffaterre's Poetics of Reading." *Diacritics*, vol. 2 (Winter 1981): 17-35.

— — —. "Sign and Symbol in Hegel's *Aesthetics*." *Critical Inquiry*, vol. 8 (Summer 1982): pp. 761-75.

— — —. *The Rhetoric of Romanticism*. New York: Columbia University Press, 1984.

— — —. *The Resistance to Theory*. Minneapolis: University of Minnesota Press, 1986.

Derrida, Jacques. *Edmund Husserl's Origin of Geometry: An Introduction* [1962]. trans. John Leavey. Stony Brook, N.Y.: Nicholas-Hays; Pittsburgh: Duquesne University Press, 1978; University of Nebraska Press, 1989.

———. *Of Grammatology* [1967]. Trans. Gayatri Chakravorty Spivak. Baltimore: Johns Hopkins University Press, 1975.

———. *Speech and Phenomena, and Other Essays on Husserl's Theory of Signs* [1967]. Trans. David B. Allison. Evanston: Northwestern University Press, 1973, 1979.

———. *Writing and Difference* [1967]. Trans. Alan Bass. Chicago: University of Chicago Press, 1978; London: Routledge and Kegan Paul, 1978.

———. *Dissemination* [1972]. Trans. Barbara Johnson. Chicago: University of Chicago Press, 1981; London: Athlone Press, 1981.

———. *Margins of Philosophy* [1972]. Trans. Alan Bass. Chicago: University of Chicago Press, 1982; Hassocks: Harvester Press, 1982.

———. *Positions* [1972]. Trans. Alan Bass. Chicago: University of Chicago Press, 1982; London: Athlone, 1982.

———. *Glas* [1974]. Trans. John Leavey and Richard Rand. Lincoln: University of Nebraska Press, 1986.

———. *Adami*. Paris: Galerie Maeght, 1975.

———. *The Archeology of the Frivolous: Reading Condillac* [1976]. Trans. John Leavey. Pittsburgh: Duquesne University Press, 1980.

———. *The Post Card: From Socrates to Freud* [1976]. Trans. Alan Bass. Chicago: University of Chicago Press, 1987.

———. *Limited Inc., a b c*. Trans. Samuel Weber. Baltimore: Johns Hopkins University Press, 1977. Published as a supplement to *Glyph 2*, Johns Hopkins Textual Studies. Republished by Northwestern University Press, 1988.

———. *Spurs: Nietzsche's Styles* [1978]. Trans. Barbara Harlow. Chicago: University of Chicago Press, 1979. Bilingual edition.

———. *Titus Carmel* (The pocket size Tlingit Coffin). Paris: Centre Pompidou, 1978.

———. *The Truth in Painting* [1978]. Trans. G. Bennington and I. McLeod. Chicago: University of Chicago Press, 1987.

———. *The Ear of the Other: Otobiography, Transference, Translation: Texts and Discussions with Jacques Derrida* [1982]. Trans. Peggy Kamuf. New York: Schocken Books, 1985.

———. *Affranchissement du transfert et de la lettre* (Colloquium on Jacques Derrida's *La carte postale*, April 4th and 5th, 1981. Comments by Derrida.) Paris: Confrontation, 1982.

———. *Otobiographies: l'enseignemnt de Nietzsche et la politique du nom propre*. Paris: Galilée. 1984.

———. *Feu la cendre*. Firenze: Sansoni, 1984; Paris: Des femmes, 197.

———. *Signéponge/Signsponge*. Trans. Richard Rand. New York: Columbia University Press, 1984 (parallel French and English translation).

———. *Droits de regards*. Photographs by M. F. Plissart with an essay by Jacques Derrida. Paris: Minuit, 1985.

———. *Parages*. Paris: Galilée, 1986.

———. *Mémoires: For Paul de Man* [1986]. Trans. Cecile Lindsay, Jonathan Culler, and Eduardo Cadava. New York: Columbia University Press, 1986.

———. *Ullyse gramophone: deux mots pour Joyce*. Paris: Galilée, 1987.

———. *For Nelson Mandela*. Jacques Derrida and Mustpha Tilli, eds. Trans. Phillip Franklin et al. New York: Henry Holt, 1987.

———. *Psyché. Inventions de l'autre.* Paris: Gallimard, 1987.

———. *De l'esprit: Heidegger et la question.* Paris: Galilée, 1987.

———. "Fors: The English Words of Nicolas Abraham and Maria Torok." trans. Barbara Johnson. *Georgia Review,* vol. 11, no. 1 (Spring 1977): 64-116.

———. "Coming Into One's Own." In Geoffrey Hartman, ed. *Psychoanalysis and the Question of the Text.* Baltimore: Johns Hopkins University Press, 1978.

———. "The Retrait of Metaphor." Trans. F. Gasdner et al. *Enclitic,* vol. 2, no. 2 (1978): 5-34.

———. "Living On: Border-lines." Trans. J. Hulbert. In *Deconstruction and Criticism.* Harold Bloom et al., eds. New York: Seabury Press, 1979.

———. "Title (to be announced)." *Substance,* no. 9 (1979): 3-40.

———. "The Law of Genre." Trans. Avital Ronnell. *Critical Inquiry,* vol. 7 (1980): 55-81. And in *Glyph 7.* Baltimore: Johns Hopkins University Press, 1980.

———. "Economimesis." *Diacritics,* vol. 11, no. 2 (1981): 55-93.

———. "Choreographies." Interview with Christie V. McDonald. *Diacritics,* vol. 12 (1982): 66-76.

———. "The Time of a Thesis: Punctuations." In Alan Montefiore, ed. *Philosophy in France Today.* Cambridge: Cambridge University Press, 1982.

———. "The Principle of Reason in the Eyes of its Pupils." *Diacritics,* vol. 13, no. 3 (1983): 3-20; *Graduate Faculty Philosophy Journal* (New School for Social Research), vol. 10, no. 1 (1984): 5-29.

———. "*Geschlecht*—Sexual Difference, Ontological Difference." *Research in Phenomenology,* vol. 13 (1983): 65-83.

———. "Of an Apocalyptic Tone Recently Adopted in Philosophy." Trans. John P. Leavey, Jr. *Semeia,* vol. 23 (1982), and *Oxford Literary Review,* vol. 6, no. 2 (1984): 3-37.

———. "Mes Chances/My Chances." In Joseph Smith and William Kerrigan, eds. *Taking Chances.* Baltimore: Johns Hopkins University Press, 1984, pp. 1-32.

———. "Devant la loi." A. Phillips Griffiths, ed. In *Philosophy and Literature.* Cambridge: Cambridge University Press, 1984.

———. "Deconstruction and the Other." Interview with Richard Kearney. In Richard Kearney, ed. *Dialogues with Contemporary Continental Thinkers.* Manchester: Manchester University Press, 1984.

———. "No Apocalypse, Not Now (full speed ahead, seven missiles, seven missives)." Trans. Catherine Porter and Philip Lewis. *Diacritics,* vol. 14, no. 2 (Summer 1984): 20-31.

———. "Interview with Derrida." In David Wood and Robert Bernasconi, eds. *Derrida and Différance* (Coventry: University of Warwick/Parousia Press, 1985), pp. 107-27. Republished by Northwestern University Press, 1988.

———. "Letter to a Japanese Friend." In David Wood and Robert Bernasconi, ed. *Derrida and Différance* (Coventry: University of Warwick/Parousia Press, 1985), pp. 1-8. Republished by Northwestern University Press, 1988.

———. "Racism's Last Word." Trans. Peggy Kamuf. *Critical Inquiry,* vol. 12 (Autumn 1985): 290-99.

———. "Des Tours de Babel." Trans. Joseph F. Graham. In Joseph F. Graham, ed. *Difference in Translation.* Ithaca and London: Cornell University Press, 1985, pp. 165-207 (also includes French text, pp. 209-48).

———. "The Age of Hegel." Trans. Susan Winnett. *Glyph*, vol. I, new series (1986): 3-43.

———. "Shibboleth" (on Paul Celan). In Geoffrey Hartman and Sanford Budick, eds. *Midrash and Literature*. New Haven: Yale University Press, 1986.

———. "Like the Sound of the Sea Deep within a Shell: Paul de Man's War." Trans. Peggy Kamuf. *Critical Inquiry*, vol. 14, no. 3 (Spring 1988): 590-652.

———. "The Deaths of Roland Barthes." Trans. Pascale-Anne Brault and Michael B. Naas. In *Philosophy and Non-Philosophy since Merleau-Ponty*. Hugh J. Silverman, ed. *Continental Philosophy—I*. New York and London: Routledge, 1988, pp. 259-96.

Descombes, Vincent. *Modern French Philosophy*. Trans. L. Scott-Fox and J. M. Harding. Cambridge: Cambridge University Press, 1980.

———. "The Fabric of Subjectivity." In Hugh J. Silverman and Don Ihde, eds. *Hermeneutics and Deconstruction*, pp. 55-65.

Donato, Eugenio, and Macksey, Richard, eds. *The Structuralist Controversy*. Baltimore: Johns Hopkins University Press, 1970.

Eagleton, Terry. *Criticism and Ideology*. New York: Schocken, 1978.

———. *The Function of Criticism from the Spectator to Post-Structuralism*. New York: Schocken, 1984.

———. *Literary Theory: An Introduction*. Minneapolis: University of Minnesota Press; Oxford: Basil Blackwell, 1984.

Eldridge, Richard. "Deconstruction and its Alternatives." *Man and World*, vol. 18 (1985): 147-70.

Fekete, John, ed. *The Structural Allegory: Reconstructive Encounters with the New French Thought*. Minneapolis: University of Minnesota Press, 1984.

Felman, Shoshana, ed. *Literatuare and Psychoanalysis: The Question of Reading—Otherwise*. Baltimore: Johns Hopkins University Press, 1982.

Felperin, Howard. *Beyond Deconstruction: The Uses and Abuses of Literary Theory*. Oxford: Clarendon Press, 1985.

Fish, Stanley. "With Compliments of the Author: Reflections on Austin and Derrida." *Critical Inquiry*, vol. 8, no. 4 (Summer 1982): 693-721.

Foucault, Michel. *The Order of Things*. Trans. Alan Sheridan-Smith. New York: Pantheon, 1970.

Fuller, Steven. "A French Science (with English Subtitles)." *Philosophy and Literature*, vol. 7 (April 1983): 1-14.

Gale, Richard. "Propositions, Judgments, Sentences, and Statements." In *Encyclopedia of Philosophy*, vol. 6. Paul Edwards, ed. New York: Macmillan, 1967.

Gasché, Rodolphe. " '*Setzung*' and '*Übersetzung*': Notes on Paul de Man." *Diacritics*, vol. 11, no. 4 (Winter 1981): 36-57.

———. *The Tain of the Mirror: Deconstruction and the Philosophy of Reflection*. Cambridge: Harvard University Press, 1986.

———. "Deconstruction as Criticism." *Glyph* 7 (1979): 177-216.

———. "Quasi-metaphoricity and the Question of Being." In Hugh J. Silverman and Don Ihde, eds. *Hermeneutics and Deconstruction*, pp 166-190.

Graff, Gerald. "Deconstruction as Dogma, or 'Come Back to the Raft Ag'in Strether Honey.' " *Georgia Review*, vol. 34 (1980); 401-21.

Green, Michael. "Response to Cynthia Willet-Shoptaw's 'A Deconstruction of Wittgenstein.' " *Auslegung*, vol. 19 (Summer 1983): 82-85.

Hans, James. "Hermeneutics, Play, Deconstruction." *Philosophy Today*, vol. 24 (Winter 1980): 299-317.

Hartman, Geoffrey. "Monsieur Texte: On Jacques Derrida, his *Glas*." *Georgia Review*, vol. 29, no. 4 (1975): 759-97.

———. "Monsieur Texte II: Epiphany in Echoland." *Georgia Review*, vol. 30, no. 1 (1976): 169-204.

———. *Saving the Text: Philosophy/Derrida/Literature*. Baltimore: Johns Hopkins University Press, 1981.

Harvey, Irene E. *Derrida and the Economy of Difference*. Bloomington: Indiana University Press, 1986.

Heidegger, Martin. *Being and Time* [1927]. Trans. J. Macquarrie and E. Robinson. New York: Harper & Row, 1962.

———. *Kant and the Problem of Metaphysics* [1929]. Trans. James S. Churchill. Bloomington: Indiana University Press, 1962.

———. "The Origin of the Work of Art" [1935-36]. Trans. Albert Hofstadter. In *Poetry Language Thought*. New York: Harper & Row, 1971.

———. *The Essence of Reasons* [1949]. Trans. Terence Malick. Evanston: Northwestern University Press, 1969.

———. *Introduction to Metaphysics* [1953]. Trans. Ralph Manheim. New Haven: Yale University Press, 1954.

———. *What is Called Thinking?* [1951-52]. Trans. J. Glenn Gray. New York: Harper & Row, 1968.

———. *On the Way to Language* [1950-59]. Trans. Peter D. Hertz. New York: Harper & Row, 1971.

———. *Nietzsche* [1961]. Four Volumes. Trans. David Farrell Krell. New York: Harper & Row, 1971

———. *Time and Being* [1969]. Trans. Joan Stambaugh. New York: Harper & Row, 1972.

———. "The Overcoming of Metaphysics." In *The End of Philosophy*. Trans. Joan Stambaugh. New York: Harper & Row, 1971.

———. "The Age of the World View." Trans. Marjorie Grene. In *Martin Heidegger and the Question of Literature: Toward a Postmodern Literary Hermenuetics*. William V. Spanos, ed. Bloomington: Indiana University Press, 1976.

———. "What is Metaphysics?" In *Basic Writings*. David Farrell Krell, ed. New York: Harper & Row, 1977.

Henning, E. M. "Archaeology, Deconstruction, and Intellectual History." In LaCapra, Dominick, and Kaplan, Steven, eds. *Modern European Intellectual History: Reappraisals and New Perspectives*. Ithaca: Cornell University Press, 1982.

Hindess, Barry, and Hirst, Paul Q. *Modes of Production and Social Formation*. London: Macmillan, 1977.

Hirst, Paul Q. *On Law and Ideology*. London: Macmillan, 1979.

Hobson, Marian. "Deconstruction, Empiricism, and the Postal Services." *French Studies*, vol. 36, no. 3 (July 1982): 290-314.

Holland, Nancy. "Heidegger and Derrida Redux: A Close Reading." In Hugh J. Silverman and Don Ihde, eds. *Hermeneutics and Deconstruction*, pp. 219-26.

Hoy, David Couzens. "Deciding Derrida: On the Work (and Play) of the French Philosopher." *London Review of Books*, vol. 4, no. 3 (February/March 1982): 3-5.

Jacobs, Carol. "The Monstrosity of Translation." *Modern Language Notes*, no. 90 (1975): 755-66.

Janicaud, Dominique, and Matte, J.-F. *La Métaphysique à la limite*. Paris: P. U. F., 1983.

Johnson, Barbara. *The Critical Difference: Essays in the Contemporary Rhetoric of Reading*. Baltimore: Johns Hopkins University Press, 1985.

Kant, Immanuel. *Critique of Judgment*. Trans. J. H. Bernard. New York: Hafner Press, 1951.

Kearney, Richard. *Dialogues with Contemporary Continental Thinkers. The Phenomenology Heritage*. P. Ricoeur, E. Levinas, H. Marcuse, S. Breton, and J. Derrida. Manchester: Manchester University Press, 1984.

Krupnick, Mark, ed. *Displacement: Derrida and After*. Bloomington: Indiana University Press, 1983.

Kuhn, Reinhard. "Michael Riffaterre: *Semiotics of Poetry,*" *Modern Language Notes* (1979), pp. 1119-1202.

Lacoue-Labarthe, Philippe, and Nancy, Jean-Luc, eds. *Rejouer le politique*. Paris: Editions Galilée, 1981.

– – –. *Les fins de l'homme: A partir du travail de Jacques Derrida*. Paris: Editions Galilée, 1981.

Lacoue-Labarthe, Philippe. "Typographie" In *Mimesis des articulations*. Paris: Aubier-Flammarion, 1975.

– – –. *Le sujet de la philosophie*. Paris: Aubier-Flammarion, 1979.

– – –. "La fable (Literature and Philosophy)." Trans. Hugh J. Silverman. *Research in Phenomenology*, vol. 15 (1985): 43-60.

Laruelle, François, *Machines textuelles: Déconstruction et libido d'écriture*. Paris: Editions du Seuil, 1976.

Leavey, John P., Jr. "Four Protocols: Derrida, His Deconstruction." *Semeia*, vol. 23 (1982): 42-57.

– – –. "Jacques Derrida's *Glas*: a Translated Selection and Some Comments on an Absent Colossus." *Clio*, vol. 11 (1982): 327-37.

– – –. *Glassary*. Lincoln: University of Nebraska Press, 1987.

Leitch, Vincent B. *Deconstructive Criticism: An Advanced Introduction and Survey*. New York: Columbia University Press, 1982.

Lentricchia, Frank. *After the New Criticism*. Chicago: University of Chicago Press, 1980.

Lingis, Alphonso. "The Pleasure in Postcards." In Hugh J. Silverman and Don Ihde, eds. *Hermeneutics and Deconstruction*, pp. 152-64.

Liszka, James Jakob. "Derrida: Philosophy of Liminal." *Man and World*, vol. 16 (1983): 233-50.

Llewelyn, John. "Derrida: The Origin and End of Philosophy." In *Philosophy and Non-Philosophy since Merleau-Ponty*. Hugh J. Silverman, ed. *Continental Philosophy—I*. London and New York: Routledge, 1988, pp. 191-210.

– – –. *Beyond Metaphysics?* Atlantic Highlands, N. J.: Humanities Press, 1986; London: Macmillan, 1986.

— — —. *Derrida on the Threshold of Sense*. London: Macmillan, 1986.

Loesberg, Jonathan. "Intentionalism, Reader-Response, and the Place of Deconstruction." *Reader*, vol. 12 (1984): 21-38.

Lusthaus, Dan. "Ch'an and Taoist Mirrors: Reflections on Richard Garner's 'Deconstruction of the Mirror.'" *Journal of Chinese Philosophy*, vol. 12 (June 1985): 169-78.

Lyotard, Jean-François. *Discours, figure. Un essai d'esthétique*. Paris: Klincksieck, 1971.

— — —. "The Sublime and the Avant-garde." *Paragraph* (October 1985): 1-18.

Magliola, Robert. *Derrida on the Mend*. West Lafayette: Purdue University Press, 1984.

Magnus, Bernd. "The End of The 'End of Philosophy.'" In Hugh J. Silverman and Don Ihde, eds. *Hermeneutics and Deconstruction*, pp. 2-10.

Margolis, Joseph. "Deconstruction: Or the Mystery of the Mystery of the Text." In Hugh J. Silverman and Don Ihde, eds. *Hermeneutics and Deconstruction*, pp. 138-51.

Marx, Karl. *Grundrisse*. Trans. Martin Nicolaus. Harmondsworth: Penguin Books, 1973.

McDonald, Christie V. "Rereading Deconstruction (Today?)." In Hugh J. Silverman and Donn Welton, eds. *Postmodernism and Continental Philosophy*, pp. 180-92.

McFadden, George. "Review of *Allegories of Reading*," *Journal of Aesthetics and Art Criticism*, vol. 39, no. 3 (Spring 1981): 337-41.

Melville, Stephen. *Philosophy Beside Itself: On Deconstruction and Modernism*. Minneapolis: Minnesota University Press, 1986.

Merrell, Floyd. *Deconstruction Reframed*. West Lafayette: Purdue University Press, 1985.

Miller, J. Hillis. "The Critic as Host." In *Deconstruction and Criticism*. New York: Continuum, 1979.

— — —. "The Function of Rhetorical Study at the Present Time." In *The State of the Discipline 1970s-1980s*. Jaspar P. Neel, ed. New York: Association of Departments of English, 1979.

— — —. *The Ethics of Reading: Kant, de Man, Eliot, Trollope, James, and Benjamin*. New York: Columbia University Press, 1987.

Montefiori, Alan, ed. *Philosophy in France Today*. Cambridge: Cambridge University Press, 1982.

Nietzsche, Friedrich. *The Will to Power*. Trans. Walter Kaufmann and R. J. Hollingdale. New York: Random House, 1967.

Norris, Christopher. *Deconstruction: Theory and Practice*. London: Methuen, 1982.

— — —. *The Deconstructive Turn: Essays in the Rhetoric of Philosophy*. London: Methuen, 1983.

— — —. *The Contest of Faculties: Philosophy and Theory After Deconstruction*. London: Methuen, 1985.

— — —. "Names." *London Review of Books*, vol. 8, no. 3 (1986): 10-12.

— — —. *Derrida*. London: Fontana Modern Masters, 1987.

O'Neill, John. "Deconstructing Fort/Derrida." In Hugh J. Silverman and Donn

Welton, eds. *Postmodernism and Continental Philosophy*, pp. 214-26.

Olkowski, Dorothea. "If the Shoe Fits—Derrida and the Orientation of Thought." In Hugh J. Silverman and Don Ihde, eds. *Hermeneutics and Deconstruction*, pp. 262-69.

Ormiston, Gayle L. "Binding Withdrawal." In Hugh J. Silverman and Don Ihde, eds. *Hermeneutics and Deconstruction*, pp. 247-61.

Pratt, Mary Louise. *Toward a Speech Act Theory of Literary Discourse*. Bloomington: Indiana University Press, 1977.

Pressler, Charles A. "Redoubled: The Bridging of Derrida and Heidegger." *Human Studies*, vol. 7 (1984): 325-42.

Ray, William. *Literary Meaning: From Phenomenology to Deconstruction*. Oxford: Basil Blackwell, 1984.

Riddel, J.N. "From Heidegger to Derrida to Chance: Doubling and (Poetic) Language." In *Martin Heidegger and the Question of Literature: Towards a Postmodern Literary Hermeneutics*. W. V. Spanos, ed. Bloomington: Indiana University Press, 1976, pp. 571-92.

Riffaterre, Michael. *The Semiotics of Poetry*. Bloomington: Indiana University Press, 1978.

———. *La Production du texte*. Paris: Seuil, 1979.

———. "Sémiotique intertextuelle: L'Interprétant." *Revue d'esthétique: Rhétoriques, sémiotiques*, vols. 1-2 (1979): 128-50.

———. "Syllepsis." *Critical Inquiry*, vol. 6, no. 4 (Summer 1980): 625-38.

———. "La Trace de l'intertext." *La Pensée*, no. 215 (October 1980): 4-18.

———. "L'Intertexte inconnu." *Littérature*, no. 41 (February 1981): 4-7.

———. "Interpretation and Undecidability." *New Literary History*, vol. 12, no. 2 (Winter 1981): 227-42.

Rorty, Richard. "Philosophy as a Kind of Writing." In *Consequences of Pragmatism*. Minneapolis: University of Minnesota Press, 1982, p. 89-109.

———. "Deconstruction and Circumvention." *Critical Inquiry*, vol. 11, no. 1 (Sept. 1984): 1-23.

Rosmarin, Adena. "Theory and Practice: From Ideally Separated to Pragmatically Joined." *Journal of Aesthetics and Art Criticism*, vol. 43 (Fall 1984): 31-40.

Ryan, Michael. *Marxism and Deconstruction: A Critical Articulation*. Baltimore: Johns Hopkins University Press, 1982.

Said, Edward. *The World, the Text, and the Critic*. London: Faber and Faber, 1984.

Sallis, John. "Heidegger/Derrida—Presence." *Journal of Philosophy*, vol. 81 (Oct. 1984): 594-601.

———. *Delimitations*. Bloomington: Indiana University Press, 1986.

———. *Spacings*. Chicago: University of Chicago Press, 1987.

———, ed. *Deconstruction and Philosophy: The Texts of Jacques Derrida*. Chicago: University of Chicago Press, 1987.

Salusinsky, Imre. *Criticism in Society: Interviews with Jacques Derrida, Northrop Frye, Harold Bloom, et al.* London: Methuen, 1987.

Schapiro, Meyer. "The Still-Life as a Personal Object—A Note on Heidegger and Van Gogh." In *The Reach of Mind: Essays in Memory of Kurt Goldstein*

(New York: Springer, 1968), p. 203-09.

Schrag, Calvin O. "Subjectivity and Praxis at the End of Philosophy." In Hugh J. Silverman and Don Ihde, eds. *Hermeneutics and Deconstruction*, pp. 24-32.

Schreber, Paul. *Memoirs of My Nervous Illness*. Ed. and trans. I. Macalpine and R. Hunter. London: Dawson, 1955.

Schrift, Alan D. "Language, Metaphor, Rhetoric: Nietzsche's Deconstruction of Epistemology." *Journal of the History of Philosophy*, vol. 23 (July 1985): 371-96.

— — —. "Reading, Writing, Text: Nietzsche's Deconstruction of Authority." *International Studies in Philosophy*, vol. 17 (Summer 1985): 55-64.

— — —. "Genealogy and/as Deconstruction: Nietzsche, Derrida, and Foucault on Philosophy as Critique." In Hugh J. Silverman and Donn Welton, eds. *Postmodernism and Continental Philosophy*, pp. 193-213.

Schurmann, Reiner. "Deconstruction is Not Enough: On Gianni Vattimo's Call for Weak Thinking." *Graduate Faculty Philosophy Journal*, vol. 10 (Spring 1984): 165-77.

Sheehan, Thomas J. "Derrida and Heidegger." In Hugh J. Silverman and Don Ihde, eds. *Hermeneutics and Deconstruction*, pp. 201-18.

Silverman, Hugh J. *Inscriptions: Between Phenomenology and Structuralism*. New York: Routledge and Kegan Paul, 1987.

— — —. "Self-Decentering: Derrida Incorporated." *Research in Phenomenology*, vol. 8 (1978): 45-65.

— — —. "Phenomenology." *Social Research*, vol. 47, no. 4 (Winter 1980): 704-20.

— — —. "The Limits of Logocentrism (On the Way to Grammatology)." In David Wood, ed. *Heidegger and Language*. Coventry: Warwick/Parousia Press, 1981, pp. 51-70. Reprinted in J. N. Mohanty, ed. *Phenomenology and the Human Sciences*. The Hague: Nijhoff, 1985, pp. 107-19.

— — —. "Writing (On Deconstruction) at the Edge of Metaphysics." *Research in Phenomenology*, vol. 13 (1983): 97-110.

— — —. "Phenomenology: From Hermeneutics to Deconstruction." *Research in Phenomenology*, vol. 14 (1984): 19-34. Reprinted with "Afterthoughts," in Amedeo Giorgi, ed. *Phenomenology: Descriptive or Hermeneutic?* Pittsburgh: Duquesne University Phenomenology Center, 1987, pp. 19-34 and 85-92.

— — —. "The Autobiographical Textuality of Nietzsche's *Ecce Homo*." In Daniel O'Hara, ed. *Why Nietzsche Now?* Bloomington: Indiana University Press, 1985, pp. 141-51.

— — —. "Interrogation and Deconstruction." *Phaenomenologische Forschung*, vol. 18. Freiburg: Alber, 1986, pp. 113-27.

— — —. "Readings of Texts/Authors of Works." *Journal of Philosophy* (1986): 14-15.

— — —. "Textuality and the Origin of the Work of Art." In Hugh J. Silverman et al., eds. *The Horizons of Continental Philosophy*. Dordrecht: Nijhoff-Kluwer, 1988, pp. 153-67.

Silverman, Hugh J., ed. *Philosophy and Non-Philosophy since Merleau-Ponty* (Continental Philosophy—I). New York and London: Routledge, 1988.

— — —. *Derrida and Deconstruction* (Continental Philosophy—II). New York and London: Routledge, 1989.

Silverman, Hugh J., and Ihde, Don, eds. *Hermeneutics and Deconstruction*. Albany: SUNY Press, 1985.

Silverman, Hugh J. and Welton, Donn, eds. *Postmodernism and Continental Philosophy*. Albany: SUNY Press, 1988.

Smith, Joseph, and Kerrigan, William, eds. *Taking Chances: Derrida, Psychoanalysis and Literature*. Baltimore: Johns Hopkins University Press, 1984.

Spanos, William V., ed. *Martin Heidegger and the Question of Literature*. Bloomington: Indiana University Press, 1976.

Staten, Henry. *Wittgenstein and Derrida*. Lincoln: University of Nebraska Press, 1985.

Taylor, Mark C., ed. *Deconstruction in Context: Literature and Philosophy*. Chicago: University of Chicago Press, 1986.

— — —. *Errings*. Chicago: University of Chicago Press, 1984.

Terdiman, Richard. "Deconstruction/Mediation: A Dialectical Critique of Derrideanism." *The Minnesota Review*, no. 19 (1983): 103-11.

Thiher, Allen. *Words in Reflection: Modern Language Theory and Post-modern Fiction*. Chicago: University of Chicago Press, 1984.

Ulmer, Gregory L. *Applied Grammatology: Post(e)-Pedagogy from Jacques Derrida to Joseph Beuys*. Baltimore: Johns Hopkins University Press, 1985.

Wimsatt, W. K. *The Verbal Icon*. London: Methuen, 1970.

Wood, David. *Deconstruction of Time*. Atlantic Highlands, N.J.: Humanities Press International, 1989.

— — —. "Introduction to Derrida." In *Radical Philosophy* (Spring 1979), pp. 18-28. Reprinted in R. Edgeley and Osborne, eds. *Radical Philosophy Reader*. London: Verso, 1985.

— — —. "Derrida and the Paradoxes of Reflection." *Journal of the British Society for Phenomenology*, vol. 11, no. 3 (October 1980): 225-38.

— — —. "Metametaphysical Textuality." In David Wood, ed. *Heidegger and Language*. Coventry: University of Warwick/Parousia Press, 1982, pp. 71-100.

— — —. "Heidegger after Derrida." *Research in Phenomenology*, vol. 17 (1987): 103-116.

— — —. "Beyond Deconstruction?" In A. Phillips Griffiths, ed. *Contemporary French Philosophy*. Cambridge: Cambridge University Press, 1988.

Wood, David, and Bernasconi, Robert, eds. *Derrida and Difference*. Coventry: University of Warwick/Parousia Press, 1985; Republished; Evanston: Northwestern University Press, 1988.

Wurzer, Wilhelm S. "Postmodernism's Short Letter, Philosophy's Long Farewell . . . ." In Hugh J. Silverman and Donn Welton, eds. *Postmodernism and Continental Philosophy*, pp. 243-50.

— — —. "Heidegger and Lacan: On the Occlusion of the Subject." In Hugh J. Silverman et al., eds. *The Horizons of Continental Philosophy*. Dordrecht: Nijhoff-Kluwer, 1988, pp. 168-89.

Contributors

DAVID B. ALLISON is associate professor of philosophy at the State University of New York at Stony Brook. He is editor of *The New Nietzsche* (MIT Press, 1977, 1985), co-editor of *Psychosis and Sexual Identity: Toward a Post-Analytic View of the Schreber Case* (SUNY Press, 1988), and translator of Derrida's *Speech and Phenomena* (Northwestern University Press, 1973).

BRIAN G. CARAHER is associate professor of English at Indiana University in Bloomington, Indiana. He is author of various articles on Paul de Man.

TINA CHANTER is assistant professor of Philosophy at Louisiana State University. She taught previously at the University of Essex and at Thames Polytechnic (London) and has published articles on French Feminism, Levinas, and Heidegger.

PAUL DE MAN was Sterling Professor of Humanities at Yale University when he died in 1983. His books include *Blindness and Insight*, second edition (University of Minnesota Press, 1983), *Allegories of Reading* (Yale University Press, 1979), *The Rhetoric of Romanticism* (Columbia University Press, 1984), and *The Resistance to Theory* (University of Minnesota Press, 1986).

EUGENIO DONATO was professor and chair of the Department of French at the University of California at Irvine when he died in 1983. He was co-editor of *The Structuralist Controversy* (Johns Hopkins University

Press, 1970) and contributor to *Velocities of Change* (Johns Hopkins University Press, 1974). He is also author of many articles in the areas of comparative literature, literary theory, and the philosophy-literature interface.

ANTONY EASTHOPE is senior lecturer in English and cultural studies at Manchester Polytechnic (England). His publications include *Poetry and Discourse* (Methuen, 1983), *The Masculine Myth in Popular Culture* (Paladin, 1986), and *British Post-Structuralism* (Routledge, 1988). His *Poetry and Phantasy*, a study of poetry, ideology, and psychoanalysis, is to be published by Cambridge University Press in 1989.

HOWARD FELPERIN is professor in the School of English and Linguistics at Macquarrie University in New South Wales (Australia). He is author of *Beyond Deconstruction: The Uses and Abuses of Literary Theory* (Clarendon Press, 1985).

CHRISTOPHER FYNSK is associate professor of comparative literature at the State University of New York at Binghamton. He served as *maître de conférences associé* in the Department of Philosophy at the University of Strassbourg (France) for 1985-87. He is author of *Heidegger: Thought and Historicity* (Cornell University Press, 1986).

MICHAEL FISCHER is associate professor of English at the University of New Mexico. His publications include *Does Deconstruction Make Any Difference?* (Indiana University Press, 1985) and *Literary Skepticism: Stanley Cavell and Contemporary Criticism* (University of Chicago Press, 1989).

JOSEPH F. GRAHAM teaches French literature at Tulane University. He is editor of *Difference in Translation* (Cornell University Press, 1985). His articles concern primarily theories of language and literature.

IRENE E. HARVEY is assistant professor of philosophy and Director of the Center for Psychoanalytic Studies at Pennsylvania State University. She is author of *Derrida and the Economy of Difference* (Indiana University Press, 1986) and has published articles on contemporary French thought and the history of philosophy.

RODOLPHE GASCHÉ is professor of comparative literature at the State University of New York at Buffalo. His publications include *Die hybride Wissenschaft, System und Metaphorik in der Philosophie von Georges Bataille*, and *The Tain of the Mirror: Derrida and the Philosophy of Reflection* (Harvard University Press, 1986).

GREGORY JAY is professor of English at the University of Wisconsin at Milwaukee. He taught previously at the Universities of Alabama and South Carolina. He is author of *T.S. Eliot and the Poetics of Literary History*, editor of *Modern American Critics: 1920-1955* and *Modern American Critics since 1955* (Gale Research), and co-editor of *After Strange Texts: The Role of Theory in the Study of Literature*.

KATHRYN KINCZEWSKI is associate professor in the Department of Foreign Languages and Literatures at the University of Denver.

JOHN P. LEAVEY, JR. is associate professor of English at the University of Florida in Gainseville. He has translated Derrida's *Edmund Husserl's "Origin of Geometry": An Introduction* (Nicholas-Hays, 1978; Nebraska, 1989), *The Archeology of the Frivolous: Reading Condillac* (Duquesne University Press, 1980), and with Richard Rand, *Glas* (University of Nebraska Press, 1986). He is also author of a companion volume to *Glas* entitled *Glassary* (University of Nebraska Press, 1986).

ARNAUD VILLANI teaches philosophy at the Lycée Masséna in Nice (France). His publications include *Kafka et l'ouverture de l'existant* (Berlin, 1984), *Beaumarchais* (Berlin, 1985), and numerous articles on topics such as Deleuze, Kafka, Roussel, Nietzsche, Kenneth White, Hölderlin, and artificial intelligence.

DAVID WOOD is senior lecturer in the Department of Philosophy at the University of Warwick (England). He is author of *The Deconstruction of Time* (Humanities Press, 1989), editor of *Heidegger and Language* (Parousia Press, 1981), and coeditor of *Time and Metaphysics* (Parousia Press, 1982), *Derrida and Differance* (Northwestern University Press, 1988), and *Exceedingly Nietzsche* (Routledge, 1988).

WILHELM WURZER is associate professor of philosophy at Duquesne University in Pittsburgh. He is author of *Spinoza und Nietzsche* (Hain, 1975) and various articles on Nietzsche, Heidegger, Lacan, and postmodernism. He is currently completing a book-length study on filming.

Editors

HUGH J. SILVERMAN is professor of philosophy and comparative literature at the State University of New York at Stony Brook. He has taught at Stanford University and has been visiting professor at Duquesne University, New York University, and the University of Leeds (England), and visiting senior lecturer at the University of Warwick (England) and the University of Nice (France). He served as executive co-director of the Society for Phenomenology and Existential Philosophy for six years (1980-86) and is currently executive director of the International Association for Philosophy and Literature. Author of *Inscriptions: Between Phenomenology and Structuralism* (Routledge and Kegan Paul, 1987), editor of *Piaget, Philosophy and the Human Sciences* (Humanities, 1980), coeditor of *Jean-Paul Sartre: Contemporary Approaches to his Philosophy* (Duquesne, 1980), *Continental Philosophy in America* (Duquesne, 1983), *Descriptions* (SUNY, 1985), *Hermeneutics and Deconstruction* (SUNY, 1985), *Critical and Dialectical Phenomenology* (SUNY, 1987), *The Horizons of Continental Philosophy: Essays on Husserl, Heidegger, and Merleau-Ponty* (Nijhoff, 1988), *Postmodernism and Continental Philosophy* (SUNY, 1988), and translator of various works by Merleau-Ponty, he is editor of *Continental Philosophy*, the first volume of which is entitled *Philosophy and Non-Philosophy since Merleau-Ponty* (Routledge, 1988), and the second, *Derrida and Deconstruction* (Routledge, 1989).

GARY E. AYLESWORTH is assistant professor of philosophy at Eastern Illinois University in Charleston, Illinois. He taught previously at Siena College (1986-89). His doctoral thesis, which he completed at the State University of New York at Stony Brook in 1986, is entitled "From Grounds to Play: A Comparative Analysis of Wittgenstein and Heidegger." He is currently preparing a translation of Martin Heidegger's *Grundbegriffe* for Indiana University Press and is a contributor to the forthcoming *Continental Philosophy-IV* (Routledge, 1990) volume on the topic of "Gadamer and Hermeneutics."

Index

271